D1095188

PAPPY'S BOYS

THE ROSE BOWL YEARS
1948 - 1949 - 1950

Edited and with an Introduction by

RON FIMRITE

Production Manager

DICK ERICKSON

1996
First Edition
Printed in the United States of America

ACKNOWLEDGEMENTS

No book of this sort could come together without the thought, assistance and real commitment of a great number of people. The original concept came from Roy Muehlberger, and after several telephone conversations I note the first written communication about it was dated April 19, 1991.

As a group of amateurs, there was no way we were going to pull this together without professional guidance. Former *Daily Cal* Sports Editor and long time senior writer for *Sports Illustrated*, Ron Fimrite, accepted our invitation to be the Editor. Without him there would be no book.

Another essential ingredient was a typist who knew the demands of the printing business and had the talent and ability to produce what was wanted in the form that it was wanted and in the required time frame. We are indebted to Lisa Zemelman from the Graduate Group in Ancient History and Mediterranean Archaeology on the campus who always seemed to be a step ahead of us.

We always felt that pictures were important to this book, and our grateful thanks to Ed Kirwan and Kirwan Graphics for not only locating the desired photos but also printing them for us. Kevin Reneau, Sports Information Director for the Athletic Department, always provided or confirmed needed historical information. With absolutely no knowledge of the business of book printing or bookbinding, we are truly grateful to Dan Gulart and American Lithographers, Inc. for assuming this entire responsibility.

It is imazing how much one can forget or be confused about after the lapse of forty-eight years. Refreshing our memories and providing great input were Jim Cullom, Ray DeJong, Wes Fry, Dick LemMon, and Carl Van Heuit. Pardon me, I know there must be a number of others deserving of credit who have not been mentioned, but playing in those old leather helmets with no face mask has taken its toll.

Last and certainly not least, I must give my wife, Jan, much credit and thanks for her ideas, feelings for what was right and what was not right and most particularly for her patience and understanding over these past four years.

Dick Erickson

This book is dedicated to
our beloved coach
Lynn O. Pappy Waldorf

TABLE OF CONTENTS

⌘

INTRODUCTION
by Ron Fimrite

⌘

In the pages to follow, you will read, in the participants' own words, of a most extraordinary time in the history of the University of California. Lynn O. "Pappy" Waldorf, a rotund and jolly man with a bass voice that came from deep within his capacious belly, came west to Berkeley in 1947 from Northwestern University with a reputation for coaching excellence already firmly established. He had been college football's Coach of the Year in 1935 and his 1936, '38 and '43 teams had been nationally ranked. But at Cal he would face the challenge of his career. The Bears had not had a winning team in eight years and had rounded off a dreadful two-win-seven-loss 1946 season with an embarrassing, 25-6 Big Game loss to Stanford, which had not even fielded a team in three years because of World War II. Cal students were so agitated by this defeat that, as the game wound down to a desultory conclusion, they maniacally ripped apart the seats in their own rooting section. It seemed a proper metaphor for the state of Cal football at the time.

But Pappy, undeterred by the dismal past, announced upon his arrival that what he had inherited in Berkeley was not a football weakling but, instead, "a sleeping giant." Indeed, the situation was far from hopeless. The Cal student body in those immediate post-war years was swollen to nearly 30,000 by the return of so many service veterans. These men, eager to work, eager to play, suffused the campus with a verve and sense of purpose it had never before experienced. But they also created, by the sheer weight of their numbers, considerable confusion, not the least of it on the football practice field, where as many as 200 varsity candidates might appear at a single session. To sift the wheat from the chaff in such a crop required organizational genius, a faculty which Pappy Waldorf had in abundance.

His very first team, in '47, finished 9-1 and was ranked 15th in the nation. It was an unprecedented turnaround. The giant had truly awakened. But not completely, for Pappy knew this was but a beginning, that his next team was made of championship material.

That 1948 team would, in fact, become, in all probability, the best that had yet represented the university. This was a college team of uncommon maturity. Of a varsity squad of 57 players, all but nine had been veterans of the war and many had played on crack service teams, often with seasoned professionals. Twenty-six of the players were 23 years of age or older; only four were under 20. These were men, not boys, taking the field for the Blue and Gold.

And there were giants among them --- guard Rod Franz, already an All American; tackle and team captain Gene Frassetto, at 26 a veteran of pre-war football; tackle Jim Turner, a 230-pound All America candidate; guard Jon Baker, later a professional star with the New York Giants; Jack Swaner, a stocky, punishing running back, and Bob Celeri, a "mad engineer" of a quarterback whose favorite play, beyond the touchdown pass, was the bootleg run. There were also on that roster such steadying hands as quarterback Dick Erickson, tackle-placekicker Jim Cullom and linemen Bobby Dodds, Doug Duncan, Forrest Klein and Ray DeJong.

But far above all in this elite company was one of the most amazing athletes ever to wear a Cal jersey --- "the Golden Boy", Jackie Jensen. This Triple Threat star --- runner, passer, punter --- had shown flashes of brilliance the previous season, while sharing playing time with Johnny Graves at fullback. His pass to Paul Keckley on an 80-yard play had won the Big Game in the final minutes and he had set a school record with his seven pass interceptions. He had also led Cal to the first NCAA baseball championship with his pitching and power hitting. The university had not seen an athlete of such virtuosity since Brick Muller of the Wonder Teams. And 1948 would truly be the year of the Golden Boy.

In the opening game, a 41-19 win over Santa Clara, Jensen reeled off three runs of more than 60 yards, two for touchdowns, and finished with 192 yards on just 12 carries. In a 42-0 win over Oregon State, he completed both of his pass attempts for a total of 73 yards and one touchdown. He scored both Cal touchdowns and gained 132 yards in a 13-7 win over perennial conference champion USC. He ran for 170 yards, had a 77-yard punt and ultimately saved a 7-6 win over Stanford when, trapped trying to punt on fourth and 31 late in the game, he miraculously dodged his way straight up the middle of the field for 32 yards and a first down. He set a new Cal single season rushing record by gaining 1080 yards on 148 carries, an astonishing average of 7.3 yards per carry. He was an overwhelming All America selection. Waldorf called him the greatest player he had ever coached, better even than Otto Graham at Northwestern. He was such a remarkable broken field runner, said Pappy, that, "he eluded the hand he could not see."

The powerful Swaner was a perfect complement to the dancing Jensen in the backfield. In fact, he led the conference in scoring with 11 touchdowns and was second to Jensen in rushing yardage. Cullom led the PCC with 35 of 40 successful points after touchdown. The Bears went undefeated in ten regular season games, outscoring opponents, 277 points to 80. They were ranked fourth in the nation.

Alas, their only loss came in the Rose Bowl, to the Big Ten's Northwestern, 20-14. Bad luck, which would become a Cal Rose Bowl tradition, had more to do with that defeat than the opponent. After running 67 yards for a touchdown in the first half, Jensen pulled up lame with a muscle pull early in the third quarter and did not play again. And Northwestern's winning touchdown, on a one-yard plunge by Art Murakowski in the second quarter, may have been a phantom score since newspaper photos seemed to show that the runner had fumbled the ball before he crossed the goal. But even this unfortunate loss could not tarnish one of the greatest seasons Cal had yet experienced.

Expectations did not run nearly so high for 1949. In fact, this team seemed cursed from the start. Jensen passed up what would have been his senior season to sign a professional baseball contract with Oakland of the Pacific Coast League. He would be a major league player within a year and in 1958, as a Boston Red Sox outfielder, would become the American League's Most Valuable Player. Swaner, scheduled for heavy-duty ball-carrying in Jensen's absence, was injured early and carried the ball only 21 times all season. And after the fourth game, the team lost scatback Charley Sarver, who had been averaging 9.9 yards per rush and 29 yards on pass receptions. Star linemen Turner, Baker and Frassetto had all graduated. Franz was there for another All America season and an impressive newcomer, Les Richter, would make up for some of the loss up front, but this did not look at all like the dominating team of the year before.

As a matter of fact, the Bears would fall behind in six of their ten games and yet, led by such newer stars as Jim Monachino, Pete Schabarum and Frank Brunk, finish undefeated again. Monachino gained 781 yards rushing and had 15 touchdowns and Schabarum and Brunk would both gain 400 yards or more. Quarterback Celeri would have his best year, passing for 1081 yards and nine touchdowns.

But it would be Brunk, who had played behind Jensen in '48, who would bring off one of the most electrifying plays in Cal history. In a game that would decide the conference championship and, therefore, the Rose Bowl invitation, USC took a 10-7 lead six minutes into the final quarter on a field goal by Frank Gifford, the future NFL Hall of Famer and football broadcaster. On the ensuing kickoff, Brunk fielded the ball two yards deep into the end zone and, on a return play practiced for the first time that week, steamed directly into the gut of the S.C. defense. Behind superb blocking, the Bear back shot quickly into the clear and evaded the last man who could have caught him, Gifford, to complete a heart-stopping 102-run as the crowd of 81,500 went delightfully mad.

Once again, bad luck struck in the Rose Bowl. With less than two minutes remaining to play and the score tied, 14-14, Ohio State's Jim Hague kicked the winning field goal from the Cal 19 yard line. The winning kick was made possible when the Buckeyes forced Celeri into a left-footed fourth down out-of-bounds punt that gave them the ball on the Cal 12. The Rose Bowl blues were back. They would continue for one more year.

The 1950 season would give Waldorf a third straight undefeated record, a 7-7 Big Game tie the only imperfection. This was a powerhouse team reminiscent more of 1948 than '49, and it, too, would have its superstar, sophomore fullback Johnny Olszewski, the inimitable "Johnny O." The '50 team may have lacked the quarterbacking skills of Celeri, but with Olszewski, Monachino and Schabarum carrying the ball, a passing game was, at best, irrelevant. Johnny O. finished with 1008 yards, Monachino with 754 and Schabarum with 647 --- a total of 2409 yards for just the three of them! The highlight of the season was a crushing, 35-0, defeat of UCLA in which Olszewski scored twice, once on a 73-yard tackle-breaking dash. Olszewski was not the elusive swivel-hipped runner Jensen had been, preferring a rather more straightforward approach to advancing the ball. Instead of "eluding the hand he could not see," Johnny O. looked for bodies to barge into, but few opponents could hold his powerful charges.

And yes, the Rose Bowl luck continued. This time, Big Ten champion Michigan was the beneficiary, winning, 14-6, after a 73-yard Schabarum touchdown run was called back on a penalty and after Monachino missed scoring a certain T.D. when, with two blockers ahead of him and clear sailing to the goal line, he slipped and fell on the damp turf at the Wolverine five-yard-line in the closing seconds of the first half.

Still, these Waldorf Bears, undefeated in three successive regular seasons, must rank with Andy Smith's Wonder Teams as the greatest of all at Cal. They breathed new life into athletics there and charged the atmosphere on campus with their energy and spirit. But their success on the field is not what gives them lasting importance. It's what they did with the rest of their lives that is their true legacy to the university.

As you, the reader, will soon discover, Pappy Waldorf was much more than a coach to these players. He was their mentor in life as well, and with his keen intellect, his innate sense of decency and his good-humored faith in the human spirit, he shined a beacon light into their future.

And for this, he is touched with greatness.

FOREWARD - STUDENTS AT BERKELEY AFTER WORLD WAR II
by Clark Kerr

⌘

Three groups of students in the history of the University of California have had the greatest impact on the campus.

The first was the entering class in the fall of 1869 and its immediate successors. The 1869 entering class was, per capita, the most famous of all classes in terms of subsequent achievements--one governor of the state, three future regents, and several faculty members out of a graduating class of 12! This class established two facts: one was that Berkeley could attract very able young people; and the second was that it could give them an excellent education. This was the first triumph of Berkeley as a campus. The entering class of 1869, and the other pioneer classes, started housing "clubs" and then fraternities and sororities, a student newspaper, informal athletic teams and, in other ways, started to build the instrumentalities of student life at Berkeley.

The third group of students was composed of the radical activists of the middle and late 1960s and early 1970s. Their contributions have been, and still are, variously appraised. They attacked the alleged neglect of undergraduates in the classrooms by the faculty, the rules which sought to restrict "action associated with speech" (free speech already existed as events in Sproul Plaza during the fall of 1964 so clearly demonstrated), national policies in the areas of race relations and the war in Vietnam; and they introduced new approaches to personal conduct in the use of drugs and in other ways.

The second group, and the one to which I wish to turn my attention, was the GI-dominated student body after World War II. These students came back more experienced, more mature, more highly motivated than any group we ever had before or since. Many had held positions of greater responsibility, in terms of impact on life and death, than most of their professors. They made their classes more dynamic than ever before or since. They asked more questions. They challenged more positions. They probed more deeply. They were a delight to work with, and when they left, the quality of classroom life deteriorated quite noticeably. As a young faculty member after World War II, I considered them, by all odds, my favorite students of all time. And so would say most of my colleagues of those years. The GI wave made us into better teachers than we had been before or ever would be again.

This second group had another, more lasting, impact. Half of its members came from families from which no college students had ever emerged before. This began the movement toward universal access to higher education and with federal financial support (the GI Bill of Rights). Nationwide, enrollments went from 1.5 million in 1940 to three million in 1950. This second group, with its concurrent impact on the birth rate, gave rise, in turn, to the tidal wave of students in the 1960s and 1970s, and enrollments in 1980 totaled 12 million. Greater equality of opportunity through higher education than the nation, or the world, had ever seen was a dramatic result of the GI wave. To preserve this movement into the future was one of the purposes of the California Master Plan for Higher Education of 1960.

At Berkeley, in particular, the GI wave of students had further permanent consequences. Berkeley was in a special situation. It still was a German-type university as had been all of the original land-grant universities. This meant that the institution provided classrooms and laboratories, and then left the students on their own. This pattern was particularly endorsed by Benjamin Ide Wheeler as president (1899-1919), himself a graduate of German universities and a great admirer of them. This meant no residence halls, few if any intramural sport fields, only a minimum provision for student activities and for cultural affairs. Most land-grant universities, including those in the Big Ten, had moved away from the German model toward the British (and Ivy League) model by World War II; but not Berkeley.

Then came the GIs. Many had gone to universities and colleges with more provisions for total student life than at Berkeley. And there were in Berkeley outside the campus too few rooms to rent, too few places to eat, too few fields on which to play, almost no cultural programs. (Enrollment had jumped from 15,000 to 22,500 students.) They griped. As a young faculty member, I heard their gripes and sympathized with them. I had gone to a British-type college--Swarthmore.

It all came to a head in the fall of 1946. It was a lousy season in football (seven defeats, two victories) and, after a defeat by Stanford in Memorial Stadium (November 23--The Big Game), the protest took the form of burning trash (and some seats)--the "rooting section . . . celebrated by tearing up the bleachers" (S. Dan Brodie, 66 Years on the California Gridiron, 1882-1948 [Oakland: Olympic Publishing Co., 1949]). This quickly attracted the attention of the alumni. What had gone wrong? The returning warriors were in revolt!

The result was a report called Students at Berkeley. The Alumni Association appointed a committee to investigate the trouble. And it was a top-flight committee. Stanley Barnes, a star on the Wonder Teams of the early 1920s and then a federal judge, was the first chairman. Other members included Cort Majors, captain of the Wonder Teams and later a Vice President of Crown Zellerbach, and Jean Witter, Class of 1916, of the All-Cal Witter family, who was the immediate past president of the Alumni Association.

A report was submitted in May 1948. It concluded:

> "To put it bluntly, the student body is not served outside the classroom in a manner consonant with the size and importance of the University. Student interests have not been anticipated or fully considered in the development of either campus or student neighborhoods."

Then followed many recommendations, including:

Residence halls
A modern student social center
More cultural facilities
Intramural sports facilities
Parking
Better campus paths (no more walking in the mud)
More attention to landscaping

This report lay untouched for four years. When I became the first chancellor at Berkeley in 1952, I resurrected it, and with essential help from leaders of the Alumni Association and the ASUC, every single recommendation was accomplished; and, in the course of doing that, new policies were set that came to guide development on all nine campuses of the university--old and new. As I walk the Berkeley campus today, I often think of what the GI wave of students set in motion and how much better student life became for its many successors on all nine campuses.

This GI effort to elevate student life carried over into intercollegiate athletics, and Berkeley entered a Golden Age of intercollegiate competition.

Berkeley became a far, far better place for undergraduate students while Group II (the GI wave) was here. And, because of it, it has remained a better place ever after.

PREFACE
by Glenn Seaborg

⌘

I am pleased and honored to be asked to write a preface to this book featuring the contributions of Lynn O. (Pappy) Waldorf to the reputation of the University of California at Berkeley. He was an extraordinary person with dimensions far beyond those of a football coach, the profession in which he excelled.

Following Coach Frank Wickhorst's disastrous 1946 season, Pappy Waldorf transformed the team to the achievement of a 9-1 record in 1947 (his first year) as the coach at Berkeley. Then followed the amazing three-year regular season records of 10-0, 10-0, and 9-0-1. This was followed by an 8-2 record in 1951. Thus during his first five years as Cal coach, Waldorf had a remarkable regular season record of 46-3-1, second only to the record of Cal's Wonder Teams of the early 1920s. His record during the three Rose Bowl years was marred only by the three close losses in the January 1 classic. Except for the 1958 Golden Bear team which lost to the Iowa Hawkeyes in the 1959 Rose Bowl, no Cal football team has played in Pasadena since on New Year's Day. And Pappy's Big Game record (7-1-2) is unmatched by any Cal coach, including the legendary Andy Smith and "Stub" Allison.

The son of a Methodist minister, Pappy was also a humble man who credited his success at Cal to his assistants, his players, the organization of the football program, the alumni and boosters — basically, almost everyone but himself. However, Pappy was clearly the driving force in bringing together all the components that led to the Bears' success.

My wife Helen actually became aware of his prowess as a football coach before I did. During World War II, we were living in Chicago where I worked on the Manhattan Project at the University of Chicago. Helen saw Lynn Waldorf and one of his teams, which featured Otto Graham, in action there as early as the fall of 1943. She attended a football game at Northwestern at a time when Pappy was making his reputation as coach there.

I recall one of my first meetings with Pappy Waldorf when he spoke at the southern California annual alumni day at the Ambassador Hotel in Los Angeles on February 4, 1951. His topic was, "Rose Bowl, 1951, and Future Football Prospects." I was amazed by his erudition and articulate presentation on this occasion; he went far beyond the confines of an exposition on football. I have fond memories of my contacts with him and my enjoyment as a spectator of his football teams. During the ten seasons of Pappy Waldorf's tenure as football coach at Berkeley, I attended his first game and his last game and the majority of the home games in between.

In 1952 Clark Kerr, then the first chancellor of the Berkeley campus, asked me to serve as Berkeley's faculty athletic representative to the Pacific Coast Intercollegiate Athletic Conference. Kerr, an avid Bears fan, had a particular interest in Cal athletics but an even greater commitment to maintaining the tradition of academic excellence of which Cal is so justifiably proud. Knowing that I shared his convictions, I was happy to accept his appointment to this position. Hence, I became well acquainted with Pappy and his boys. I shall quote from my journal in order to give much of the flavor of my contacts with our football teams during this time.

I'll start with a description of my attendance at Pappy's first game as Berkeley's football coach.

Saturday, September 20, 1947

I made the usual rounds of the labs during the morning and, in the afternoon, went to the first football game of the season. California has a new coach — Lynn O. "Pappy" Waldorf — and this year's team looks promising. It beat Santa Clara 33 to 7. Waldorf comes to us from Northwestern University, where he developed such outstanding players as quarterback Otto Graham and established a reputation as a fine leader of men and molder of character, the type of coach we want at Berkeley.

Helen and I missed Pappy's first Rose Bowl game because she was pregnant and expecting soon. However, listening to the radio broadcast was the highlight of this New Year's Day.

Saturday, January 1, 1949

New Year's Day was highlighted, not by a holiday dinner, but by the radio broadcast of the Rose Bowl game between the Northwestern Wildcats, coached by Bob Voights — who played under Lynn Waldorf — and the California Bears, under Waldorf himself. Although Cal lost, 20 to 14, it was a tremendously exciting game with long runs — Frank Aschenbrenner of Northwestern ran 73 yards in the first quarter for a touchdown, followed by a 67-yard touchdown by Jackie Jensen. The game was not without controversy: the referee ruled that Art Murakowski of Northwestern crossed the goal line in the second quarter before losing the football, a ruling disputed by Cal's Will Lotter. Despite the injury to Jackie Jensen in the third quarter that forced him to leave the game, the Bears played extremely well.

Helen and I attended the Rose Bowl game in the next two years.

Monday, January 2, 1950

In South Gate. Leaving the children with their grandparents, Helen and I went to the Rose Bowl game — we had high hopes for the Cal Bears since they had a 10-0 season while Ohio State had a 6-1-2 season. California scored first on Jim Monachino's touchdown. After two touchdowns by Ohio State and another by California, Ohio State finished the game with 1:57 minutes left with an 11-yard field goal by Jim Hague. The final score was 17 to 14 in favor of Ohio State. It was rather sad.

Monday, January 1, 1951 — New Year's Day

In South Gate. Helen and I left the children with their grandparents and rode with Jeanette, Eino, and Bill Jenkins to the Rose Bowl in Pasadena. Before taking our seats at the game, we visited the restrooms and, while waiting for Helen and Jeanette, I saw Senator Richard Nixon, whom I have known since 1948 when we were both honored by being chosen among the nation's ten most outstanding young men. For some reason whenever I think of Richard Nixon, I am reminded of Dr. James Nickson, whom I knew during my Met Lab years, so I introduced Bill to "James" Nixon. When Nixon moved on, Bill remarked that he thought Nixon's first name was Richard.

The game was quite exciting since California scored first in the second quarter by a 39-yard pass play from quarterback Jim Marinos to end Bob Cummings. Unfortunately, Michigan's Don Dufek made two touchdowns in the fourth quarter, and Michigan won, 14 to 6.

During Pappy's Rose Bowl years, Helen and I were privileged to see the game in which Frank Brunk made his miraculous touchdown run.

Saturday, October 15, 1949

In the afternoon Helen and I went to Memorial Stadium to watch the Southern California-California football game, which Cal won 16 to 10. After USC scored and appeared to have won the game, our Frank Brunk caught the kickoff at our goal line and ran through the entire USC team to score a touchdown. Helen and I were sitting in the end zone, watched Brunk receive the kickoff in front of us, and clearly saw his miraculous run down the field.

Another notable occasion during these Rose Bowl years was the game with the University of San Francisco featuring the running of USF's outstanding Ollie Matson.

Saturday, November 18, 1950

After a number of routine tasks and conversations, I had lunch at home and then went alone to Memorial Stadium, in spite of very heavy rain, where California played the University of San Francisco. The USF team is very good and features the running of Ollie Matson. The score was 13 to 7, in favor of California. Helen decided, because of the rain and the fact that some kids are a bit under the weather, that this was a good day to stay home.

The spirit of team unity that Pappy instilled in "Pappy's Boys" was evidenced by a reunion which featured Pappy's Rose Bowl squads on September 22, 1989 at the Berkeley Marina Mariott. I was proud and honored to be a participant in this event:

Friday, September 22, 1989

Helen and I left our Lafayette home at about 6:15 p.m. to drive to the Berkeley Marina Marriott Hotel, where we arrived at about 7 p.m. Here we attended the reception and dinner for "Pappy's Boys," the football players who played at Berkeley during the ten years that Lynn "Pappy" Waldorf was the football coach (1947-1956). The evening was directed toward honoring the three Rose Bowl teams, and a large number of the members of those three teams, as well as other Cal football players, who played both on the Waldorf teams and other teams, were present.

Helen and I sat at a table with Bob Karpe, "Eggs" Manske (one of the coaches, and the only surviving coach of the Waldorf era), Mary Louise Osborne and her husband (she is the daughter of Lynn and Louise Waldorf), and Ed Bartlett and his wife (he played end on three of the Waldorf teams). In the course of the evening we met and talked with a large number of the football players of the Waldorf era.

The after-dinner program began with some short introductory remarks by Jack Hart (co-captain of the California 1958 Rose Bowl team). He introduced Dick Erickson, who served as master of ceremonies. Erickson introduced and called for remarks by Ed Bartlett, Bob Karpe, Mary Cole (Matt Hazeltine's sister), "Eggs" Manske, and Waldorf's other daughter, Carolyn Pickering. He then called on me for remarks, representing the University administration.

I began by expressing the appreciation of Helen and me for being included in this reunion of Pappy's Boys. I said that, in representing the administration, I wanted to say how proud we were of the scholar athletes who had represented the University during the Pappy Waldorf era. I then called attention to the fact that "Seaborg" is an anagram for "Go Bears." I mentioned that I had seen the first football game between Berkeley and UCLA when I was a student at UCLA in 1933 — a game that resulted in a 0-0 tie. I also mentioned the fact that, soon after I started as a graduate student at Berkeley, I went back down to Los Angeles to watch the Berkeley-USC game which was won by California due to the efforts of Arleigh Williams. I said that Helen and I had seen nearly all of the home games played by the football teams during the ten years of the Waldorf era, missing essentially only those games when I was out of town. Also while serving as Faculty Athletic

Representative during part of the Waldorf era, I had on several occasions traveled with the football team. I concluded by reminding them that I served as Chancellor of the Berkeley campus from 1958 to 1961, and it was during this period that the California Bears last appeared in the Rose Bowl.

After my remarks, there were further remarks by "Eggs" Manske. Then the team captains from teams playing in the Rose Bowl in 1949, 1950, and 1951 were introduced, and each took charge of introducing consecutively the players on their teams. The players stood up as they were introduced. The concluding speaker, Pete Schabarum, gave an emotional response on behalf of the players. After the program was over, I went around to talk to Charlie Sarver, the scat back who played on the 1948 and 1949 Waldorf teams. Then, Helen and I drove home, arriving at about 11:30 p.m.

REMEMBERING PAPPY
By Paul Christopulos

⌘

I learned from Pappy Waldorf how to lose with dignity. It is a virtue that many among us sorely lack. Pappy lost three consecutive Rose Bowl games, but each time he stood tall and congratulated the winner.

While I was probably the closest person in the Athletic department at Cal to Pappy, I didn't participate in football. But during the off season I spent more time with him, outside of his family of course, than anyone else. So, I was able to observe Pappy in a variety of different circumstances.

One night Pappy and I had dinner with Frank Spenger, the owner of the famous restaurant in Berkeley. We closed the place down and the three of us sat in a corner and reminisced. At one point, Mr. Spenger pulled out a check, signed it with an "X" and said to Pappy, "You fill it out for whatever you may need [legally, of course] in the Athletic Department." I practically jumped across the table to accept the check. Pappy restrained me, saying, "Frank, the Department has plenty of money. We are not short of funds" (the ASUC in those days had over $3,000,000 in reserves). I told Pappy later, we could have used some additional funds for tutoring money, which came from the outside, and only amounted to about $500 - $600 per year. Pappy cautioned me not to accept anything (and take advantage of anyone's generosity) if it wasn't truly needed.

Throughout the years I was with Pappy, I never once saw him say anything or do anything that was unsportsmanlike. I recall one particular incident where his true sportsmanship came into play.

We were playing UCLA in the Los Angeles Coliseum. Several days before the game, Clark Kerr, chancellor of the University of California at Berkeley, called me (Greg Engelhard, the Athletic Director was out of town), and asked me to bring Pappy and Red Sanders, the UCLA football coach, together before our game to tell them he wanted their teams to play a "clean" game that day. There had been an unfortunate incident the year before, and Kerr did not want it repeated. "I don't want this University to be embarrassed on the football field," Kerr told me. I mentioned this to Pappy before the game, and he agreed to come out of the dressing room and meet in the foyer of the Coliseum. When I went in to ask Coach Sanders to come out, he hesitated but did agree to meet. When the two met, Pappy put his one hand out and the other around Coach Sanders and said, "Red, clean football is the only kind of football you and I coach." "You're right, Lynn," Sanders replied. That was a first rate example of Waldorfian sportsmanship.

Pappy went without hesitation into the visiting dressing rooms of Northwestern, Ohio State and Michigan to congratulate the coaches and players to whom he had just lost three heartbreakers. I remember Pappy telling me later, "It's easy to congratulate your opponent when you're the victor, but it takes a lot of inner strength to be the first one to shake the hand of the winner when you're the loser."

When Pappy had that great winning streak going, he handled his accolades with great modesty. To the media he always spoke of his opponents with respect, no matter what the pre-game odds were (and sometimes the odds were overwhelming.) One columnist in San Francisco wanted to do a piece on Pappy comparing him with the legendary Andy Smith, but when Norrie West, the Sports Information Director, approached Pappy on the subject, he flatly refused. He later told me that Smith should remain beyond comparison. "Honestly," he said, "I don't deserve to be in the same category as Smith."

During the off season Pappy made it a point to be in contact with opposing coaches. One basic reason was to offer assistance or moral support to those whose jobs might be in jeopardy. When Marchie Schwartz seemed about to lose his job at Stanford, Pappy met with him several times during the off season and spoke to Alfred Masters, the Athletic Director at Stanford, on his behalf. The same was true of Jeff Cravath at USC. Pappy and I spent three full days and nights at the West Coast Relays one year with Jeff. And I recall how Jeff poured his heart out to Pappy, and Pappy volunteered to come to his assistance.

And the same was true of a coach at Kansas State at that time and a couple of coaches elsewhere, whose names and schools I can't recall at the moment. I remember Pappy telling me, "Always offer yourself to be of help to others. Don't look for any recompense. That will come when the person you helped does a good turn for somebody else along the way. Good deeds will make the world a better place."

Pappy was an absolute master at dealing with the media. He taught me several things about these relationships:

* Always return the calls you get from media representatives.

* Always be truthful.

* If possible, be as general as you can, after you've given them what they want to know.

* Spend time with media representatives during the off season. This will hold you in good stead when you're talking with them in the heat of battle.

Both in our travels and at home, Pappy and I would philosophize about life in general, about philosophical subjects (we spent a whole weekend once discussing Plato's "Republic" which I had read in my Philosophy 6A class at Cal). And Pappy said one of the main characteristics of famous men is that they showed initiative. They were creative.

I had shown some creativity when I first met Pappy in his first spring football practice in 1947. I had just returned from the east coast where I had received a Masters Degree from Johns Hopkins University. I asked Pappy if I could stop in and see him the following Monday, and he said, "Of course." So over the weekend, I wrote a nine-page paper on what I thought the Athletic Department should be. Let me say at this point, that I often visited the Athletic Department when I was in high school in Stockton, so I was familiar with the coaches, Athletic Directors (Ken Priestly, Bill Monahan) and others. So I knew what was missing.

Pappy read the paper, and that's how I was hired at Cal. Pappy never forgot that story, and he repeated it to groups all over the state when we travelled. "But don't just rest on your laurels," he would admonish me, "Just keep being creative in your life, and you'll succeed."

Pappy was a fierce believer in making sure that his football players graduated. That was his long-term goal, and he, and we in the department, always worked to that end. When we travelled, he would take pride in the successes of his former athletes at schools like Northwestern and Kansas State. Every time we went to Chicago, he would look up Bill DeCorrevant, the great star from Austin High whom Pappy coached at Northwestern. (At Austin High School in one game, DeCorrevant carried the ball nine times and scored nine touchdowns). He was successful at Northwestern. too, but Pappy was interested in Bill's business accomplishments more than he was in his athletic achievements. And people like Bill and others, especially around Chicago, just loved our Pappy. The graduation rate of the players on Pappy's Rose Bowl teams was 98.9 per cent.

Concern for the environment and ecology is a relatively new phenomenon. Pappy and his wife, Louise, were in the forefront of this development. On our travels throughout California, Pappy took time off, especially if Louise was along, to go inland to see waterfalls, or meadows with tall grass or special kinds of trees. One day we were in the southeastern part of the state, and I recall Pappy and Louise walking through a meadow about three miles long because they were told a certain kind of bird nested there. I, of course, remained in the car for a nice nap. But after that I too became interested, and we visited many areas of the state to search out special geological, ornithological and special natural points of interest. And Pappy would talk about how the environment was being desecrated.

If Pappy hadn't been a coach, he would have made a superb history professor. His knowledge was uncanny. During our travels together when we weren't talking about football, our conversation always turned to history. Pappy was a real Civil War buff. He told me once he had read every book that was published on the Civil War.

But he also knew world history as well. He would talk at great length about the Treaty of Brest-Litovsk (in which the Russians pulled out of World War I). He knew all about the Geneva Conference. He knew about the French Revolution and the steps by which the Ancien Regime evolved into the Jacobin Republic.

I had taken Diplomatic History of the United States (History 167) from the Renowned UC Historian, John D. Hicks, but Pappy knew even more than Hicks did about the Reconstruction Era, the Louisiana Purchase and the War with Mexico. He often talked about what an outstanding Secretary of State John Hay was and how the Hay Treaty helped to reshape U.S. policy in Europe.

I had minored in history at Cal and taken an M.A. in International Business at the School of Advanced International Studies at John Hopkins. And yet, I learned more history from Pappy than in all those courses put together, only because he had a more practical understanding of historical events. I was absolutely fascinated by his description of the Battle of Stalingrad in Russia, for example. I hadn't realized how pivotal that great battle was in re-shaping the map of Europe.

Pappy taught me patience and perseverance. I'll never forget how patient he was when daughter Mary Louise became partially paralyzed, shortly after the Waldorfs moved to California. He knew it was a severe illness, but he didn't panic and he kept Louise, his wife, and daughter Carolyn from panicking as well. He put his faith in the doctors who were treating Mary Louise, and he cautioned them to be understanding and, above all, patient. And Mary Louise recovered.

Pappy always reminded me that we represented a great and renowned academic institution and that we had to be open to all attitudes and viewpoints. We had to be especially careful not to offend alumni and others who were recommending guards who stood 5'6" and weighed 145 pounds, because the following year these same people might be recommending a 6'0", 215-pound running back who placed second in the 100-yard dash in the state track and field meet.

One early evening Pappy and I boarded the Lark, the train from Jack London Square in Oakland to Los Angeles, for one of our recruiting forays in Southern California. We had planned to have dinner on the train, retire early and arise fresh the next morning for a full day's work. Shortly after we took our seats at a table in the dining car, a gentleman walked up to us and said, "May I join you gentlemen?" Pappy said, "Yes, of course." The gentleman took his seat, opposite Pappy and said, "You're Pappy Waldorf, aren't you?" Pappy replied, "Yes, and this is Paul Christopulos who works with me." Then Pappy looked at our visitor and said, "And you're Ty Cobb, right?" "Yup, that's me," the guest replied. Well we had a nice dinner, and great conversation followed. Later we retired to the club car for an after -dinner drink, and at about 10:30 p.m. Pappy left us to go to his stateroom, leaving Cobb and me alone. Well, all my life, and especially as a youngster, I was a Detroit Tiger baseball fan. So, here was my opportunity to talk to my life-long baseball idol. And, of course, I asked a hundred-and-one questions. The next thing I saw was Pappy coming down the aisle. It was 7 a.m. and the train was about to pull into Union Station in Los Angeles. "Are you guys still here?" Pappy asked. I was so embarrassed, but Ty Cobb excused the two of us by saying, "Pappy, I've had a fascinating evening here with your colleague." Later, Pappy told me in a nice way that maybe Cobb was saying he had a "fascinating" evening just to exonerate me.

But Pappy did enjoy some "fascinating evenings" of his own. Whenever we played an intersectional team in Berkeley, Pappy would have me wait in the press box until the visiting sportswriters had filed their stories. I would then bring them to the Waldorf home, where he and Louise acted the perfect hosts. One day after our Cal-Wisconsin game, Pappy asked me to bring Wilfred Smith, Sports Editor of the Chicago Tribune, over to his home on LeRoy Avenue. Smith was a great piano player, and after making the rounds and introductions in the Waldorf home, Pappy asked him to play. The evening became a marathon sing-a-long of college songs and old time favorites. Then at one point, Pappy took me into the kitchen and said that it was now seven o'clock Sunday morning, and would I be good enough to drive Smith to the San Francisco airport for his 9 a.m. flight to Chicago. Obviously, I couldn't (and wouldn't) say no. So off to San Francisco we went.

Pappy and I always attended Big C Board of Directors meetings at the Claremont Country Club together. On one occasion, following the meeting, several of us adjourned to Bud's Tavern nearby. When we closed Bud's at 2 a.m. we went over to the home of Nibs Price (Brick Muller and Harold Breakenridge made me call and awaken him) just down the street in Piedmont. So Muller, Breakenridge, Waldorf, Tessier (line coach Bob Tessier) and I arrived at 2:30 a.m. at the home of poor Nibs. Then before I knew it, Brick Muller dialed the Breakenridge's home, also in Piedmont, and when the lady at the other end of the line answered, Brick handed me the telephone receiver. Of course, it was Mrs. Breakenridge, and Brick yelled into the telephone speaker after I had apologized to Mrs. B. profusely, "We want to come over for breakfast." I was stunned and embarrassed. But gracious as she was, Mrs. Breakenridge said, "I would love to have you all over for breakfast." What else could the poor woman say? And, off we went to the Breakenridge home and had a delicious 4 a.m. breakfast of pancakes, ham, bacon, eggs, sliced potatoes, coffee, and hot chocolate.

And, I drove the troops home.

THE CAL COACHING STAFF
1947-48-49-50
by Edgar (Eggs) Manske

⌘

As the last remaining member of Pappy's coaching staff that migrated from Northwestern to the University of California, it is indeed a pleasure and honor to write this chapter on the Cal coaches. I would like to dedicate it to their wives. I think everyone will agree that it's the wife who makes the family a liveable unit. The man undoubtedly gives it its basic roots, but it is the woman who nourishes it to maturity. I'm sure that Louise, Fran, Meredith and Jane had a lot to do with our success as coaches at Cal.

In picking a football coaching staff it's very important that the coaches be compatible with the rest of the faculty. The players they select should also meld into the regular student body and not be isolated from the other students.

When Pappy came to California in 1947, we all knew that Athletic Director Brutus Hamilton chose the right man at the right time for the right university. Both Brutus and Pappy shared the same deep feeling on how best to use Cal's student athletes. I would like to think Pappy chose his original staff for the same reasons.

My personal contact in football as a player and as an assistant coach with eight different head coaches, gives me some expertise in evaluating Pappy Waldorf as a great coach and a great human being. Pappy was a unique individual who was the son of a Methodist Bishop, a philosophy graduate and an outstanding football player at Syracuse University. Pappy was a great thinker, a great speaker and a great humanitarian. He would have been the best in any endeavor he wished to pursue. He chose football coaching because he loved the challenge of taking young college kids and developing them into good football players and outstanding men. Pappy was a man who could see the forest as well as the trees. His great success as a head coach stemmed from his ability to pick assistant coaches who were well-versed in the basic fundamentals of the game. He also gave them the authority to get the job done. His practice organizational ability was outstanding; there was no lost motion or wasted time. On game days Pappy always let the team know he had faith that it would prevail.

Pappy's success at Kansas State, Northwestern and California didn't just happen. Pappy planned it that way. Whenever Pappy took on a new assignment, he had the great ability to organize his assets and move quickly to the top. His first year at Northwestern, he beat Notre Dame, and was named "Coach of the Year." In his second year, He won the Big Ten championship. He was off to the same start at California in 1947-48-49 and 50. Pappy's regular season record in his first four years at Cal of 38 wins, one tie and one loss should be something special for all of his Boys.

Wes Fry was our offensive coordinator and backfield coach. Wes and Pappy were about the same age. Wes was a great football player at the University of Iowa and got both his bachelors degree and law degree from Iowa.

Wes was Pappy's offensive coordinator and backfield coach at Kansas State when they were Big Eight champions. When Pappy came to Northwestern, Wes took over as head coach at Kansas State and remained there for several years. He again joined Pappy at Northwestern during the war years.

Both Pappy and Wes were single wingback coaches and used that system to great success. When the Chicago Bears beat Washington, 73 - 0 in the NFL

Championship game, all the colleges became interested in the Bear T formation. Northwestern adopted it some time later with the help of Luke Johnsos who was the Chicago Bear head coach during the war years. Wes Fry's expertise in the fundamentals of offensive backfield play was the main reason why Cal's backs were so great.

Bob Tessier, our offensive and defensive line coach, had been a great player at Tulane, graduating with a degree in physical education. He had coached at the University of Idaho before World War II and had joined Pappy at Northwestern in 1946. Bob had a low key approach and great patience, and he would work long hours with individual players until a play was done correctly.

I met Wes and Bob for the first time at Pappy's home in Evanston before we all made the move to Berkeley. Pappy outlined our basic responsibilities, and then he talked about some of the problems at Cal. He felt we had to develop more alumni groups -- like the San Francisco Grid Club and the Southern Seas -- to seek out qualified student athletes. Pappy also invited Nibs Price to be a member of his staff. Nibs, Cal's head basketball coach, would not only work with us during spring training but would help in developing the sort of alumni clubs Pappy wanted throughout the state.

Since I had played four years with the Chicago Bears, had installed the "Bear T" at Holy Cross in 1941 and had been an assistant to Clark Shaughnessy, the so-called Father of the Modern T-Formation, at Maryland in 1946, I felt I knew as much about coaching that offense as anyone. But after our first meeting, it was obvious that Wes Fry would be in control of our offense. Since I was driving out to California, I offered to take Wes with me so we could discuss the offense that he and Pappy had used at Northwestern. By the time we reached Berkeley, I knew pretty well that we would be primarily a running team and that I would need to develop big ends who would be good blockers and capable short pass receivers.

The staff decided that we would not bring our families west during the six weeks of spring practice, so we all stayed at the Durant Hotel and spent a lot of time together. We had staff meetings at breakfast, lunch and dinner. Our Saturday night dinners were always in San Francisco, because Pappy enjoyed eating at fine restaurants. Somehow, though, we always ended up at Shanty Malone's bar for a nightcap.

Since Wes controlled the offense, Bob and I had to team up to get any of our ideas discussed. If Wes disapproved of our suggestions, Pappy would table them for later discussion. It took me a full year to get a buck pass into our offense.

In March of 1947, Pappy invited anyone who wanted to play football out for spring practice, and the flood gates opened wide. I had never seen such a mass of humanity on a football field before -- all walk-ons. We coaches were overjoyed when the two basketball coaches, Nibs and Zeb Chaney, offered to help out.

Right from the first day, the staff decided we would have to play our best athletes, regardless of position, on the first three teams. Personal desires had to give way. The Culloms and the Bakers had to move from fullback to tackle and guard. We didn't think they had a chance to beat out the Jensens and the Swaners. By the end of spring practice we ended up with three pretty good quarterbacks, Dick Erickson, Tim Minahen and Bob Celeri, each with different abilities. In '47 and '48 Dick always started our ball games because he was the least excitable and seemed to have a stabilizing influence on the team. Pappy was deathly afraid of fumbles in those opening minutes of every ball game.

It was a rare occasion when I had the pleasure of seeing my ends perform on Saturday. Usually, I was in Seattle, Los Angeles, Palo Alto, Madison or Minneapolis, scouting the opposition.

My briefing to the staff on Sunday evenings at Pappy's home was always a bit unusual. Pappy would be sitting back in his big easy chair, smoking his sweet-smelling pipe, with a gleam in his eye, while Wes, Bob and Nibs would be picking my brains clean. Those Sunday evening meetings were always crucial in that it set the pattern for our practice and game play for that week. Every assistant coach who scouted for Pappy had to answer one simple question: "How can we win?" and you had better have a logical answer.

Our fourth game that 1947 season was with Wisconsin, a team that had beaten Cal, 28-7, the year before. I spent a lot of time analyzing films for my week of scouting the Badgers. I wanted to make sure I was well-prepared. Wisconsin was coached then by Harry Struhldreher, who had quarterbacked Notre Dame's famous Four Horsemen backfield. When I returned from my scouting trip on Sunday, I told Pappy that Wisconsin had a weakness in the defensive backfield which we could exploit. I said that Struhldreher's defensive right half was slow reacting on pass plays and that we should be able to score a couple of early touchdowns by streaking our left end right past him.

Pappy listened for awhile and then popped up and said, "You mean to say Harry is still burying his worst defensive back at that right half spot?" I said, "Pappy, why in hell didn't you tell me that before I left?" Pappy cleared his throat and said, "Well, I was just testing to see if you could find it." Let the record show that we scored two early touchdowns over the Wisconsin right half and won the game, 48-7. After that, Pappy always respected my scouting reports.

After a few years of going with the complete team concept, the staff decided we could best use our personnel by adopting the offensive and defensive team concept. It gave us greater flexibility in utilizing the special talents of individual players. It also extended Cal's domination of the Coast Conference for an additional two years.

One sad note was sounded in those years of ringing success, the death from a cerebral blood clot of Bob Tessier on November 28, 1950, just three days after the Stanford game. Bob's association with his players was so personal that he treated them as part of his family. His death was a devastating blow to all of us, and I feel certain the grief his players suffered had a great bearing on the outcome of the Rose Bowl game, which we lost to Michigan, 14-6.

In my six years at California, I was amazed by the cooperation and the dedication of its people to the University. It was my pleasure to have known President Sproul and his booming voice, Dr. Kerr, Dean Freeborn and Dr. Seaborg (our faculty advisors); Professors Garff Wilson and Dr. Palm, Vice President Jim Corley and alumni Executive Secretary Stan McCaffrey.

The University of California has had its great days in the sun. The Andy Smith, the Stub Allison and the Waldorf dynasties will always be a source of pleasure to all the Old Blues. There is no doubt in my mind that Pappy's Boys hold a very special place in the hearts of all who coached them. It may be said of them that:

They walked through the front door at Cal like other students.
They worked their way through Cal like other students.
They graduated in four years like other students.
They are all very successful in their chosen professions.
They have accomplished it all! What else is there?

In closing, I would like to pay special tribute to the 1947 football squad. Many were war veterans who were at Cal to get an education and to enjoy playing football. They set the standards for the 1948-49-50 Rose Bowl teams.

OUR FATHER, LYNN O. (PAPPY) WALDORF
by Carolyn Waldorf Pickering and Mary Louise Waldorf Osborne

⌘

> "It is my conviction that nearly every boy playing football, on whatever level, enjoys the game. If a player does not derive some enjoyment from both the practices and the games, then certainly he is missing the most important part of football. Every player should be able to look back on incidents in his football career that made him a stronger, wiser, finer person. The humorous incidents, of which there should be many, are as valuable as any others."
>
> Lynn O. Waldorf, This Game of Football

Dedicated to his wife, Louise:

"To my wife Louise
Who, for twenty-seven years has provided
Appreciation in victory
Support in defeat, and stability
in an unstable profession."

When Horace Greeley wrote in the mid-19th century, "Go West young man, go West", little did he know the response he would get! One who heeded that call in the spring of 1947 was Lynn O. Waldorf. Born the son of a Methodist minister in Clifton Springs, New York in 1902, he had lived his entire life east of the Mississippi before 1947. He graduated from Cleveland's East High School in Ohio, then went on to Syracuse University. His father had graduated from there in 1900 and lettered in baseball. The senior Waldorf went on to become a minister, starting at Century Methodist Church in New York, then to Wichita, Kansas, Cleveland, Kansas City, Missouri, before becoming Resident Bishop for the Chicago area in 1931, where he remained until his death in 1943.

Our father grew up in a family of five -- a sister and three brothers. It was hoped that each son would become a minister, but all three became coaches instead. Sister Ethel Margaret did, however, marry a Methodist minister, letting the boys off the hook.

John Waldorf coached football and basketball a few years at Nebraska Wesleyan University while serving as athletic director. He graduated from Missouri where he lettered in basketball and football (Captain in 1929 as fullback and linebacker) for Coach Gwin Henry. He was twice a member of the All Conference team in football and was second team All League in basketball. In 1930, he played in the East-West Shrine game. He officiated for 26 years for the Big Eight and became the only man to officiate in five major Bowls: Orange, Sugar, Cotton, Gator and Rose. John was also a member of the NCAA Rules Committee. He and Dad would see each other over the years at conventions, each always working to improve the game.

Paul Waldorf coached at McKendree College in Lebanon, Illinois. He then went on to teach Spanish at a college in Mankato, Minnesota.

Robert, nearly 20 years younger than Dad, graduated from Missouri in 1940. He was a second string All American that year. He was picked for the Big Eight All Star team and played in the College All Star game in Chicago that year. His coaching career began at Marquette in Milwaukee, followed by two years in the service in World War II. He went on to coach at various high schools and colleges in Maryland and Virginia until he retired in 1976 to live in Arlington, Virginia.

Early on, Dad developed a great fondness for books. Perhaps this stemmed from an after-school job stoking coal at the local library, where he often conversed with the janitor on many subjects, or so the story goes.

Dad played and loved football since high school days at Cleveland, where his team won the City title his senior year. It was on to Syracuse University in 1920, where he played football and was a member of the rowing team until he grew too heavy. As a sophomore, Dad was a varsity lineman substitute, but he wanted to do better, so in the spring he asked his father to help him find the hardest work he could for vacation. This resulted in his employment with the C.H. Voel Construction Co. where he carried bricks for the entire summer. He lost 15 pounds but went back hard as nails. He wrote his father that the opposing players felt like "featherbeds" to him. He won a starting position in the line at right tackle. This team was unbeaten and defeated powerful Nebraska. He went on to be named second string All American on Walter Camp's team in 1922 and again in 1924.

Although he rarely talked about football at home, he did tell us how his story related to two of his own Cal players who worked in the woods during the summer running five miles to and from their jobs to condition themselves for football.

Dad and Mom, Louise Jane McKay, were married in La Grange, Illinois, August 14, 1925. They had met in college at Syracuse University as freshmen. They were both active in student life, Mother being a Tri Delta sorority member and Dad, a Pi Kappa Alpha. Dad was to be invited many times to the Berkeley Chapter and we lived next door to a former housemother, Mrs. Camper, on LeRoy Avenue. Also, over the years, Dad developed a close friendship with Berkeley Chapter member and Dramatic Arts Professor at Cal, Garff Wilson.

Our parents' courtship took place mostly on the Syracuse campus. They spent much time strolling through Morningside Cemetery which borders the campus. Later both Bishop and Mrs. Waldorf were buried there, as are now Dad and Mother.

Their Midwest background would produce strong feelings of character. Dad used to say, "If you say you will do something, do it!" To be faithful and trustworthy was important to both parents and your word on anything was to be kept. This no doubt has rubbed off on all who knew them. This wasn't to say Dad was harsh; quite the opposite. When we got into trouble for picking on each other, or being picked on, or any other childish infractions, Dad would hear what happened, then send the offender outdoors to pick a switch. Of course we would come back with the puniest of twigs. We both laughed and then a small lecture would follow...the point was made and remembered.

The Waldorf family got its German understatement from the Bishop and its wonderful Scottish candidness from my five-foot Grandmother who kept all that Waldorf beef in line. Grandfather advised, "Don't be a herd thinker, yet don't be 'agin' 'em' (the majority) just to be 'agin' 'em'." He cited the example of the goose..."Draw a circle around a goose, and put food on the outside of that circle...The goose won't cross the line to get it. If you have the conviction of right in your heart and mind, don't be afraid to cross the line." Because of his calling he used a biblical parallel..."When the Israelites, who had fled Egypt and were in the desert, were nearing the promised land, twelve spies were sent out to see if Israel could win the fight for the land. Ten came back and said, 'No way...That land has a fellow bigger than Primo Carnera,' but two others, Joshua and Caleb, said, 'Let's take 'em,' and that was the decision taken, and it was the correct one." Such was the decision by Dad to leave Northwestern and go West to meet the challenge as only he could have done. He also had the ability to choose his assistant coaches well during his career.

Upon graduation in 1925, our father began as head coach at Oklahoma City University. Not only that, but he got to help build and paint the locker rooms before classes and the season began. From that time on he did little of that sort of thing at home until retirement. All the coaching staff at Northwestern during the war years had "victory gardens" on the outskirts of Evanston on special plots. Carolyn learned to dislike summer squash then, and it stayed with her until we moved to California with all its wonderful fruits and vegetables. Oklahoma City University won the conference championship in 1927 with an 8-1-2 record after going 4-6-0 in 1925 and 5-4-1 in 1926.

In 1928 he moved on to Kansas as line coach. Mary Louise was born by then. From 1929-1933 he coached at Oklahoma A&M (now Oklahoma State University) where his teams went 4-3-2 the first year and then went on to conference championships every year except 1930 when they were co-champions. During this time Carolyn arrived on the scene in Stillwater, with its dust storms--Mother used to line the window sills with wet towels. Carolyn also remembers Mary Louise's kindergarten burning down.

It was during this period that Dad became acquainted with Wesley "Plowboy" Fry, and a long a fruitful friendship and coaching association would develop for both. Wes was born in Iowa. His parents died when he was fairly young, and he was brought up by various family members and friends. He carried the nickname "Plowboy" through college. He played football well, presumably, since he went on to play professional ball with Red Grange and the New York Yankees after graduation. He married Fran, also from Iowa, in 1927, and went on to graduate from law school in 1928. He then coached at Classen High School in Oklahoma City and Oklahoma City University in 1932. It was during this time, while Dad was at Oklahoma A&M that he and Wes met. Dad went back to Kansas State University in 1934 as head coach, and Wes joined him there. Kansas State went on to win its only Big Six Championship ever. All American tackle George Maddox played that year. At the 50th reunion of that 1934 Championship team, former player Myron Rooks said Dad "was one of those congenial coaches who could get right with you and play football. He had charisma and charm, and he could really get the most out of his players." The thing Rooks remembers most about Coaches Bo McMillin the year before and Lynn Waldorf in 1934, is that neither one of them ever, ever, said a cuss word. Except for one time! "It was the Nebraska game when we won the championship and we were getting whipped at the half, 7-0. We had our halftime briefing and at the end of it, Coach Waldorf said, 'Now get the hell out of here.'"

Wes and Fran had two boys approximately the same ages as we Waldorf girls. Later at Northwestern daughter Meredith was born. It was at the end of that year, 1934, that Dad moved us to Wilmette, Illinois, where he became head coach of Northwestern University in Evanston. Wes stayed on as head coach at Kansas State until 1940 when he rejoined Dad's staff at Northwestern.

Dad was elected the first Coach of the Year in 1935. The next year Northwestern won the Big Ten Championship. While at Northwestern he helped develop eight All American players: 1935 Paul Tangora, Guard; 1936 Steve Reid, Guard; 1938 Robert Voigts, Tackle; 1939 John Haman, Center; 1940 Alf Bauman, Tackle; 1943 Otto Graham, Halfback, and Herb Hein, End; and 1945, Max Morris, End.

Carolyn was only fifteen when Dad took the Cal job. The decision to go to California and leave all her friends and New Trier High School seemed unbearable. But survive she did, and very well, for change and opportunity were really ahead. During this era she acquired the name, "Pepper", from either Waldo Fisher or Wes because she was the official greeter for the coaches as they arrived for meetings at our home. Carolyn's main interest in those days was horses. During the season she would be dropped off in the morning and spend the day at the stables and be picked up at five. This pleased everyone. It was all English riding style. No one rode Western, except West of the Mississippi. It was a wonderful way to spend the Saturdays of football weekends.

When the City of San Francisco pulled into the Berkeley station in February of 1947, and Dad got off, he was greeted by Brutus Hamilton, the athletic director whom then-President Robert G. Sproul had sent out to find a coach meeting the high standards of the University of California. Brutus was the ideal athletic director and represented the University well. Dad was quoted as saying, "I'm delighted to be connected with a school where the students take an active interest in athletics. That's a healthy set-up." Two sportswriters were at the station, Bob Brachman of the San Francisco Examiner, and Ed Schoenfeld of the Oakland Tribune. Ed and Dad would host a Sunday noontime radio show for a number of years. Dad always had good relations with the sportswriters. There were many who came to the house. Dad was back and forth that Spring between Illinois and California along with Wes Fry (the only other Northwestern staff member), and they were joined by Eggs Manske and Bob Tessier. These wonderful men went west to bring the Bears to life, and were assisted by UC'ers Nibs Price and Zeb Chaney. Hal Grant was brought up from Southern California to coach the freshmen. Over the years numerous student coaches were added, including Frank Van Deren, Rod Franz, Jim Cullom, John Ralston, Ray Willsey, Mike White and others who in turn went on to their own coaching careers. What a fine tribute to the game and to Dad.

We came west as soon as school was out. Mary Louise was a junior at Syracuse by then. We stayed at the Durant Hotel and Pixie, our dog, stayed at the vet's until the house we rented was ready. We lived there until 1954 when the family moved up to the Grizzly Peak home in Berkeley. Mother sold this home in 1985 when she moved into the Santa Rosa retirement complex.

While Dad and staff were busy organizing the 260 or more players who came out for spring practice, we got acquainted and marveled at all the wonders of California.

At the fall scrimmage before the season began, Mother had a luncheon for all the players' and coaches' wives, and then they went over to watch the scrimmage. This became a wonderful tradition that continued until most of the married veterans had graduated. Carolyn, of course, got to help in the kitchen, along with Thelma Kearns, who became Mother's caterer for most of the many parties held at the house after home games. Upwards of 90 invitations would be sent to different alumni and Bear Backers. Mother managed so well. People looked forward to these gatherings, and they played a part in the over-all plan of building alumni relations and University pride.

It was a great time and place to be in. Carolyn graduated from Berkeley High along with some future Cal greats, the Ricksen twins and tennis star Hugh Ditzler. She first went to The University of the Pacific, and then transferred to Cal, graduating in 1954.

1947 and 1948 were exciting years, and Carolyn went to all the home games. The Rose Bowl of 1949 was especially exciting. Just-wed Mary Louise and her husband came out for Christmas and the festivities. We all stayed with the California contingent at the lovely Mission Inn in Riverside, California. We were treated to wonderful luncheons and sightseeing trips, while the team was practicing. In 1949, as a high schooler, Carolyn was feeling a bit awkward, and Jack Swaner, whose kindness she won't forget, bought several of the group a Coke shortly after arrival at the Mission Inn. This made Carolyn feel part of the group, even though she was the coach's daughter. Everyone enjoyed the pool, where Zoe Ann Olsen, fiancee of Jack Jensen and an Olympic diver, and Jane, Eggs Manske's dear wife, also an Olympic swimming and diving star, put on the most beautiful diving exhibition you could imagine. Jane was so talented. She did unique and beautiful ceramics as well as paintings and bronze sculpture. Later, she was commissioned to do the bust of Dad that rests in the Stadium Hall of Fame Room. The bust was dedicated in 1985, and Jane and Carolyn did the unveiling, with a few remarks from Carolyn.

The team appeared twice on the Bob Hope Show during the Rose Bowls and watched the Ralph Edwards "Truth or Consequences" show. We saw the Queens crowned and were bused to the Rose Bowl Parades, where we sat in the bleachers, were served orange juice and given corsages to wear. The only imperfect things were the scores. But everyone still enjoyed victory celebrations, and one alumnus sent up a washtub of champagne that first year.

The years 1947 to 1956 were golden at the University. One cannot write about Cal without mentioning the great Cal Band. The musicians were so spirited. They used to gather below the dressing room balcony after the games and serenade until Dad and some of the players came out and talked to the fans. They even came up several times to serenade Dad at the house, and we lived six blocks from North Gate, all uphill. They presented him with a silver cigar box he would always cherish.

Dad learned early just how important the Big Game was. The Bears were 40 point favorites in 1947 -- going in with one loss to USC. But they were behind when Jackie Jensen threw a wobbly pass that Paul Keckley caught and ran for 80 yards and the touchdown that gave us a 21-18 win. We learned right then what can happen in the Big Game. Dad's record against Stanford was 7-1-2.

Dad's biggest source of pride was that so many of his players graduated with degrees. "Players should enter school in the same manner as the non-athletes," he always said. "They should continually progress towards graduation. Players should have fun playing football. If a player, four years after graduation, is making progress in his career, then he and the school can take credit."

Dad was very proud of the fine All Americans he coached, but he knew and appreciated all those who helped get them the recognition. Long after retirement he could remember almost every freshman and Rambler by name.

Dad had wonderful assistants who were so much a part of Mom's and Dad's life, as well as ours. Carolyn felt like the daughter in an extended family. Bob and Meredith Tessier were part of that family, and his unexpected death in 1950 left a sad void. Meredith was quite an artist, and Mom and Dad had several of her pictures in their home. She even taught Mother to paint, and Carolyn has that picture in her home. Jane and Eggs Manske were special; Jane had such a flair for life.

After Dad retired from coaching, he and Mom were perfectly happy to remain in the Bay Area, which they loved. He had a long association with the Shrine game, and chaired its Selection Committee for the West in the early 70's. He worked for the San Francisco 49ers as Personnel Director and Scout for nearly 15 years. He had a great respect for the Morabito family and Lou Spadia. He was able to go to schools to find talent that no other professional could get to, and this must have helped the relations between college and pro ball. One of his projects was to help players plan for the future in both college and pro ball whenever he could. He retired in 1972, and the 49ers put on a civic dinner in his honor at the Fairmont Hotel which was attended by nearly a thousand people. He traveled a lot during his years with the 49ers, occasionally to Preservation Hall for jazz, in New Orleans. As a Civil War buff, he had respect for the South and its heritage. He worked as a U.C. fund raiser in the early days of the Robert Gordon Sproul Associate program. His greatest reward was working with and developing his players at California. It was a unique time and experience for all. That the players went on to form "Pappy's Boys" shows the mutual respect and admiration that they shared. The support Pappy's Boys have so successfully given to the football program and the University is a credit to all. The Waldorf family is very proud and grateful.

Mom and Dad had been out for dinner with Jim and Marty Cullom and Dick and Jan Erickson to celebrate their 56th wedding anniversary. They had such a wonderful time. The next day, Dad went for his daily walk, and he died. A very meaningful Memorial Service was held in Memorial Stadium on August 26, 1981 with players and coaches and friends well represented. He was buried back in Syracuse, where a poem he had written was read:

"TO WHOM IT MAY CONCERN"

From those who talk and will not do,
From those who take and will not give,
Deliver us.
From over-kill and under care,
From lack of water and polluted air,
Spare us.
To walk a ways in the other man's shoes,
Lead us.
For this small stagnant pool from our river of dreams,
Forgive us.

And here is Carolyn's small limerick for Pappy's Boys:

There once was a man of renown,
Who went west where fame would be found
With his boys most remarkable,
Built a legacy unstoppable,
And a bond that went on and on.

The following excerpts were taken from an audio taped interview between Pappy Waldorf and Assistant Coach (under Marv Levy) Rocky Carzo three days prior to Coach Waldorf's death in August, 1981.

On his college playing days at Syracuse University:

"I played three years as a regular under (Coach) Chick Mean, who was a wonderful man and, I think, a great coach...The three years I played I weighed 197, 195 and then came back weighing about 230 my senior year. Chick got me down to 198 and then I leveled off at about 210...I'm very proud of our record in 1923. We lost one game to our rival, Colgate, but we won all the others...We had a strong defensive team. And I enjoyed football very much. I was, I guess, what you would call a walk-on...My father being a Methodist minister, I got half my tuition from the church and eventually I did get some help, my junior year, I guess, with the other half of my tuition. That's all I ever got. But there wasn't much heavy recruiting in those days."

On his first coaching job at Oklahoma City University, 1925 through 1927:

"I majored in philosophy at Syracuse, minored in sociology, and I never took any physical education courses or education courses, or anything on how to coach football...In fact, I never could have coached in high school because I didn't have the necessary degrees...I didn't know what I was going to do when I graduated...My father was a Methodist bishop and I think President Antrum of Oklahoma City University knew I'd played football at Syracuse, and so he inquired whether I was interested...I didn't know what I was getting into. I became a head coach because I had to...My first practice, 14 guys showed up...We finally scrounged around and got a few more people out, but when we finally got a team together, six out of the starting eleven had never played in high school and our line averaged 158 pounds from end to end...Oklahoma City had been in the Oklahoma Collegiate Conference for four years and it had never won a game in the conference. We won a couple that first year....By my last year we had a pretty good team. We won the conference championship---tied for it. Won eight games I think it was, something like that. We beat Haskell University, which at that time had a record of 26 unbeaten games....The second year we broke the school's record for gate receipts by taking in $87.50"

On coaching at Oklahoma A & M (now Oklahoma State), 1929 through 1933:

"We just won 34, lost 10 and tied seven. But the thing I was proudest of, we had two big rivals---Tulsa and Oklahoma. And on the first play in the second quarter of the first year, Oklahoma scored on us and never again...Oklahoma A & M then had 2200 students, I recall, and we did not get the top athletes. So we went for numbers. I learned how to handle numbers. In the average year there we would have 120 freshmen and 80 varsity candidates. That's in the fall. We had more in the spring. and we had one freshman coach and three volunteer coaches. One was head of the agronomy department, one was the YMCA secretary."

On coaching at Kansas State, 1934:

"We had an interesting team at Kansas State. It looked like you reached into the student body blindfolded and grabbed the first eleven guys you could find. We had one end who was 166 pounds, the other was 220...The left guard was Dan Partner, with a club foot. He later became the science editor of the Denver Post...Well, the thing I loved about that team was that in all of our ten games, no one scored on us in the fourth quarter. We scored 77 points in the fourth quarter and won most of our games. We won the championship, incidentally---the last championship Kansas State has won."

On coaching at Northwestern, 1935 through 1946:

"At Northwestern, we had 13, 14, 15 players just about as good as anybody else. But after that, it dropped off...In 1935, we had an average season, although we beat Notre Dame for the first time since 1902. In 1936, we won the championship, the only undivided championship Northwestern has ever won, I believe...In '46, my last year there, we had a pretty good team. We started off real well, tied Michigan and beat Minnesota. The first five games we did real well and then we had a few kids hurt and so Illinois beat us toward the end and then Ohio State. But we had a pretty fair team. Then I had a chance to come to California."

On coming west to Cal:

"We liked San Francisco very much. And I always had it in the back of my mind that if ever I had the chance to come to the coast and coach at either California or Washington, I would take it. So we came to California, and, again, this was just after World War II when there was a tremendous number of veterans back. My first spring, we had 255 out for spring training. They weren't all football players...Anyway, they were a fine group...I thought, 'We're gonna go someplace'..."

On Cal academics:

"In the ten years I was there we graduated 96 per cent of our lettermen, and they were fine people. When I came from Northwestern I was a little concerned about the ASUC running things, but I never had any trouble...The thing that was great was that our athletic director was Brutus Hamilton, one of the finest people who ever lived...Herman Spindt was the director of admissions when I was there. And he was tough, but he was fair. One time I went to his office with two transcripts. He looked at the first one and said, 'If this individual will come to summer school and get a B and a C, I'll admit him.' He looked at the other one and said, 'No, I can't admit this individual---must go to a junior college. The first one was Johnny Olszewski, the second one was my daughter."

JACKIE JENSEN

by Katharine Jensen

⌘

Jackie Jensen died on July 14, 1982. He was buried on a hilltop in Amherst County, Virginia overlooking the Blue Ridge Mountains on a windy summer day. As the ropes lowered the plain wood casket into the red earth a thought struck me: it was like the creaking of a ship's rigging. So this descendant of Vikings left a rather short and storm-tossed life when he'd at last found a safe haven. His tombstone reads VIR FORTIS ET CLEMENS ERAT (He was a strong and gentle man).

In the spring of 1973 Jack left Nevada to coach baseball at Cal Berkeley. He went eagerly as to a meeting with a sweetheart of one's youth, only to find her much changed. Irreconcilable differences prevailed and after a few years Jack was forced to see what to me had seemed inevitable. The lingering tone of the sixties and the tighter structure of college athletics had not married well with Jack's background and personality. So, regretfully leaving many excellent friends and what had basically been a delightful life, Jack survived a time which I so feared would prove fatal to him, as several years earlier he'd had a major heart attack.

As we drove across the country to find a small farm in Virginia, he kept asking, "What will it be like?" Drawing on childhood memories of farm life, I described how we would have an orchard, grapevines, a vegetable garden and how we could warm ourselves by a wood fire.

And so it was. We found a lovely old plantation house, formerly known as Oakland, in Fluvanna county, and worked hard together to do all the things we'd dreamed of. We had a firewood business and Jack worked as a carpenter and read about Jefferson and the Civil War. We cleared fields to establish a Christmas tree plantation, and Jack helped with the baseball program at the nearby Fork Union Military Academy.

Like Jefferson, he kept a daily record of weather and work done and garden notes. He maintained a wide correspondence, and became enamored of simple country ways. In the mornings he drove his '68 Ford pick-up truck to the small town of Scottsville on the James River to have coffee with the guys. Jack shot groundhogs to protect our beautiful garden and kept the plantation neatly groomed. We canned vegetables, cracked nuts, split firewood, went to church and had the fulfilling joy of sitting among our white columns, sipping juleps, knowing we were using mind and body to create beauty and productivity on what had been a quasi-abandoned property.

Finding the administration of the academy to be like-minded, he was invited to start a baseball camp there. This was the best of all worlds. It went well. He played in "Old Timers" games around the country and caught up on old times with Ted Williams, Joe DiMaggio, Yogi Berra, Mickey Mantle and went home to tie up his tomato plants. His favorite song was Hank Williams Jr.'s "A Country Boy Can Survive."

He was asked to serve on the President's Council for Physical Fitness. He had lunch at the White House where he and (then) Vice President George Bush exchanged autographs. They had been opponents in the Yale-Cal encounter during the first College World Series of Baseball in 1947. Back on the farm, his peacocks hatched their first brood. As the peahen strode out of her nesting area of our hay field (which Jack had protectively fenced) with tiny peeping peachicks behind her, Jack rushed into the kitchen with twinkling eyes. "We're grandparents!!"

Fit and tan, broad-shouldered and narrow-hipped at 55 he was prepared for his second baseball camp, and looking forward to playing in the first all star old-timers game in Washington D.C. The third day of the camp he unexpectedly came home to watch the Major League All Star game with me. "Why not with the coaches at camp?" I silently wondered.

I think he knew he was going to die that night. At 2 am he had pains in his chest, and I called the rescue squad. He walked to the ambulance and advised me to follow in the car. I felt paralyzed. I seemed to know too. In what seemed an eternity I called the hospital in Charlottesville, found his wallet and clothes. I walked out into the night and heard a bobcat scream at the edge of the woods. Jack was gone. In the best possible way. He "quit winners" as the gamblers in Nevada used to say.

He had conquered his fear of flying. He had made an old plantation come back to life. He had created a successful business. He never stopped growing intellectually and had the stated personal goal of helping someone each day of his life.

He was a rare sort of man. We may all be created equal, but some grow closer to heaven.

DICK ERICKSON

⌘

My saga begins back in the 1930's in the California valley town of Stockton. This was a true Sinclair Lewis town complete with a Main Street. Although the country was suffering from the granddaddy of all depressions, I truly was not all that aware of it. It seemed to me that the parents of all our friends and neighbors were gainfully employed. Next door was a barber; on the other side was an elderly lady living by herself; down the other side of the block was the owner-operator of a tire store; a real estate lady lived a few doors down, and we even had an attorney living across the street for awhile.

Looking back on it now, those who did work, worked mighty hard and for long hours. During most of the 30's my Dad always had at least two jobs going. Except for Sunday morning church, Dad worked a seven-day week, and there were also plenty of nights when he was gone.

Recalling my elementary school days two things stand out--first, school and grades were of the utmost importance and second, athletic competition (really play at that age) was a constant. The desire or determination to "meet the kids" so we could get on with the game was a great motivating factor to get that homework done or the piano or trombone practicing completed.

Then it was into the street, over to a vacant lot, or into the large backyard of a neighbor for a game of baseball or football. It's a funny thing, but I really can't recall playing much basketball. I think there might have been a hoop above the garage door in our home out by the College of the Pacific, but my older brother and I rarely used it. Our younger brother, however, obviously found a hoop somewhere as he became an outstanding basketball player.

Baseball (almost always played in the street) started as soon as two guys could get there. You pitched or played the outfield until you could catch a fly ball, and then it was your time to hit. As more guys showed up we would get into a more conventional kind of game. By chalking out a base path on the curbs on both sides of the street and in the middle of the street approximately equidistant from the curb bases we had a "perfect" diamond. Balls tended to wear out fast, and some good black auto repair tape usually extended their lives considerably.

In the late Spring all the way through Summer these pick-up games would go on. Around 5:30 or 6:00 PM the Dads would begin to come home, and, as they joined us, we really got into some serious baseball.

Once August was over, our attention turned to football. The base paths gave way to chalked goal lines, and we developed phenomenal variations on the kick, pass and run games. At a rather young age (around seven or eight, it seems to me) I can remember getting into some great games of tackle football. A friend's grass backyard became our Bowl. Our Moms pretty much ruled against any form of tackle games so we didn't talk much about them around home. One afternoon I got a foot in the mouth, and sure enough a lower front tooth had been chipped off. Mom could not learn about this so I developed a very effective way of talking without moving my lips, or, alternatively, with a hand over my mouth. This was a success for about two days before she learned the truth, and off to the dentist we went for what ultimately became a gold cap in the lower front of my mouth.

This is jumping way ahead (and you will be relieved to know that I do not intend to go into much more about my growing-up years), but let me follow through with this tooth story. In the Fall of 1944 I found myself at the Naval Training Center in San Diego. I had just completed boot camp and was admitted to Quartermaster School. Fall is synonymous with football, so naturally I turned out for the Training Center team. Although I was just over eighteen and most of the team members had two or more years of college competition and several of them had semi-pro experience, I at least was fortunate enough to make the squad. This was a good football team. We beat U.S.C. and U.C.L.A. (with Bob Waterfield) and the only loss I can remember was to the El Toro Marines. At any rate, somewhere along the line (I am not sure whether it was in practice or in a game) that gold cap was kicked out, taking with it a bit more of the original tooth. You know, all that face mask stuff players wear today must save a fortune in dentist fees.

By this time I had finished QM School and received orders (not lighter than air duty which I had requested) to proceed to Camp Bradford outside Norfolk, Virginia, which was a crew organizing base for LST's. On the way there I was able to stop by Stockton long enough to visit my dentist and have an impression made for a replacement cap. Two or three weeks later when it arrived at Camp Bradford, I took it into Sick Bay and requested that it replace the temporary which I had been wearing. Fine they said, but they were not allowed to use novocaine except for extractions. It was wartime, you know. There was no alternative so I boldly told them to go ahead. Like most football players one tends to accept the realities of pain, but I was not ready for this. After removing the cap, the stub of the tooth had to be cleaned, rinsed and blow-dried before gluing on the new cap. I really think this was my worst experience with pain.

The final chapter in this long tooth tale took place on the floor of Memorial Stadium in Berkeley on a Saturday afternoon in the Fall of 1947. T Formation quarterbacks aren't (or, at least in those days, weren't) supposed to get involved in violent activity. But, coming out of some pileup as we were heading toward the South end zone, I knew from the feeling of fresh air hitting a partially exposed tooth nerve that it had happened again. For some reason I felt I should call time out, which I did. Head Trainer Jack Williamson came running onto the field and said, "Dick, what's wrong?" With some difficulty I told him that I had lost a tooth. "What the hell do you want me to do," he said, "get on my hands and knees and look for it? Play ball!" That was that and the game went on. Enough of the real tooth had gone this time that the dentist at long last simply pulled it out.

If you are still with me, let's back up to the mid to late 1930's. We had moved out to the Pacific Manor area just one block from the C.O.P campus. Amos Alonzo Stagg had been pushed out of Chicago University after reaching 65 years of age. He was already a legend to those of us whose world revolved around football. Every afternoon during the Fall (and the Spring practice period too) I would rush from school to home to the C.O.P football practice field. It wasn't long before Mr. Stagg (for some reason I don't believe anyone called him "Coach Stagg", it was always "Mr. Stagg") became aware of my hanging around there every day, and he suggested I help the managers carry the balls out to the practice field and bring them in, as well as pick up towels, dirty jerseys and pants and generally do the dirty work. I was thrilled. One day the player who usually held the ball for PAT practice hadn't shown up, so Mr. Stagg asked me to hold the ball for their fullback and kicker, Phil Martinovich. I had made it!

The Stockton High Tarzans usually played their games under the lights at Baxter Stadium on the C.O.P. campus on Friday nights and the Pacific Tigers played either Saturday afternoon or evening. Dad loved football, too, and if he wasn't working he, along with my older brother, John, would take in those games, and several times each year Dad would drive us on those two lane roads to Palo Alto and Berkeley to see the Indians and the Bears. Although the thought had, I am sure, been there much earlier, it was this exposure to big time football that made me determined beyond any doubt to play in a Rose Bowl game.

Back to Dad and Mom for a moment. Like most people during those hard economic times, I know they struggled. First Congregational Church was an extremely important part of their lives, and, although, as mentioned earlier, Dad usually had two jobs going at once, there was always time for a church committee, Community Chest assignment, some sort of benefit for Dad's Round Table Club or his Masonic Lodge. It was a fact of life that you gave back to your community and to those who needed help.

My heroic Naval career took off in a different direction at Camp Bradford a few short days before I was supposed to leave for the South Pacific aboard my LST. I was called into Headquarters where a crusty old Chief Petty Officer with an arm full of hash marks advised me that "I had my choice." I could stay with my ship or proceed to Bainbridge, Maryland, and the Toombs School which at that time was serving as a Naval Academy Preparatory School. Thinking that that wasn't much of a choice, I went to Bainbridge, and a couple of weeks later on to a hastily established preparatory school at Camp Peary, Virginia. It was a typical snafu. Several hundred of us swabbies had descended on Bainbridge, and they were not expecting us. Solution: a Quonset hut type school at Camp Peary famous for its U.S. Navy prison, an Italian prisoner of war camp and an illiterate Navy boot camp. Annapolis wasn't to be, but in late Spring of 1945 I was ordered to John Carroll University in Cleveland, Ohio, and when that V-12 program was discontinued in September of 1945, it was on to the University of Michigan.

When I first learned that I was headed to Ann Arbor, I hitch-hiked up there and boldly appeared at Coach Fritz Crisler's office to inform him that I wanted to play football for him. He said "sure", but get my "butt" up there as soon as possible. They needed a quarterback for the JV team. About my second week there, we traveled down to Columbus to take on the Ohio State JV's. This is probably hard for any of you who might be even a bit familiar with my Cal playing career, but I was playing defensive left half (left cornerback now) in that huge mostly empty Buckeye stadium when I unbelievably intercepted a pass and ran it in for a touchdown. My only career defensive touchdown!

The following Monday, back in Ann Arbor, Coach Crisler advised me that I had been moved up to the Varsity squad. At first I assumed that this move was due to my sterling defensive play in Columbus, but then I learned that Harry Ponsetto, the starting quarterback, had injured his knee in Saturday's game and was lost for the balance of the season. Howard Yerkes moved up to the starting position, and I came up as his reserve. This was a wonderful experience. Although the 1945 Michigan team was a far cry from Coach Crisler's later teams, there was some real talent there. In fact it was the beginning of the juggernauts that came along in the late '40's. Besides Yerkes, there was Pete Elliott, Dan Dworsky, Leonard Ford, and a number of other outstanding athletes.

This was a great learning experience for me, although as a T formation quarterback, I did not relish Coach Crisler's game plan that included shifting from the T to a single wing formation in short yardage and goal line situations. A blocking single wing quarterback, packing all of 165 pounds, I was not. As a matter of fact a badly executed block from this formation left me with a terribly painful right shoulder, and when the trainer and the doctors at the hospital could not diagnose the problem, it was solved by simply strapping the upper arm with tape to the shoulder each practice and game day . This took care of that deep pain. And that it did for the balance of my playing career (three years). As a matter of fact it wasn't until 1971 when x-ray and other diagnostic procedures had advanced considerably that they found that I had severely torn the tendon coming down the front of my right shoulder. A rather simple (that's what they told me) operation removed the torn portion; the good remaining end was then fed through a hole drilled in my upper arm and it was then spliced back on itself. Voilá--no more pain.

Following that season Coach Crisler called me into his office, and knowing I would soon be discharged from the NROTC unit there (the war was over), invited me to return in the Fall of 1946 and play for the Wolverines. Naturally I was flattered, but after some thought I declined. I was a California boy. Those late cold November afternoon practices in Yost Field House followed by at least a half-hour session outside on a blustery snowy field just were not fun. And besides, the Big Ten schools were not going to the Rose Bowl at that time, and I was going to play in a Rose Bowl game.

Another major event in my life took place while there in Ann Arbor. My thoughtful Theta Delta Chi brothers, following an unusually free-flowing Friday beer and spaghetti dinner at the fraternity house, decided to go to the dance at the Union, and one of them successfully got me a blind date with the roommate of his Kappa Delta girlfriend. I had a great time--at least I was told that I did. On learning that I had had such a wonderful time I thought that I should at least know what she looked like. At those Union dances a couple's picture was taken as you came in, and the following Monday you could check them out at the photography studio down in campus town. I was impressed with what I saw, and that was the beginning of a love affair with Janet Young that resulted in our marriage in June of 1947 and that, thank God, continues today. We have been blessed with four wonderful children--Sally, Hildie, John and Becky, and now six very rewarding grandchildren.

Although Jan's upbringing in Detroit, Michigan was considerably different from mine, it is absolutely amazing how similar our families and family values are. Her grandfather was a minister and her family were also very active members of the Boulevard Congregational Church. As parents they encouraged and assisted their three children to participate in all sorts of activities, and by personal example taught the lessons of service to others.

There isn't a lot to be said about my three years of competition at Cal. Needless to say 1946, with a two and seven record, was a disaster. The opening of Spring practice in 1947 with Pappy Waldorf and his assistants certainly was greeted with much enthusiasm by the sports media and us players as well. None of us, however, in our wildest dreams would have predicted the four seasons that followed. Exclusive of post-season play those seasons from 1947 through 1950 saw Cal with 38 wins, 1 loss and 1 tie.

Academically I had also been making positive progress. As a matter of fact I was on schedule to graduate from the School of Business Administration in June of 1948. Interestingly, due to military and freshman eligibility requirements at that time, I had played four years of college varsity football and still had two years of eligibility remaining. Coach Waldorf was well aware of this, and following our highly successful 9-1 season of 1947, he asked me to stop by his office one afternoon. After pointing out to me the obvious strengths of this team where most of the key players would be returning in 1948, he urged me to consider rearranging my course schedule so as to postpone graduation until January 1949. And "Dick," he said, "I think we have a good chance of going to the Rose Bowl."

Those magic words. Jan was all for it, but she insisted that I try getting into the MBA program. Thanks to some very thoughtful and helpful faculty members, arrangements were worked out, and I received my BS degree in January of 1949 and an MBA degree following the first Summer session in 1949.

Pappy was right. We went undefeated in the Fall of 1948, and Cal was selected as the Pacific Coast Conference representative to the Rose Bowl. We played Northwestern University. We lost, 20 to 14.

When Lynn and Louise Waldorf came to Berkeley there were something like nineteen players who were married. In many ways we found the Waldorfs extensions of our own families. Louise made it very clear to the wives that they needed to prepare themselves for those many nights and weekends when they would see very little of their husbands. Louise urged them to get involved. Work, volunteer, find ways to help others. These were all the same lessons, the same values Jan and I had been taught on both sides of our families.

Thanks to my faculty friends, I became a part of, and ultimately headed, the Business Administration and Economics Division of University Extension, headquartered on Montgomery Street in San Francisco. That led in 1952 to a managership of a public relations and educational organization funded by 166 stock fire insurance companies on the Pacific Coast with offices in San Francisco and Los Angeles. Then in 1957 I was invited back to Cal as the third Executive Manager of the California Alumni Association. There is no doubt in my mind but that position resulted from eight years of volunteer work as well as from my "not for pay" work. There was the alumni board of my fraternity, the board of the Big C Society, service as a volunteer coach with Pappy through 1956 with sideline telephone responsibilities on game days. Also there was the Touchdown Club of San Francisco, the Business Administration Alumni Association which Professor Ted Malm and I organized, and on numerous occasions the giving of talks for the California Alumni Association.

I shall never forget my final interview with the Alumni Association selection committee. There were four or five persons gathered in an office at Alumni House. I had been ill all week with (would you believe it) mumps, and as you would imagine, I wasn't feeling all that great. In my opinion this was really a command appearance, and I wanted that job. The interview evidently went all right; I did get the position. About the only question I remember being asked was one from Sis Collins, an extremely active and dedicated alum from the Class of 1934 who was really aware of everything going on with the University of California. She asked me why I really wanted the position and whether or not I would simply use it as a stepping stone within a year or so to go on to something else? As noted, I did get the job, and for sixteen years (the longest tenure for any Executive Manager) I was privileged to serve the Alumni Association and the University of California. In 1972 I was invited by Chancellor Al Bowker to move over with him as an Assistant Chancellor and organize and run a Development Office. This it was my pleasure to do until my retirement in 1984. At the start we brought in $900,000 and at the end we were bringing in $48,000,000.

Looking back on it all now I cannot but take great delight, pleasure, and honor from the literally hundreds upon hundreds of fantastic people Jan and I were able to get to know well and work with on what we sincerely believe were in the best interests of our Berkeley campus.

The Alumni Association presidents were all something very special starting with Cort Majors and followed by the very able Mort Smith, Jim Archer, Norrie Nash, John Mage, Bill Hudson, Wendell Witter, Chris Markey and George Link.

Then there were Ralph and Barbara Edwards. Ralph came on the Alumni Council (many thought we would be lucky if he got to one meeting a year) and over a period of four years, I do not believe he ever missed a meeting. He was asked and became the founding Chairman of the Robert Gordon Sproul Associates--our $1,000 a year donor group. As a matter of fact he named it. In January of 1959 the Bears again returned to the Rose Bowl, and it was Ralph who single-handedly organized and emceed a fantastic program of Hollywood stars in the Pasadena Civic Auditorium with all income going to the construction of the new Student Union Building.

In 1968 the University of California celebrated its 100th birthday. Under the leadership of Dramatic Arts Professor and Chairman of the Public Ceremonies Committee Garff Wilson we staged an unbelievable year of special events, programs, lectures and even produced a book entitled AND THERE WAS LIGHT. Jim Moore was Chairman of a traveling exhibit about the University which went up and down the State. An introductory film clip to this exhibit was narrated by alum Gregory Peck.

The book AND THERE WAS LIGHT was edited by Irving Stone, and, along with Garff and Public Affairs Director Dick Hafner, I served on the Publishing Committee. Some 38 prominent alumni from all walks of life were identified, contacted and ultimately submitted chapters for this book. In many ways it was that experience along with tackle Roy Muehlberger's idea that got us going on this publication.

I am sure many of you (at least those who are still reading this) probably think that I have passed up many good opportunities to conclude this treatise, and now let me try to do just that.

Service to others, volunteer work, commitment to charitable organizations, and a professional relationship to one of the world's greatest institutions of higher learning has been most self-fulfilling. Combine them, as Jan and I are able to do, with a loving and caring family, and you have two lives that are overflowing with love, joy and gratitude.

From my point of view, its genesis in many ways comes from the Rose Bowl. What a blessing. That 20-14 loss is still and always will be a curse. But as Pappy always said, "When you are knocked down, you have to learn to get up again, again and even again." I am up again; if only I could have one more chance at those guys.

JOHN RALSTON

⌘

After graduating from high school in June of 1944 (and while awaiting orders to report to Marine Corps boot camp) I decided to work in Chicago with some of my teammates. I had gone to high school in northern Michigan so working in Chicago was fairly convenient; besides, I was expecting orders at any time. However the days turned into weeks and I found myself still working in early August. Thus, it seemed natural for me and one of my teammates to visit the College All-Star Football practices at Northwestern University where the team was preparing for the annual game against the professional champions.

My teammate and I were wearing our high school letter sweaters and standing on the sidelines eating fig newton cookies when all of a sudden one of the coaches, Henry Frinka of Tulsa, came over and asked us for a cookie. We were so excited we almost dropped all of them in our anxiety to be sure he had as many as he wanted. Coach Frinka asked us where we were from and as we visited, we were joined by another coach, who incidentally was the head coach of the College All-Star team, Mr. Lynn Waldorf. You can imagine how two 17-year-olds felt in the presence of such idolized company. It was truly a "forever moment" for me since I'd wanted to be a football coach from age 11 forward. I saw my first NFL game in Green Bay when I was 13 (fall of 1940); and meeting Lynn Waldorf had to be the ultimate thrill.

My mother and father had separated in Oakland, California in the early 1930's and my mother , having custody of my brother and me, decided to take us back to northern Michigan (small town called Norway) to be raised by her parents. My father lived in Oakland and worked for the Army Engineers during and after World War II. I had planned, following discharge from the Marine Corps in early 1947, to attend the University of California. This decision was solidified when Lynn Waldorf decided to leave Northwestern and take the head coaching position at Cal, also, in early 1947. I enrolled at Cal for summer school and turned out for the frosh team in September.

At best, I was a lousy player but I knew that by participating I could become a better coach someday. And with my idol as the head coach, I felt I was truly in heaven during my four years at Cal. I later adopted a coaching philosophy patterned after Waldorf's that I employ to this day. Pappy was not only the inspiration for my life's work, but a mentor who guided me throughout his life.

All of Pappy's players in the early years will remember Spring practice in 1948. Imagine 232 players out for football! Pappy would assign the players to groups, and invariably I would be among the last few to be assigned. I can see him now trying to think of my name. Pappy prided himself on knowing everyone's name, but with so many players, he didn't have a chance to get them all. By the time he got to me and I'd helped him with the name, the drill was over and he blew his whistle and re-assigned the groups.

In 1948 and 1949, Cal invited 90 players to early training camp and 35 more after school started. I was in the latter group of 35 and played on the Cal Ramblers (J.V. team). In the fall of 1950, I wanted very much to be selected as a member of the 90 players knowing that this was my only chance to get to play in a Varsity game. I finally got up nerve enough to go see Pappy and let him know how important it was for me to be part of the early camp. By this time Pappy knew of my interest in coaching and I think he considered this as he studied the roster. As I remember, he only had seven centers on the squad list (all other positions had eight players already set) so he asked me if I could play center. Thus, I was included with the 90-man squad and before the first game with Santa Clara, found a home as a linebacker.

In the fall of 1950, we had another Rose Bowl team and an opportunity to play against Michigan on New Year's Day. We set up our southern California practices far away from L.A. in San Bernardino so as not to be distracted. After two previous losses, Pappy made this game a veritable "crusade". The preparation was meticulous and our workouts were "mankillers". Unfortunately, as I remember saying later, we peaked a little too early (perhaps our final scrimmage prior to the game) and we lost, 14 to 6, after dominating play in the first half. I remember Pappy pacing in front of the hundreds of sports writers until he had his complete composure before addressing them. Pappy was a master of the spoken word and always had the ability to say the right thing at the right time.

Spring practice of 1951 found me back in Pappy's office, this time asking to be included as a student assistant coach. Again he welcomed me, and I become Eggs Manske's "flunky". I was involved in all of the meetings before the actual practice sessions, and this was a great learning experience. Our final practice was on April 21, a day I will always remember because Patty and I were married that afternoon. I was at practice that morning, much to Pappy's surprise. But, he agreed that there was no better place for me in those "final hours" before the actual ceremony.

Pappy always felt that a young man aspiring to be a college coach should first gain experience coaching at the high school level. Thus, I joined the many Cal graduates that went into high school coaching. I took a job as an assistant to Rod Franz at Mt. Diablo High School in Concord. From there, after two years, I moved to San Lorenzo High School as head coach for three years. At every opportunity, and there were many, I approached Pappy expressing my desire to come back to Berkeley as a full time member of his staff. In 1956, my persistence paid off and Pappy hired me as the Rambler coach. I think he just got tired of saying no and finally gave in.

Pappy came to California in 1947 and coached for 10 years. I had the good fortune to be with him the first four years as a player and also the final year, 1956, as an assistant coach. This was a tough year for California football even though Joe Kapp did lead us to a Big Game win in Pappy's final game.

Some of my fondest memories of Pappy in this final year came from the staff meetings we had in the bottom floor of his home on Grizzly Peak Blvd. These meetings would start at around eight or nine p.m. and continue well into the morning. And Pappy would still be watching film even after dismissing the rest of us. Usually around one a.m., Wes Fry would say to Pappy, "Don't you think we should have a little buttermilk?" Then Pappy would call for "Louisa" (his wonderful wife Louise) and she would come down with a tray, seven glasses, a bottle of Early Times, and a bucket of ice. Pappy would thank her and then acting as bartender, fill the glasses evenly. When he had emptied the entire bottle, he would add ice only; we were all expected to consume our share. I needed the drink "like a hole in my head," but if Pappy did it, then I just followed along.

After his last game, Pappy entertained the coaches and alumni at his home. He did this after every home game, and Louise was always the gracious hostess, entertaining sometimes even the most antagonistic of alumni (Patty and I followed the same practice for nine years at Stanford, making our home available to all staff, faculty and alumni after each home game).

At his last party, Pappy, with a glass raised, sang "Que Sera"--- "Whatever will be, will be; the future's not ours to see..." I can see him now.

It wasn't very long after his resignation that Lou Spadia of the San Francisco 49ers caller Pappy, putting him back in football as their chief scout. This gave Pappy and Louise a chance to travel together, since in those days, scouts did a lot of driving from one campus to another. Pappy took special pride in the knowledge that he was always welcome on every campus and that he was frequently even asked to speak to the squads themselves. At that time there was some resentment at the colleges and universities of professional scouts but never as far as Pappy Waldorf was concerned. I know, in my own case, as the coach at Utah State and at Stanford, I was especially ecstatic whenever Pappy came to visit our campus.

Pappy was always available to me as a source of reference when various jobs presented themselves. Needless to say, he was instrumental with timely recommendations for the head coaching positions at both Utah State and Stanford, as well as in professional football.

What a wonderful responsibility in return was given to me when I received a call from Charles McClendon, Executive Director of the American Football Coaches, asking me if I would introduce Pappy as the recipient of the Amos Alonzo Stagg Award, college coaching's highest achievement award. Needless to say, I jumped at the chance and prepared diligently, hoping to say all the proper things.

Pappy gave us all a "legacy of winning" and he did it with dignity. I don't think I ever saw him lose his temper or use foul language, and he treated every player with the utmost respect. He always knew what to say and was a master at any gathering, large or small, blue collar or black tie. He epitomized the "master coach. " He was a legend in our game, and he set a pattern for us all to follow.

My final contacts with the Waldorfs came at memorial services for each of them. A beautiful service was held for Pappy on August 26, 1981 at four p.m. in the stadium at Berkeley. The entire Cal football team, as well as Head Coach Roger Theder were in attendance along with hundreds of friends, former players, alumni, faculty, and administrators from Cal. Louise was present with their daughters Carolyn and Mary Louise. Needless to say, I was honored to be asked to participate in the eulogy along with Jim Cullom, Ray Willsey, Dick Erickson, former Stanford Head Coach Chuck Taylor and Professor Garff Wilson.

Shortly after our "Pappy's Boys" was formally established, a group of us in 1978 went up to Santa Rosa to watch Cal's pre-season workouts. We decided to stop in and visit with Louise at her retirement community apartment. We had a super visit, with Louise recalling the Waldorfs' early contacts with Brutus Hamilton and their initial visit by train to Berkeley. She was so alert and seemingly getting along so well.

Patty and I both participated in the eulogy for Louise on January 9, 1992. It was a beautiful service, again attended by many in our "Pappy's Boys" organization.

Even now, so many years later, when difficult times occur, Patty and I often find solace by asking ourselves, "I wonder what Pappy and Louise would do?" They remain ultimate role models for the two of us. As a college coach once more, I still find myself twirling my whistle around my finger and calling out "two minute" time warnings to my staff. Pappy Waldorf was the greatest coach, and with Louise, he had a"perfect team."

ROY MUEHLBERGER

⌘

Life has been great so far, but, we believe, "the best is yet to be, the last of life for which the first is made." But first, to look back, I'll only touch on a two-year period in West Africa and what led up to it. Everything I did as an adult was steered by a chain of circumstances beginning with Pappy picking me out of a double line of tackles butting heads that extended from sideline to sideline. Two years of his advice, praise, instruction and encouragement to relentlessly get up and try again, determined my life. Immediately following graduation, President Truman sent me my "Greetings", and two weeks later I was in the Army to help stop the North Koreans. My contribution to the North Koreans failure was to serve on the Fort Ord football team. "Rose Bowl" was the magic qualification. It did not have to be explained. The Coach "drafted" me without a tryout and without further questions put me on the team.

After two more years of football I took new bride Nancy (college sweetheart) back to Berkeley. As an outgrowth of football, I was hired as a management trainee for the Kaiser Companies by Pappy's predecessor Frank Wickhorst. Like all Cal coaches, he was a fine role model, and he continued to be an advisor to me for the rest of his life.

Finally, the real world arrived. An exciting succession of jobs with Kaiser led from Oakland, to Fontana, Ca.; Sunnyside, Utah; Monterey, Ca.; Oakland again and finally to Accra, Ghana, West Africa. These jobs principally involved negotiating grievance and contract settlements with most of the major labor unions in the country, when labor unions were at the peak of their power. The job in Ghana was more comprehensive and very different.

Nancy, our girls and I went to Ghana a year before the new aluminum plant was built. My job was to do whatever had to be done to arrange for the 1,000 plus employees who would run the place. This included determining how much labor, especially skilled and managerial, could be obtained in Africa, how much from Europe and how much each would cost; establishing wages, salaries, safety procedures; acquiring housing, food, clothing, transportation, a newspaper, a country club; establishing security, a trade school, a school K-9 for dependents' children, and hiring the people to do whatever had to be done. It was busy, lonely and fun. The mail never arrived and the phones were non-existent. Decisions had to be made on the spot and quickly. The boss was 8,000 miles away. It was the perfect job. Besides the job, with Nancy and our girls, we had fabulous trips to remote parts of Africa and Asia, and saw the usual attractions in Europe and the Orient. The girls' education came in the school for ambassadors' children. Living was fun, exciting and unlike anything before or since.

We lived in the endless summer of the equatorial Third World. We had never heard of their four seasons, namely: the long rains, the short rains, the harmattan (hot dry dusty wind from the Sahara), and the hungry season. Excitement was always unannounced and sudden. A short nasty third world revolution was one of these. The four of us were pinned down in our house, which was in the no-man's land between the regiment protecting the dictator and the regiment that successfully threw him out. My neighbor, the American military attaché, yelled to me to leave in a hurry by car during a truce that was sure to come when the radio station was captured. This we did, driving past the casualties and debris. The afternoon was spent watching from the roof of a friend's house a few miles out of town. A company of American Marines could have decided the outcome any way they chose in a fraction of the time.

Late in the day I left with my driver, after the radio announced it was over, to return to my house to keep out looters. En route, in traffic, we were kidnapped and instructed to drive into town by two half-drunk soldiers on the losing side. This was a wild ride through masses of panicky refugees. My luck held out; someone coming down our lane the wrong way forced my driver to swerve into the parking lot of a construction firm. Lo and behold, here was Etienne Atiogby, the construction superintendent I had just hired to rehabilitate homes. He was there with some ironworkers with their belts of wicked looking tools. The soldiers melted into the crowd, but it wasn't over. Martin (driver) and I left and got home only to have the heaviest fighting of all break out. The Russian palace guards had not surrendered and were being blown out with heavy weapons. We were no longer in no-man's land, but still in the field of fire. We took off on foot in a hurry to get behind the first hill. Upon getting to a road, some refugees pulled up to us, shook their fists in my face and said, "Go home Russian."

Anybody the size of a tackle, and a little sloppy looking, was believed to be a Russian. Russians were all over the country, training guerrillas and doing what Communists do. A mile or so of walking down empty streets (the only time we have ever seen empty streets in Africa) and we were at the home of a friend. It was over. The Communists lost another of their nasty little wars.

Ghana wasn't always exciting, but it always had something to keep you awake--awake and alive all the time. Army ants, disease, parasites, snakes, riots, jungles, juju (magic), you name it. No wonder it was called "The White Man's Grave." (We also had two Kaiser doctors from Oakland on the job site.) A more pleasant part of our lives came from our horses and rides on trackless savannah for an hour at dawn almost every day. We could ride for a thousand miles without crossing a road. Kayak trips down jungle rivers were rides through a green tube of trees meeting overhead. Parrots, monkeys and drums of the natives announcing your passage downstream were always in view or earshot. Life was never dull.

After a year, we spent a month in East Africa in the game parks, riding in a big jeep-like sedan with a hatch on top, and a tribal rifleman for security. Fabulous. Short trips into the Cameroons, Togo, Nigeria or the primitive north became almost routine. Sometimes these were for business, sometimes for medical treatment, or sometimes for pleasure. Seeing caravans or unloading ships at sea into dugout canoes, proud naked natives, masses of animals--all these things are gone now, but Nancy, Marion, Frances and I were there, as the result of a long row of dominoes that started on the Cal gridiron and was propelled by Pappy's fatherly advice.

Before leaving Ghana permanently, I received a singular honor. I was elected a Chief with the formality, dress and symbols that go with it. West African Chiefs have always been elected. There was one other white Chief in Ghana. He lived in a mountain village, and like all the rest, except me, had many wives. I gratefully accepted the honor of "Chief," but they did not offer me any wives on this occasion, although previous offers were still open. We loved the Ghanaians--politest people we ever met, except when enraged.

The plant, the schools, the cafeteria, the paper, the homes, etc. and the people were there on time. It is still the biggest aluminum smelter in the world. On our way back to Oakland for reassignment, we took a six-week trip through Ethiopia, Pakistan, India, Nepal (and a trek into the Himalayas), Thailand, and Japan.

The Vietnam war wiped out the capital for additional major overseas jobs, so I left Kaiser after fifteen years to go into the resort business. My associates' comments ranged from "you have to be crazy" to "I knew you were stupid." They were half right. It was the best move we ever made.

There is not room here to go into half a life in the resort business, and, anyway, that is all in the past. The future has always been the most important part of our lives. Some of the things in the future may well be the main justification for our existence. Specifically, Nancy and I are in the process of creating the "Sewanee Prizes." These prizes will be one of the nation's foremost literary awards. They will be awarded annually to the best author under age 35 for a work in American History or for an American historical novel, as determined by the Huntington Library and the University of the South ("Sewanee"). We hope this will give gifted high school and college students a literary goal and an incentive to excel. The award will provide for speaking and teaching engagements and a stipend that will allow the winner to study or travel independently for a year. Other annual awards will go to the best student creative writer at Sewanee, and another for the best patriotic poem about America.

Another project well underway is to collect for the American History library at Sewanee and to build a suitable endowment. Libraries are the first thing to be cut during budget crunches at colleges, with the result that many colleges, even the largest, have a poor to mediocre American History section.

Possibly the most productive of our efforts may turn out to be the farm my partner and I have built in the sea to raise abalone. Abalone are now fished-out worldwide to a depth of fifty feet and are scarce. With this project we will raise them in cages in the ocean, something which has never before been accomplished commercially. We have had to continually develop new equipment, new feeding and harvesting techniques. The fecundity of the sea is something to behold. Abalone should be a major source of high quality food during the next century. We think our pioneering will be responsible for a part of this and for a partial restoration of the wild populations of the abalone as well as an ecologically friendly business.

The past has been great. The best is yet to be. Thank you Pappy and thank you Bob Tessier for bending my twig.

PETE SCHABARUM

⌘

Writing a retrospective of my life has given me a real jolt. To use a football metaphor, it has forced me to turn around and look backward at the yardage gained. And looking backward is something I don't normally do.

Football taught me that the goal line is always straight ahead. That is the direction one must go. Every step backward increases the risk of being thrown for a loss. The time for rehashing the game is after it is over.

Writing this has required that I be both player and commentator -- a situation which rarely leads to objective analysis. Even worse, it meant that I had to squarely face the fact of the almost 50 years which have passed since my days at Berkeley.

My mind is flooded with a host of memories, all good, I might say, some well before college. So let me begin with a few memories about high school, because that was a great period of my life, encompassing, as some would say, the formative years.

I attended Covina Union High School. In those days Covina was in the heart of the Citrus Belt, far out in the suburbs east of Los Angeles. The orange groves are all gone today, replaced by housing tracts as far as the eye can see and freeways clogged with commuters. Covina is a bedroom community within the vast commercial area of Los Angeles County. It's called progress, I guess, but Covina was a better place to live when I was young.

We had a small student body. I now realize that its size gave me an opportunity to do a number of things that would not have been possible were I at a larger institution. I was involved in all the athletic activities available -- football, baseball, basketball -- as well as in student government, including Commissioner of Athletics, Class President, and Student Body President. I did not think about it then, but these activities were catalysts that would propel me into other ventures in later years.

In 1947, as my senior year of high school football came to an end, I earned a certain amount of recognition but not enough to turn a whole bunch of heads my way, which, of course, was the way it was in those days anyway. During the spring of that year I began to look at which colleges were available and what might be of interest.

That summer my father, also a Cal Berkeley alumnus, a great sports enthusiast and my best fan, invited me to drive up to Berkeley with him. This was about the time a new coach and his crew of assistants signed on for the new season. It was then that I met the man who would have a profound impact on my life -- Coach Pappy Waldorf.

The long and the short of it is that I signed up -- not literally, though, since I just showed up as a freshman in the Fall. Hal Grant as freshman football coach had good players from all over the state, and not a few from Southern California.

Actually, I got a big bang out of my freshman year. I was thrilled at being at the University of California and being caught up in campus life at a time when the fortunes of football were beginning to enjoy a turn for the better.

I vividly recall two games of that particular season. One was the Navy game, in which the entire -- it seemed to me -- U.S. Fleet came into San Francisco Bay on a beautiful Saturday afternoon. There was a parade up University Avenue into Memorial Stadium, and Navy put on quite a show. But our boys won the day, and it was all a great big, beautiful event.

The Big Game that year was also a winner for Cal. It was won, as so many are, in the waning minutes of the game. Jack Jensen threw a pass to Paul Keckley who had to run back and scoop it up. Paul ran for what seemed an eternity in every direction but toward the goal line. In the tradition of great football wins, he finally found the opening he needed and ran for a touchdown.

It was one heck of a ballgame, and it set the tone, at least for me as a newcomer, to life on campus and to football for the remainder of my time at Cal.

Those were the years of the men's rooting section in Memorial Stadium. Only male students were allowed on the Cal side between the 40-yard lines. They got pretty raucous, and there were a couple of games when enthusiasm and emotion took over and the bleacher seats were torn up and passed overhead down to the bottom of the rooting section where they were neatly stacked.

My freshman year also started me down an academic pathway, which ultimately -- thank God -- led to achieving a degree, not in the School of Engineering where I began as a freshman, but in the School of Business Administration.

I realized my goal after floundering around the first two or three years trying to figure out what it took to get a degree from the University of California.

The 1947 team, made up entirely of Vets from the big war -- World War II -- started the ball rolling for what would be many good years of winning football under Pappy and his coaching staff.

The next three years were something else. We won all our regular season games, except for a tie with Stanford. It was quite a record, and I take pride in having been a member of those teams.

Why we lost three successive Rose Bowls I've never been able to figure out. That was a real disappointment, but it doesn't diminish what we accomplished. Who needs Rose Bowls when you've done so well in regular season games?

On the other hand, victory would have been sweet.

None of us will forget those tough two-a-day practices in the heat of late August and early September, getting the season started. Nor the almost eight months of each year, for three years in a row, we spent playing football. That's quite a commitment to any kind of activity, but it was well worth it.

I mentioned our tie with Stanford. That was 1950. Score -- 7 to 7. Hopefully my teammates have charitably forgotten, but I remember goofs that I committed during my playing days, and in that game I had a "beaut." Jim Marinos threw a big fat melon ball of a pass over my left shoulder. I was out behind the defensive secondary, the goal line was there for the taking, and I dropped the ball bigger than life. Had I hung onto it, we would have scored six points and, perhaps, would have won the game with that touchdown. I've kicked myself for 45 years over that play.

All of his players remember with a great deal of affection and no small amount of awe Pappy's commanding personality. He set the tone, the attitude, and the direction of the football program at Cal. His leadership was aided and abetted by a classy crew of coaching assistants who were great individuals in their own right. They included Bob Tessier, "Eggs" Manske, Zeb Chaney, Wes Fry, Hal Grant, Nibs Price, and even a few student athlete coaches.

As a running back, I came under the direct tutelage of Wes Fry. I still remember that Wes's idea of a good back was measured not just by his running ability but by his blocking as well. As a consequence, there were some mighty good blocking backs at Cal in those years.

As college came to an end, I had the good fortune of being invited to play in the Hula Bowl in Honolulu, Hawaii. "Play" is a misnomer because in fact I picked up a broken ankle bone during the Michigan Rose Bowl game the previous week. As a result I spent much of my time in Hawaii on a surfboard. Not a bad option and one that made for what turned out to be a great trip.

I was then invited to be on the Chicago All-Star Team, which that year played the Cleveland Browns. The almost 10 days of practice at St. John's Military Academy near Waukesha, Wisconsin in preparation for the game were memorably hot and steamy. Two drills a day, all of which led to naught because I didn't get a minute of play in the game.

I moved on to the San Francisco 49ers training camp in Menlo Park, having been drafted by that team, and began three great years of being part of the 49er organization.

We didn't win any championships, but we had a good team and a first class coach in Buck Shaw. We also had some fine ball players. Frankie Albert and Norm Standlee were closing out their careers. For a new boy fresh out of college it was a chance to travel and see a part of the country I hadn't visited before, to make a few bucks that could not have been earned as quickly otherwise, and to enjoy the friendship and comradeship of a lot of fine guys.

The 1951 season came and went. In January of 1952, because of the Korean War, I became a member of the California Air National Guard. I traveled to Texas for Aviation Cadet Training School where for some 13 months I went through pilot training school and subsequently washed out.

It's probably just as well. Finding an airport from the air was always problematic for me. That brought me in the Spring of 1953 to Hayward, California, where I continued service in the Air National Guard while playing for the 49ers during the 1953 and 1954 seasons.

I enjoyed the privilege of playing with the likes of Y.A. Tittle, John Henry Johnson, Joe Perry and Hugh McElhenny, who made up what is yet considered one of the finest backfields in the history of pro football. I played behind these legends on offense and even filled in at defensive wing back.

It would be remiss of me not to mention Tony Morabito, the owner of the 49ers, who took a young college boy -- myself -- and signed him to a reasonable contract. Tony was a very gentlemanly guy, and I'll always remember him for having lent me a sizable amount -- $10,000, if you will -- for one of my early real estate ventures after I finished playing pro football.

That loan, for all practical purposes, was essentially made on a handshake. It was repaid, but the point is that he made it and he had a lot of confidence in my willingness and ability to pay him back.

As the 1954 pro football season came to a close, I began thinking about what I might do in the real world after football. During the previous off-season I had begun to dabble in the real estate business, and California was in the middle of a real estate development boom. This was particularly true in the San Gabriel Valley, my old home territory. I went back there and began as a neophyte in real estate development. I quickly found that what I learned in college did nothing for me other than prepare me for the realization that I didn't know anything about anything after all.

At that point I started a three year apprenticeship in the business of learning how real estate is developed. I went to night school and took a number of courses at UCLA Extension, as well as at the University of Southern California Law School.

My efforts as a budding developer were so minimal those first three years that I had trouble deciding whether I needed to file an income tax return. But that's what the learning process is all about.

Around 1957, the picture started to change. I was getting good momentum, and it was the time during which I met and won my bride, Gerry Ann Curtice. She was a beautiful blind date. We courted for an ever so brief period, were married in December 1957, and settled down in the Covina area.

Gerry and I are the proud parents of three children -- Laura, our daughter, and two sons, Frank and Tom. They are now grown and have ended up generally staying in the greater Southern California area. We have three grandkids, and we look forward to the occasions when we all get together.

As the years went by, my real estate business became more and more successful. It came to a point where I had to choose whether I wanted to get into the real estate big leagues or remain a one-man operation. I opted to do the latter. This decision gave me time to develop interests in new fields.

I asked a friend what he might recommend in the field of public service for me. He suggested that I meet with a local Superior Court judge and ask him to nominate me to the Los Angeles County Grand Jury. I did, and he did -- and as a consequence, my name was drawn from the box and I became a member of the 1965 Los Angeles County Grand Jury. In what set the stage for a career in politics, the presiding judge appointed me as Foreman of the Jury.

My term on the Grand Jury put me in contact with an entirely different group of people than I had previously associated with, and I learned a great deal about how county government operates.

At the end of 1965, it became apparent that the then-sitting member of the California State Assembly -- our Assemblyman -- would not run for reelection. That prompted me to consider running for public office, which, as it turned out, I chose to do.

I was elected in November 1966 to what I thought would be a part-time job. To my surprise and subsequent chagrin, on that same ballot there was a proposition establishing the California Legislature as a full-time legislative body. Voters supported the proposition and, of course, now -- some 30 years later -- I suspect many of them regret it.

Slowly but surely my part-time job became a full-time commitment.

After two and a half terms, I decided it was time to return to civilian life, to get back to my family, and to eliminate the terrible commute between Los Angeles and Sacramento. The routine was: fly to Sacramento on Monday and return on Thursday each week for most of the year.

I must say, however, those years were not only exciting and challenging, but most interesting.

Ronald Reagan was in his first term as California's governor in 1967. He attracted an eager group of citizen politicians and/or aspiring volunteers who went to Sacramento with aspirations of making things better.

I had the pleasure of serving on a number of important legislative committees that exposed me to how state government operates. I became involved in the issues of the day; I traveled throughout California; and I enjoyed seeing things that one is normally not aware of as a tourist or casual observer.

Then, as now, reforming the state's welfare programs was a hot issue. I sat on the negotiating group that put together a major reform of the welfare system as it was in the 1960's. In addition, I was chairman of a subcommittee that drafted and won passage of several pieces of landmark legislation in the field of air pollution control that have been on the statute books of California since 1971.

I served on various subcommittees of the Ways and Means Committee of the Assembly with responsibility for reviewing the proposed State budget. For three years I, and a few other members of the Assembly, played a role in determining the spending program for the State of California. That was important to me and of tremendous interest.

I strongly recommend to anybody who has the inclination to get involved in politics and seek a seat in the State Legislature. Giving of oneself in public service is rewarding, and it provides an extraordinary opportunity to learn a great deal about the state in which we live.

In 1972, as my third legislative term was winding down, Frank Bonelli, the member of the Los Angeles County Board of Supervisors representing the San Gabriel Valley, died in office.

Governor Reagan appointed me to fill the vacant seat. It was March, and by law I was required to run for reelection in the June primary. I was pleased to return home sooner than I anticipated, but for three months I had to battle stiff competition to keep my new job.

As I will shortly discuss, I am a strong believer in term limits for elected officials. But there are those who point out, with justification, the hypocrisy of my position on the issue for it was not until March of 1991 -- some 19 years later -- that I retired from the office of First District Supervisor for the County of Los Angeles.They were 19 years of, in the main, interesting, challenging and satisfying public service.

My only defense for championing term limits after having remained in public office far longer than I now believe appropriate is that sometimes we learn through experience.

It is no secret that I have a conservative point of view. That fact served me well with my constituents because they, too, were generally of a conservative bent. Not so for the rest of Los Angeles County. Consequently, for the first eight years I was a conservative minority vote on a liberal majority Board. More often than I care to recall I was on the short end of the voting on many important issues.

I also seemed to have an inclination for getting too far out front on issues where it was clear that all hope was lost. This propensity caused me to get my fanny on the hot seat from time to time. Some of my press clippings from this era are better forgotten.

I remember one long day at a Board meeting when I tried to breach the liberal majority line on an item even though I knew there was little chance for success. I failed. I got my brains beat out.

When I returned to my office, a member of my staff was waiting. He was not in a good mood. He questioned why I purposely put myself in a position to be publicly mauled by my colleagues. He added insult to injury by characterizing my performance as akin to putting my head down and running into a brick wall at full speed.

In politics, as in football, I tried to reach the goal line at all costs. Sometimes I failed. My staffer stared at me in disbelief when I explained that I did it because I knew that when I picked myself off the ground I could say, "That felt good." He didn't understand how old football jocks think.

By 1980, even I was totally discontent with beating my head against the wall as a minority member of the Board. I decided that in order to have any significant impact on county government, it was necessary for me to risk my political career by helping two Republicans challenge incumbent Supervisors.

Ronald Reagan became president, swept into office on a tide of voter discontent over inflation brought on by President Carter's economic policies. Along with Reagan's victory, the Republican challengers won seats on the Board of Supervisors.

This created a new Republican majority that worked well together and enjoyed substantial success in reshaping county government.

Once the new majority was in place, I launched a long overdue government reform program that called for using the private sector to perform many county functions that historically had been the sole province of public employees.

Some functions of government can only be carried out by public employees. Others can be provided by the private sector at less cost to taxpayers. But the idea of pressing for cost-effective government using this common sense approach is a relatively recent phenomenon. Privatizing government functions is opposed by Democrats, public employee unions, and the liberal press.

Perhaps the most dramatic success in privatizing public services was in the area of transportation. We created the Foothill Transit District, a bus system that served 20 cities. The creation of this agency made it possible for us to make a serious comparison between the cost of operating a public agency operated by private enterprise against that of the local rapid transit district's bus system, which is one of your typical giant, costly bureaucracies.

In the end, it demonstrated that the Foothill Transit District was equally efficient, and it could be operated at a forty percent reduction in cost.

As I write this chapter of the history of Pappy's boys, the Los Angeles County Board of Supervisors is wrestling with a $1.2 billion budget shortfall, largely created by its own fiscal mistakes. Board members are facing onerous proposals calling for laying off some 18,000 county employees and closing county hospitals. It is with a certain amount of amusement that I watch the liberal Democrats who now control the Board turn to privatization as a means of saving money. The public employee unions, typically a Democrat constituency, are crying foul. It is truly amazing to see the press support these liberals' privatization efforts as a prudent course of public policy.

I like to think I promoted a sober approach to governance during my tenure on the Board. I believe my constituents were well-served, and I take pride in a variety of improvements in public services and facilities that were initiated under my stewardship.

My interest in development continued while I served on the Board of Supervisors. I was a builder. I built 200 miles of trails for horsemen, bicyclists, and hikers. Those who enjoy such recreation can now start out in the foothills of the San Gabriel mountains and wind their way through towns and neighborhoods all the way to the ocean.

I built parks -- some 30 regional and community parks were completed in my district on my watch.

I built fire stations, libraries, sheriff stations, courthouses, and health centers. I launched the start of the replacement of Rancho Los Amigos Medical Center, a world renowned rehabilitation hospital located in Downey.

These improvements to public services for the growing San Gabriel Valley had largely been ignored before my appointment. I found that in building these facilities I could enjoy a sense of satisfaction even when my efforts to change county government at the regular Board meetings were frustrated.

Much of my public life found me as a member of the minority. In the State Assembly the Republican Party was the minority. During my first eight years on the Board of Supervisors, in theoretically a non-partisan office, I was a philosophical minority member. That is a tough role to deal with. You learn how to get a job done in different ways. If you can't muster the votes you need from the Supervisors, you go around them. You use the bureaucracy when possible. You focus on what needs to get done, and you pursue it relentlessly. All in all, getting something accomplished in government is a lot like playing football.

There are good and bad things that come with every activity. A career in public service has its negatives, such as having to take the abuse of the public and the media that, in many cases, gets far too personal. On the plus side, there was the opportunity to be in the arena while current events and issues of the day were being debated and in some way dealt with. That makes it worthwhile.

Gerry and I participated as delegates at three different national Republican Party conventions, and we were part of two presidential inaugurations in Washington, D.C. We were invited to travel to a number of places throughout the world as the guests of various governments or organizations. So, all in all, it was a most interesting period of our lives.

I retired from the Board of Supervisors in March of 1991. Gerry and I now call the Indian Wells area of the desert near Palm Springs our principal residence. I use the word "principal" because in fact we are still very active in Los Angeles.

I have attempted to keep my hand in the political pot. I was very much involved in sponsoring two state ballot initiatives dealing with limiting the terms of officeholders in our State constitutional offices and the Legislature and, subsequently, our California Congressional delegation.

Both issues were approved by the voters of California, and we are beginning to see the final throes of entrenched, special-interest incumbents in the Legislature leaving office in 1996 as a consequence of being term-limited out.

Unfortunately, the U.S. Supreme Court declared unconstitutional the Congressional term limits initiative, so we're literally back to the drawing boards on that question.

I am convinced that one of the biggest shortcomings of good legislating on the part of either city councils, the state legislature, or The Congress of the United States is the fact that we have had people who decided to make a career out of being in government -- that is to say, an elected position in government. As a consequence, their focus is on staying elected rather than making the tough decisions that are required in dealing with important issues facing California.

I do some government consulting these days. My years of county and state experience and contacts generated during public life are useful in this endeavor. Gerry and I have also done an extensive amount of traveling over the years, and we will continue to do so as long as life, limb, and the wallet allows.

Both Gerry and I are extremely fortunate to be in good health. Thank God I have no serious injuries from ten years of playing football. No bad knees or other physical problems appear to be present.

There are those who would suggest that the football helmets of my gridiron days did not provide the protection of modern helmets and that is reflected in some of the legislative decisions I made over the years -- but that's another subject.

Over the years, I as well as many others who played football at California have had a continuing interest in and loyalty to its football fortunes, as well as to the University of California in general. I owe a great deal to many people for providing me with the tools to go forward in life. Much of that help came from classmates at Berkeley.

I want to give a great deal of credit to Bob Karpe and others who were the instigators in bringing Pappy's Boys together as an organization. It has become the vehicle for those of us who were Pappy's players to join together periodically, to reminisce, and to remind ourselves of the "good old days," and to consider, by way of a pay-back, doing our part to foster the interests of athletics at Berkeley.

Toward that end, I came up with the idea several years ago of creating a life-size bronze statue of Pappy that we could put on campus. I discussed it with a number of our teammates at one of the annual reunions, and the idea was well received. So I began then to bring together the ingredients necessary to make it happen.

Some months later I was on a goose hunting trip with a bunch of hunters, one of whom was a well-regarded sculptor by the name of Doug Van Howd. During the bus trip back from our hunt, Doug and I got into an extensive conversation, which led to our negotiating an agreement that called for his creating the bronze statue. My role was to pursue all the other details, not the least of which was raising the funds to cover the cost of his work.

That deal having been made, he proceeded to do his work, and I began fund-raising. I called on a number of our teammates, many of whom contributed , and in due course we raised the necessary money to not only have a sculpture created, but also enough to have it installed on campus.

Getting the site approved, along with other things related to the campus, was no small task given the fact that Berkeley, like every other institution, has its bureaucracy.

It took well over a year to get campus approval of what turned out to be a magnificent site in Faculty Glade, to have the plans completed and approved for installation, and to obtain committee approval for the exact language to be used on the plaque at the foot of Pappy's statue.

All this having been pursued and ultimately accomplished, we were able to have what turned out to be a wonderful unveiling in September of 1994, where a crowd of a couple of hundred of our teammates, friends, and family gathered. It was an impressive get-together with all those present well pleased with the outcome.

If you haven't seen Pappy's statue, next time you're on campus, make an effort to go by and take a look.

I relish the times when Pappy's boys get together, and the activities that these events foster. I have enjoyed this opportunity to share a few memories from the days of our youth.

It's the third quarter. I've enjoyed the game of life. I thank God for my years at Berkeley and the friendships made there. I expect that life will be as it has been -- a real challenge and of tremendous interest. I look forward to the future.

FRANK BRUNK

⌘

The first eleven years of my life were spent in Mexico. My grandfather and his cousin, were in the real estate business in Berkeley when they saw a flyer advertising available land in the Yaqui River valley of the Mexican state of Sonora. They knew the land to be very fertile, but it was full of mesquite and had no water control. Winters were mild and fairly dry, but the summers were very rainy and floods were the norm.

Nevertheless, a few Americans, including my grandfather, took a chance and bought land and started farming rice and wheat. When my father graduated from high school in 1918, he was informed that he was to report to the U.S. Army. Fortunately, World War I ended and he went off to college. But the lure of great adventure in a foreign land was too great so he went to Mexico to join his father. Dad and his brother helped my grandfather clear several thousand acres of land and develop an irrigation system for the crops.

Cajeme was the nearest town--later the name was changed to Ciudad Obregon, after one of the Presidents of Mexico. My brother Don and I were both born in Berkeley but were taken immediately after birth to Mexico. We attended school in our home with the aid of a tutor.

It was near the end of 1937 when my brother and I were told that we were going to Los Angeles and would be seeing the Rose Bowl. Of course, that didn't mean a lot to us because we had no idea what the Rose Bowl was. But on January 1, 1938 we saw California beat Alabama, 13 to 7, and Don and I were hooked on Cal! After the game I became an imaginary Vic Bottari and Don became Sam Chapman, the two biggest stars on that great Cal "Thunder Team." We played many make believe games of football in our backyard in Mexico.

It was soon after that the Mexican government determined that Mexicans and not Americans, or any other foreigners, should own land in Mexico. The Great Agrarian Movement had taken place and my father and his brother were forced to give away the farm land they had worked so hard for. It would take a year or two for my parents to settle their affairs and leave Mexico, so they decided to put Don and me in private school in San Rafael, the Tamalpais School For Boys. That was real culture shock for us, but our sports interest and our private tutoring had prepared us to relate to a new world. Don and I went out for everything we could, even though we didn't know how to play the games. We played football, basketball, and tennis. We tried track and swimming. And we were obliged to attend church services on Sunday mornings.

That was the beginning of my nomadic school life. Our parents did get out of Mexico after two years and bought a home in Oakland. The ninth grade at Claremont Junior High School became my first public school experience, another culture shock. After graduating from Claremont I went to Oakland Technical High School, but after two weeks I was able to transfer to Berkeley High. Both my parents had gone to Berkeley and I suppose that was how I was allowed to attend while still living in Oakland.

World War II broke out in 1941, and because of gas rationing and all the other restrictions, Dad decided to go back to what he knew, which was farming. A close friend from Mexico had settled in Willows in the Sacramento valley and convinced Dad to go there to resume his farming life. Away we went to yet another school.

Two years later I graduated from Glenn County High School (Willows High). Some sort of service responsibility was ahead of me so I took the Navy V-5 tests, passed and was allowed to attend classes at the University of California in Berkeley. I was lucky because most other V-5 inductees were sent to schools like the University of Idaho. My dream of going to Cal was coming true.

The war years were unusual in that players like Bill Hachten, Dick Madigan and George Quist all earned letters at Cal as Navy trainees, then after the war attended Stanford and achieved stardom. All these guys left in mid summer of 1944 and the season started with almost no players.

Bob Celeri had enrolled in the summer as a 16-year-old out of Fort Bragg High School but was not eligible to play football. There was no one to play tailback so Coach Stub Allison put me there. It didn't matter that I had never played the position before because I was just happy to be playing. We practiced for a week, and I tried to learn how to pass and to do all the other things required of a single wing tailback. Our second game was against UCLA. The papers got wind of something happening that was different and Stub referred to it as his "secret weapon". I really think he was trying to throw UCLA off by mentioning this, trying to worry them. In practice, I ran a play into the line and broke three metacarpals in my left hand, and the next day the headlines screamed that Cal's "secret weapon" was hurt. Somewhere in the small print they mentioned my name. What a start for the next "Vic Bottari" at Cal! Needless to say, I was crushed beyond words, lost interest in school and shortly thereafter left for sea duty in the China Sea.

When World War II ended, I came home and re-entered Cal and, of course, went out for football. Frank Wickhorst was the coach in 1946, and he had many former players who had returned for a final year or two in order to graduate. I was relegated to the Ramblers. Our roster had some pretty good names for awhile--Rod Franz, George Fong, Bill Montagne, to name a few. Rod and George did find their way up to the varsity after two or three games. We had a great Rambler team, a great schedule and we always played the preliminary to the varsity game. We always won while the varsity was going two and seven. In fact the stands would fill up early just to see our games, and toward the end of the season, fans began chanting "Ramblers to the Rose Bowl" out of frustration over the losses by the varsity. It certainly was some consolation for not having made the varsity team. We did have fun, maybe the best fun year of football in our lives.

Pappy Waldorf arrived on the scene the next year, 1947, and the competition began all over again. It seemed like every young man who had ever thought of playing football was there that spring. I don't know how Pappy, Wes Fry, Bob Tessier and Eggs Manske were able to cut through all the contenders and settle on a squad for the fall, but there I was, on the team with a real uniform and a real chance to play football for Cal! The only problem was, I was going to play the same position as Jackie Jensen.

Jack was such a great player I knew that I would not get to play a lot. We did become very good friends and fraternity brothers and eventually, roommates. I learned so much from Jack. We would sit and talk about the game and he would tell me how he would fake and cut and score touchdowns. He expected 100-yard games and would anticipate them by saying that he might carry the ball about twenty times for a few yards but then he would go for a couple of "30-yarders" to get his 100-yard game. I think Jack Jensen was the greatest athlete I ever saw. In football he could make incredible runs and fabulous blocks. He could throw passes, punt and play defense with the best. He could shoot a basketball with great accuracy and was a

fabulous ping pong player. Jack could do anything with ease that required physical dexterity. I took him to Mira Vista Country Club and Tilden Park golf courses and showed him how to play that game. Jack went from playing in the 100's to the 80's, completely skipping the 90's! But baseball was his game. His exploits in baseball are well known, but I have a special appreciation for the fact that he signed a baseball contract after his junior year. By not being at Cal as a senior he made it possible for me to play.

In that junior year I was not playing very much, though, and Eggs Manske could sense my frustration. He took me aside and convinced me to continue working hard. He told me my time would come and that I needed to be ready. In the Rose Bowl of January 1949 against Northwestern, Jensen badly pulled his hamstring on the opening play of the second half. Pappy turned around and yelled for me to go in. How could Eggs have known this would happen? I was in a daze when I got to the huddle, but Cullom brought me back to my senses. He said, "Well here's Brunk, I guess we have to start blocking!" I had a pretty good game in that second half, thanks to Cullom and all the linemen blocking so well. After the game I was awarded the Vard Stockton Memorial Award for the outstanding performance on offense.

My senior year at Berkeley was the highlight of my college football career. Backing up Jensen, playing a little here and there, playing in the Rose Bowl on January 1, 1949, were realizations of dreams come true. But my senior year as a starter was something I will never forget, seeing my name in the program as the starting Left Half. And, even without Jensen the team won. We were ranked nationally in the top ten of the country. How could it get any better than that?

It did get better than that. I had gotten hurt in the first game of the season against Santa Clara and Charlie Sarver took over at Left Half. He did a great job. I don't think I have ever seen any one who had better ability to run the ends than he did. He was great at catching passes and then running with the ball. Tragically, his career ended in Wisconsin when his knee was torn up by a devastating tackle. My own knee injury had healed enough for me to make the trip and I was sent into the game. I scored my first intercollegiate touchdown that day, we won and we went home to begin preparations for the USC game on October 15.

We practiced hard all week, but on Friday we held a light workout which consisted mostly of running. The coaching staff had decided we should try going up the middle on kickoffs as a change of pace. We must have practiced up-the-middle returns ten or twelve times; I know because Jim Monachino and I were runnin[illegible] them back each time to the goal line. The next day we started the game by receivin[illegible] the kickoff and the return was up the middle, but I got creamed! Their kicker was [illegible] strong that he could kick off into the end zone and we had blocked way too early; [illegible] players who were blocked had time to recover and by the time I got to them th[illegible] was nowhere for me to go.

We scored in the first half and led 7-0 going into the third quarter. [illegible] scored a touchdown in the third quarter to tie the score. Midway into the fo[illegible] quarter Frank Gifford kicked a field goal and USC led 10-7. Southern Cal's McGee kicked off, deep again--two yards into the end zone. The ball was heade[illegible] Jim Monachino this time and I was all set to yell "You take it" when it start[illegible] curve back to me, so I took it. I caught the ball and Jim went ahead to blo[illegible] another up-the-middle return. Blocks were delayed properly this time and a [illegible] alley opened up for me. Monachino blocked, Franz blocked two players, Jim [illegible] Bob Minahen, Carl Van Heuit, Len Jones, Jim Turner, Ray DeJong, George S[illegible]

and others all made perfect blocks as I kept going up the middle. At about the 45 or 50 I veered to the right to avoid Gifford and outran the rest of the USC players to the end zone. It was bedlam! I didn't feel tired even though the game had been a difficult one to play with lots of hard hitting. I felt totally light in weight, and then the rest of the team arrived. It was survival time! The play was perfect, just as it had been drawn up with everybody blocking. I was the lucky guy who got to carry the ball!

This was the first game that Cal was on TV, and Pappy had a TV set sitting on the end of the Andy Smith bench. As my runback began the players moved to the sideline and Pappy couldn't see anything so he turned around to look at the TV. Boots Erb and Pappy watched the play on television while the rest of the team crowded the sideline. The crowd was so excited about the runback that one person threw his new cashmere sweater into the air and lost it and to this day blames me for it. I was told about a pregnant lady who wet her pants, and my brother found himself hugging Marty Cullom in the middle of the men's rooting section. The next day my father reminded me that this should not go to my head, that the runback might open a few doors for me in business, but once I was in I was on my own. I came back to earth.

All of this started from long ago at Cal, so many of these dreams came true, thanks to Pappy, my coaches and my teammates. Pappy was such a wonderful man, a father figure, full of humor, compassion and a love for coaching. He had a passion for New Orleans Jazz and his limerick recitations were legendary. He was a great part of my life, and I think of him often. He encouraged competition, and we were better players for it. I also treasure the friendships cultivated on those teams. We are very fortunate to have an annual reunion to sustain these wonderful memories.

Other passions have entered my life since graduating from Cal. I am a proud man because of my wife Jenifer, and our terrific children and grandchildren. Although I started playing golf at about age twelve I didn't get serious about the game until after college. I was very fortunate to become involved with the Northern California Golf Association and to be elected its President. It was greatly satisfying for me, but it was also a great honor to have been elected to head this incredible group of 165,000 golfers. It was in this period that I became aware that the Athletic Department had eliminated golf as a recognized sport at Cal. With the help of some other dedicated people, we have not only resurrected golf at Berkeley, we have restored it to prominence. We have insisted that Cal Golf be available to students who want the benefit of a great competitive experience in a very wholesome sport. We are currently working toward establishing a complete endowment for both men's and women's golf. It is something we will accomplish, I have no doubt.

This has been a wonderful reminiscence and it has brought me to the realization that life has truly been good to me. I have been blessed with marvelous support all around me throughout my life, not only on the football field but with my family, too. My dreams are still being realized every day in all the things I do. Pappy Waldorf was a tremendous influence on me. His life concepts are with me every day: compete fairly and well, have concern for your associates and remember that while the thrill is in winning, it has to be done with dignity. And, of course, it rains on both sides of the line of scrimmage.

ROD FRANZ

⌘

As long as I can remember I have always been keenly interested in sports and physical activity. Growing up I used to fight occasionally with my brother who was three years my senior. He would always beat me at first, but then I would get him in a head lock and not let go until he cried "uncle". In grammar school, Bill Ray, Cecil Edwards and I formed a tackle football team at Funston Playground. We called ourselves the Yellow Jackets because somehow we obtained yellow sweatshirts with black markings on them. We played all comers.

At Marina Junior High School, I played two years at left half-back on our intra-city soccer team. We had a wise Scottish coach, Frank Zanazzi, who taught us how to kick and trap a tennis ball before we moved on to a soccer ball. My last year at Marina, we tied for the city championship. A star teammate on the team was Dan Begovich who later joined with me as a great end on the Cal Rose Bowl teams of 1949 and 1950.

At Galileo High School I played three years of football, first on the "Goof Team" (reserves), then as a back-up right guard, and finally as the first string right guard. We won the "Goof" championship. Our varsity teams were not very good and by my senior year, with less than 24 players, we had no wins and one tie.

What I really enjoyed in high school was crew! We had lightweight and varsity 12-man crew boats birthed at the Marina Yacht Harbor. I rowed two years first string on the lightweight crew as number five port my first year and as stroke and captain my second year. We took second place in the first year and won the city championship my years as stroke. We perfected a new technique in rowing by sprinting the entire course rather than starting with a sprint and then going into a long stroke. The next year, as a senior, I stroked the varsity crew to another city championship. You could actually feel the boat leap ahead as all twelve crewmen made the vessel cut the water on each stroke. If anyone goofed off you could feel it in your oar during practice. It never occurred in a race. Dan Begovich rowed in the bow and my lifelong friends, Bill Ray rowed port five behind me on the varsity and Judge Jack Ertola rowed port five in our lightweight crew.

During my senior year in high school, I enlisted in the U.S. Army Air Corps during World War II. Upon graduation, I was called to active duty in March 1943. After basic training at Jefferson Barracks, Mo., in the Army Air Corps ground crew, I became a drill instructor, teaching platoons of 48 soldiers their basic training. At this time in my life, I was 18 years old, and weighed 165 lbs. I had not fully matured and, frankly, did not even have to shave on a daily basis. I had hoped to qualify for officer's training school, but after a year as a drill instructor, the Army had enough 90-day wonders. I volunteered for an overseas outfit. I was placed in a truck company of an Air Service Group, and after additional training we shipped out to the China-Burma-India Theatre. We were stationed in the Assam valley near the Himalayas to service flights supplying arms and materials to the Chinese Army fighting the Japanese invasion of China.

Upon the surrender of the Japanese to end World War II, my outfit was transported by air directly to Shanghai, China, and to the Japanese Air base north of Shanghai to occupy the field and open it for future occupation. My last assignment at the Shanghai air base was to form a Chinese Officers' truck driving and maintenance school to teach the Chinese to take over and maintain our U.S.

military vehicles. I set up the school using German, Jewish, and White Russian refugee interpreters who had escaped persecution years before in their native lands. I finally was shipped home and discharged in April 1946 with the grade, Motor Transportation Staff Sergeant.

By the time I was discharged from the service, I had grown to my full height of 6'1" and weighed 200 pounds. I always worked out in the service by doing push-ups and sit-ups and by boxing. I even made a set of bar bells out of a pipe and two gasoline tanks filled with concrete, which I used for weight-lifting while in Assam.

With the availability of the G.I. Bill of Rights, my goal was a college education. I also decided to try out for the football team. Like almost everyone in the Cal football program, I was a "walk on". I had no idea of how good or bad I would do. I did meet the 1946 coach, Frank Wickhorst, and his backfield coach, Vic Bottari. Vic was kind enough to check my high school transcript and tell me I needed a science course and a make-up geometry course with a B and C grade to qualify for the University. I achieved the necessary grades to enter in the fall of 1946.

Football practice had already been well under way. When I came out, I started on the last string of the Ramblers. I had very little technique, but a tremendous amount of desire. It became apparent that you could use your aggressive desire to its fullest extent on defense. I rapidly worked my way up to the varsity prior to the opening game against Wisconsin. By making the varsity my freshman year, I thought I had died and gone to heaven. Along the way I had knocked out the first string guard (without really knowing what I had done), and one of the regular quarterbacks was infuriated with me because I would tackle him too many times before he got the ball away. In the opening Wisconsin Game at Memorial Stadium, Cal lost, but I received my first test. Coach Wickhorst sent me in the game. I didn't have a regular helmet so I just grabbed an extra one and away I went. When I got down in my stance, the helmet came down over my eyes and I could not see. Wickhorst took me out and yelled, "What is the matter?" I told him the helmet was too big. He said, "Get one that fits and get back in there!" From that moment on, I became Cal's right guard for the next four years, playing both offense and defense as necessary.

With the departure of Coach Wickhorst, Athletic Director Brutus Hamilton chose Lynn "Pappy" Waldorf to become the new football coach for the 1947 season. The spring practice of 1947 was a real eye-opener. With about 250 potential candidates out for the squad, each practice was highly organized so that every minute was accounted for. The spring practice encompassed the basic fundamentals of the game and team development. None of the players stood around--all were kept busy in one capacity or another learning the intricacies of the game.

It was in the spring practice of 1947 that I became well acquainted with the tremendous coaching talent of our line coach Bob Tessier. Bob taught us, the linemen, all of the things that are essential to becoming a superior player and member of a great team. I learned to jolt, to follow through, gain the line of scrimmage, split a double team, obtain critical angles when blocking an opponent and above all, to "get-off", "get-off", "get-off"! (During my time at Cal, there were many complaints about the way we would "beat the ball" on the line of scrimmage. We were simply taught repeatedly to get off with the ball.) This was one of the most important factors in our winning record. Bob also taught us to stay low, gain ground, get the angle on an opponent and follow through. These techniques became automatic and were usually easier accomplished in a game than in practice where your opponent could anticipate your moves.

Lynn Waldorf was a wonderful and exceptional man. He was just what the doctor ordered when he came to Berkeley. I had the honor of meeting and greeting him when he and Bob Tessier first arrived in Berkeley by train. I also had the pleasure of driving him home after his retirement party at the Bow and Bell Restaurant, which was organized and attended by his former Pappy's Boys players. We didn't just like him, we loved him.

In my lifetime, I have had several important accomplishments. In some cases they are of record and in some cases, they are not.

Receiving All American recognition for three years is one distinct honor of which I am very proud. I realize, however, that this honor is no more nor less than a reflection of the fine teams I played on and upon the whole organization headed by Pappy which developed "A Legacy of Winning." We had many fine student athletes who were teammates of mine who could also have qualified for this honor. Being elected to the National Football Foundation and Hall of Fame in 1977 and being inducted into that prestigious group at a black tie affair at the Waldorf Astoria in New York was an additional highlight of my career.

The greatest Honor I have received from the University was my selection as a charter member of the University of California Hall of Fame.

After receiving my general secondary teaching credential at Cal, I accepted my first job as football coach at Mt. Diablo High School. I was fortunate to have my teammate at Cal, John Ralston, as our backfield coach for the first two years. Our three-year record was two losses the first year, and undefeated championships the second and third years. It is my opinion that coaching high school young men is the most rewarding and fulfilling experience any coach can have. You take what you have, work with these young men and watch them grow and develop.

In the spring of my last term at Mt. Diablo, I was selected to coach the Northern All Stars along with John Giannoni from Lodi High School in the annual Shriners' North-South Game at the Los Angeles Memorial Coliseum. Over 50,000 attended. Final score, South 7, North 6.

After three years at Mt. Diablo, I moved on to accept the head football job at the University of California Riverside. U.C.R. was a brand new branch of the university system and I was the school's first football coach. We played the first year with students who were a little short on speed and ability, but we did manage to win the first varsity game of any team at U.C.R.

From U.C.R. I received a call from Pappy to coach at Cal. Pappy assigned me to coach the freshman team (his last year of coaching). John Ralston joined our staff as the Rambler Coach. On our freshman team we recruited many talented players who later went on to become Rose Bowl players as seniors against Iowa during Pete Elliot's tenure. Our abbreviated freshman schedule included wins over U.S.C. and U.C.L.A., whose varsity teams were powerhouses of the era.

With Coach Waldorf's retirement, the university selected Pete Elliott as his replacement. Pete hired John Ralston and me as assistants on his staff. Although Pete had a fine staff and I enjoyed the camaraderie, I began to have doubts that I wanted to continue coaching as a career. I thoroughly enjoyed the coaching, but more and more the other necessary facets of the business, including recruiting and the necessity of being away from home continually, led me to the decision to change careers. Our family was growing and I had little time to participate in a regular family life.

For the next nine years I worked in a totally different world--the world of fabricated steel for Consolidated Western Steel and the American Bridge Division of the U.S. Steel Corporation.

For the past 25 years, I have been involved in matters dealing with the management of publicly owned water supplies. Prior to my retirement, I was the Manager of Legislative Affairs for the East Bay Municipal Utility District, which serves domestic and municipal water to 1.2 million people in the East Bay. During my tenure as the District's advocate with the State Legislature, I guided 48 pieces of E.B.M.U.D.-sponsored legislation through the process in 23 years and saw every one of them become law; not one of the proposals sponsored by "East Bay Mud" failed.

Included in this group of legislative accomplishments were SCA 20 (Mosconi) which set reasonable guidelines for assessment of taxes on publicly-owned property outside a public agency's boundaries, thereby settling a state-wide dispute with the mountain counties; the establishment of the Bay Area Sewage Services Agency to develop and implement a regional water quality management program for the San Francisco Bay; gaining authority for the District to issue revenue bonds without an election; and the authorization and implementation of the first state-wide water conservation plan.

For the past four years I have been on the Board of the Arcade Water District in Sacramento. Arcade, a public agency, serves some 100,000 people. I am the president of the district.

What do I consider the single most important accomplishment of my life? It involves my lovely wife, Lois, and our wonderful family.

Lois and I met at Cal in our freshman year. By our sophomore year she had accepted my fraternity pin. We became engaged and were married in January of 1949. We have been blessed with seven wonderful children.

Rod, our oldest, teaches theatre arts and speech classes to high school and college students in Fairfield, Iowa. His productions are well attended and play an important part in the community.

Rick, our second son, and his wife, Mary, live in the Sacramento area. They have two little ones, Kala and Patrick. He is employed by Home Depot.

Beth, our oldest daughter, resides in Glenshire near Truckee with daughters Sarah and Serena and her husband, John Dill, a Sales Representative in Nevada.

Linda is married to Scott Lasher. Scott is owner and manager of Wes Lasher Inc. of Sacramento, dealing in automobile sales and service. They have three delightful children, Emily, Rodney, and Blythe.

Jeffrey is our engineer. He is a program manager with INTEL Corporation based in Folsom. Jeff and his wife Mary have two lovely little daughters, Marin and Marissa.

Michael, our youngest son, and his wife Sheila have a handsome young boy, Mikey, and daughter, Alexandria. Mike is Sales Manager of Wes Lasher Inc. Sheila continues to model on a part-time basis.

Jodi, our youngest, is married to Bill Palmer, a young attorney in Sacramento, who is Deputy Commissioner and General Counsel of the Department of Insurance for the state of California. Jodi and Bill are the proud parents of little William Rodney.

I am proud of each and every one of them. We are a close and loving family. My grandchildren bring me great joy.

I have been the provider for our family, but Lois is the heart. She does it all without fanfare. She runs our house, but always has time for family requests for baby-sitting, paper-hanging or whatever. In her busy schedule she finds time to work out on a regular basis, doing aerobics, swimming, tennis and power-walking with me. She is known to the grandchildren as "Nonna", and each grandchild will seek her out to play games, draw, or read stories.

I read with pleasure in the June 1992 edition of the California Monthly that Lois Richter Franz "looked more beautiful at the class reunion than on campus." Lois' real beauty goes well beyond her appearance, as friends and family will attest. I am a very happy and fortunate man.

WILLIAM T. (BILL) PANTTAJA

⌘

I was born in Dinuba, Ca. (that was where the hospital was--my family lived in Reedley) on May 19, 1930. My father moved the family to Oakland when I was five years old so that I would have a better chance of going to Cal. I attended Fremont High School (with Bob Fitzgerald) and in our senior year we took second place in football in the Oakland Athletic League. I was offered a grant-in-aid to go to Stanford along with some of my teammates but I just could not do that.

As a Frosh I had the pleasure of getting to know a lot of great guys and playing in the line with Ed Hart, John Ralston and Bob Witter. We had a good team but we didn't win them all. The next season (1948) "Pappy" asked me to save my eligibility because I was only eighteen and had some growing up to do. He had some of the other young players stay back because he wanted to keep them after the older players left. I practiced all that season with the Ramblers, gaining experience and size, but did not play in any of the games.

In 1949, I played with the Ramblers and got some much-needed game experience and my Rambler "C". Late in the season, a minor knee injury kept me out of the game with the Stanford Braves.

In the spring practice of 1950, I felt that I was doing well and would make the Varsity in the fall. In the last week of the spring session, I had a second knee injury which kept me out of the final scrimmage. In the summer, I was happy to be called back for the early practice and, after getting a knee brace, began to learn the position of defensive tackle. A week before the season opener, I had a third knee injury which Dr. Brick Muller said finished any chance I had of contributing to the team. The biggest disappointment for me was not being able to earn a "Big C".

In June 1951, I graduated with a BA in History and entered the US Army as a Regular 2nd. Lieutenant. After a short period of training at the Field Artillery School in Oklahoma, I was sent to Korea, arriving during the winter of 1951-52. During the war there, I served first as an artillery aerial observer directing fire and then as a staff officer. I had planned to resign my commission at the end of the Korean War and return to Berkeley for an advanced degree. About that time, I was made commander of an artillery battery at Fort Hood, Texas, and put on the promotion list for captain. I served as a battery commander for three years and then returned to the Artillery School as a student and stayed on as an instructor. In 1958, I was sent to study Japanese at the Defense Language School at the Presidio of Monterey, Ca. I did well in the year there and the Army sent me to Tokyo to continue my studies for three more years. While in Tokyo, I helped the college football team at Waseda University as a line coach. At the end of the Japanese language and area studies program, I graduated from *Rikkyo Daigaku Daigakuin* (St. Paul's University) in Tokyo with a Masters Degree in Japanese History.

My next stop was Okinawa where I served as the aide-de-camp and interpreter for Lt. General Paul W. Caraway, the High Commissioner of the Ryukyu Islands. The service there at that time was very useful to me for the role I was to play in the return of Okinawa to the Japanese. After two very interesting years, I returned to the Field Artillery in the First Armored Division, Fort Hood, Texas. In 1965, I attended the year course at the US Army Command and General Staff College, Fort Leavenworth, Kansas, and then was sent to the Army General Staff at the Pentagon. This was a difficult time due to the military buildup in Vietnam and the widespread opposition to US involvement there. My duties in the Pentagon were to analyze the political impact of proposed military actions in Asia and make policy recommendations to the Chief of Staff, US Army, and through the Joint Chiefs of Staff, to the President.

After three years in the Pentagon, I was assigned in 1969 to command a field artillery battalion in the DMZ in Korea. It was an excellent unit and I was proud to be the commander for a year. I also served as the commander of Camp Pelham and regional coordinator for all the Army forces in their dealings with the towns in the area near the DMZ.

I was sent directly from Korea to become the Chief, J-5 Section (Government Affairs) of US Forces, Japan. In that position, I had responsibility for all coordination and negotiations between our headquarters, the Government of Japan, and the US Embassy in Tokyo. I had responsibility for the organization and activities of the US side of the US-Japan Joint Committee for the Status of Forces Agreement contained in the US-Japan Security Treaty. During my assignment as Chief, J-5 Section, the United States negotiated the historic return of the Ryukyu Islands (Okinawa is the main island) to the Government of Japan. This voluntary action by the United States is the only instance, so far in recorded history, of a conqueror transferring sovereignty to a former enemy of lands and people taken by military action.

The international political benefits to the US of this action outweighed the extensive military value of air and naval bases there in the western Pacific under US control. Long and delicate negotiations were conducted to ensure continued US access to bases and facilities essential to the continuation of the Vietnam War and future military requirements in Asia. The US had occupied the Ryukyu Islands for over 25 years and had installed US laws, rules and regulations as well as an economic structure; all of these systems had to be changed to conform with Japanese law and practice in the "home islands". A three-part negotiating team was established to solve the problems: the Japanese government team consisted of representatives of all ministries concerned; the US Embassy team had State Department specialists; the US Forces military team had the problems of maintaining the work force of Okinawans, ensuring the use of essential bases and facilities, and related problems of the security of the bases against all forms of intelligence activity.

My role as the head of the third team was to make sure that the needs of the US military were not overlooked or negotiated away for some political gain. As the promised deadline in May, 1972 approached, the pressure grew on the US military to make concessions on things the military felt were essential to its mission in Asia. Fortunately, the Japanese negotiators wanted the return of the Ryukyu Islands for domestic political reasons and backed down on their demands at the last moment. The documents were signed in a dramatic midnight meeting and then-Vice President Agnew turned the islands over to the Emperor of Japan in a formal ceremony the next day (May 15, 1972).

In 1973 I moved downtown to the US Embassy in Tokyo where I became the US Army Attache. I served in that capacity for three years and, when I was not selected for promotion to brigadier general, I requested early retirement to enter business in Japan. Upon retirement, The Japanese government awarded me the Order of the Sacred Treasure medal for my activities in furthering US-Japan friendship and cooperation.

I decided to stay in Japan after my military service to use my knowledge of the Japanese and their language in business. In addition to the fact that the language was very difficult to master, I felt that over the years I had developed an insight into the Japanese mind. I had come to respect the serious and careful way that the Japanese approach problems and seek solutions. They are very pragmatic and always keep their own interests foremost in their minds. The actions they take are sometimes considered to be arbitrary, illogical or even unfair by people with Western backgrounds. But once you know the Japanese and their way of thinking, it is not too hard to determine how they will act. Of course, knowing the language is a big help, but anyone can master the art of working effectively with the Japanese.

In 1976, I began my civilian career as the Executive Director of the American Chamber of Commerce in Japan. I managed the office with a staff of ten persons and did the administration for the elected officers from American businesses in Japan. The job involved dealing with the Japanese ministries controlling business in Japan and with the US Embassy. After four years at ACCJ, Borg-Warner Corporation of Chicago hired me to run their operations in Japan (1981). I had over 30 subordinates and in four years the business increased from $10 million a-year to over $50 million a-year. The firm sold Borg-Warner parts in Japan and manufactured a specialty pump in our factory there. In addition, I was a director on six of the Borg-Warner joint ventures with Japanese companies. I trained one of my Japanese subordinates to take over and, in 1985, left the company to become a consultant in Hawaii.

In 1987, I was selected to be the Executive Director of the Japan-America Society of Honolulu. In that position, I acted as a go-between for the people of Hawaii with the Japanese businessmen there. While in Hawaii, my wife and I helped in the rebuilding of the Cal Alumni Club of Honolulu and we both served on its board of directors.

In the summer of 1990, we had an offer from German friends in Japan to sit their house in Germany (near Frankfurt) and we moved from Hawaii to Germany. We travelled Europe for almost a year and a half before returning to the US and settling in the State of Washington. I remain active as a member of the Board of Directors for NCR Japan in Tokyo and plan to work as a consultant for companies doing business in Japan. I also have a contract with the State Department to serve as an escort and interpreter for Japanese visitors in a VIP program.

My most important accomplishment was learning the Japanese language and putting it to use for our government and myself. I am probably the only one of "Pappy's Boys" who can carry on a conversation in Japanese!

JIM MONACHINO

⌘

As a youngster, I always had the desire to become an athlete. I would compete in foot races at my Dad's company picnics with older kids since I was faster than most children my own age.

As a grade-schooler, I used to watch my cousin, who was a star quarterback at John Adams High School in Cleveland, Ohio, play and wanted to be as good as he was. Whenever he would come over to our house, he would always take me out in the backyard and throw to me.

In the summer, I would get involved in sandlot baseball and as an eighth grader, play for the American Legion--no Little League in those days. In the fall, it was sandlot football. Some guys had equipment and some didn't, it didn't matter. We just wanted to play. We would have as many as 15 on a side. Great times! My dad would always have to come looking for me as I was usually late for supper.

When I was in the sixth grade, I contracted rheumatic fever and was restricted to the classroom during recess and excused from any gym classes. This was a very difficult time for me because I didn't know if I would ever be able to compete again. Just before entering junior high, my homeroom teacher asked me if I wanted to take part in recess activities. My doctor had finally given me the o.k. Boy, was I ever excited! Thank God, the illness was never a factor in my future.

My first year in high school (10th grade) was a very memorable one. A neighborhood friend who was in the 11th grade had taken me to the athletic field to sign up for football. The coach was calling out names and issuing uniforms. It seemed as if there were 100 athletes waiting in line. When he handed out the last uniform, I was still waiting at the gate. He said that was all he had and there would be no more available. I was crushed!

I thought for sure, that as a cousin to the star quarterback who had graduated, I would certainly be picked to try out for the team. My friend said to wait for him, and in a little while he came to me and said to go to the equipment room and get into anything I could find. The tears dried up, and I was on my way. By the time the season started, I was running with the first team.

The next summer, 1945, my dad returned from a trip to the West Coast and informed us we were moving to California, like NOW! He was having health problems and his doctor recommended that he move west. Another blow! All my friends, some as far back as kindergarten, were going to be left behind. And where was I going to go to school? What kind of team did they have? How good were the players there? Would I be able to make the team? All kinds of questions popped into my mind. I knew it was best for my dad, but I was really angry.

After spending most of the summer with family friends, my dad finally found a place for us to live, and after checking the area out, I was enrolled at Redondo Union High School in Redondo Beach, Ca. It was like starting all over again. The first few days of practice were a little awkward, to say the least. I was this 'hot shot' from the East who was going to replace someone on their team. An outsider! It took a while, but I finally convinced them that I was capable of playing their kind of ball and that I was not such a bad guy after all.

The two years there were fruitful for me. We had a very successful football team, two losses in two years, and also went to State with our baseball team. I played third base and was named to the All CIF team in both sports. I was Boy's League

President my senior year and Homecoming King. All in all, it turned out to be a good move Dad made and I *didn't* have to play ball in the snow!

Hal Grant was coach when I arrived at Redondo. He was filling in for Russ Seifert who was still in the service. Coach Grant was a great coach and a gentleman in the truest sense of the word. I've never known him to utter an off-color word. And, he knew how to motivate boys.

I remember our pre-game meeting before our first game. He advised us that our opponent had a very large defensive line and that it was virtually impossible to run up the middle. His plan was to send one halfback around one end and the other around the other end. And then, send Monachino up the middle! That brought guffaws of laughter. Coach looked at us and said if we thought it was that funny, then he had nothing else to say, and he walked out of the room. Dead silence! We won the game.

My senior year, Coach Seifert returned and took over the football program. It was like day and night, the difference between him and Coach Grant. Fire and brimstone were his tactics. Kick 'em in the butt and run till you drop. But we won.

At the end of the season, Coach Seifert asked what plans I had for college. I said, none, as I was planning on helping Dad, who was having health problems, in a small business he had started. Coach Seifert would hear none of it and took it upon himself to write to the major colleges. I was soon contacted by UCLA, USC and California. After visits to their respective campuses, I was leaning toward Cal but UCLA really put some pressure on me to attend. When I learned that Coach Grant was hired to be the Freshman Coach at Cal, it cemented my decision to enroll. Before leaving to register, I played in an All Star baseball game at Wrigley Field in Los Angeles. After the game, I was approached by scouts from the Boston Red Sox organization who wanted to offer me a contract if I would not play football at Cal. I, of course, said I couldn't do it, and that ended my baseball career, if in fact there ever was one.

Going to Cal made my parents very happy and proud since I was the first member of our family to attend college. But more challenges were now facing me: meeting new friends, competing with great athletes, living away from home for the first time. I remember my first visit to the campus. I was awe-struck: the Campanile, the magnificent buildings, the athletic facilities and the grounds. Really beautiful. And Memorial Stadium. What a sight! Nestled in Strawberry Canyon, a sprawling 80,000 seat bowl. There was no doubt in my mind that this was where I belonged.

Fall practice. More than 150 players signing up. Scary? You bet! Talent? You bet! Freshmen like Pete Schabarum, Charlie Sarver, Carl Van Heuit, Bob Minehan and many more. And the veterans, both past players and returning war veterans: Jack Jensen, Jack Swaner, Rod Franz, Jim Cullom, Jon Baker, Bud Van Deren, Bob Celeri, just to name a few. You think, "How in the world will I make the squad?" But you work hard and you enjoy the competition and there you are, first string on the Freshman team. Freshmen were ineligible to play varsity in 1947.

The acceptance of the freshmen by the veterans was gratifying. They took us under their wings and guided us through some very difficult times. I believe the credit goes to Pappy and his staff. They never made you feel as though you didn't belong. Everyone was part of the "*Master Plan*". Their ability to understand the differences between players and jell them into a winning team was uncanny. It was a lesson we all learned. As we moved into the business world later on and became managers, owners and leaders, we would like to think we were as successful in our pursuits as Pappy and his staff were in theirs.

The next three years were fantastic. Three conference titles, three Rose Bowls and many honors were received and many friends made. I was drafted by the San Francisco 49ers, and making that team was a great thrill since the competition there was even more talented than that I faced in high school or college. A short tour of duty with the Navy in San Diego interrupted my professional career, although while on the San Diego Naval Training Center team I played against many of the professional draftees I would face in the future.

Upon my return to the 49ers, I finished out the 1954 season and was released. I signed a contract with the Washington Redskins in 1955 and was considered the starting halfback until a knee injury sidelined me. It wasn't until the final game of the season against the Steelers that I worked my way back into the lineup. Although selected as Offensive Player of that game by Washington sportswriters, contract differences with the owner, George Preston Marshall, influenced me not to return to the team in 1956. Besides, my family was living on the West Coast, and I would have had to live on the East Coast during the season. We had three children at the time, and it was too costly to move back and forth.

I was about to enter the business world! After bouncing around Southern California in the insurance business for three years, I decided that was not for me. I applied for a sales position with a major clay pipe manufacturing firm and took over the Northern California territory, based in San Jose. Although we increased sales 100% four years in a row, there did not seem to be any potential for job or professional growth with that company. An opportunity to take over as sales manager for a clay pipe company in the Midwest prompted our move to Des Moines, Iowa in 1967. This was a five-year plan before a move back to California. We are still trying to get to that 'fifth' year.

There were some moments of indecision. The firm that recruited me decided to sell out to a large corporation. I would manage the Iowa and Minnesota locations. Competition from the plastics industry over the years forced us to close both operations. Now the question was, "Do we stay or return to California?" With our children well into their educations, and having established ourselves in the community, we decided to stay.

In 1983, I became Vice President and General Manager for a Des Moines concrete block manufacturing company, and I look forward to retiring with this firm in a few years. In addition to my business responsibilities, I accepted the 1992-93 presidency of the West Des Moines Chamber of Commerce. I enjoy the interaction of the Chamber in promoting economic development, and supporting the business community and city government.

Sharing in these accomplishments is my wife, Marjorie, my greatest fan and supporter. She backed all my business decisions, right or wrong, and picked up and moved countless times, always encouraging me to take on more challenges. Together, we raised five children, all of whom are busy pursuing careers and raising families of their own. I would like to think I was a positive role model for them.

Maybe what I've described here represents not so much accomplishment as challenge. I do believe that my background in athletics and my training under such great coaches as Hal Grant and Pappy Waldorf have helped me face these life challenges and, with the support of my wife and family, to have conquered them to the best of my ability.

DR. JOHN S. NAJARIAN

⌘

At a very young age, I became quite enamored of the sport of football. I was involved in a park league and would play touch football games with my peers at any opportunity. In the 1930s no professional football team existed west of Chicago, so my football fantasies were clearly focused on the University of California in Berkeley. As soon as I could find a way to get transportation, via streetcars and buses, I began going to Memorial Stadium in Strawberry Canyon as often as possible to watch the Golden Bears play football.

I vividly remember sitting on Tightwad Hill, below the area where the large cement 'C' was embedded in the ground. Although it was not the best seat in the house, it was certainly one that fit my financial situation. Later on, with the bravado and foolishness of youth, my friends and I sometimes found ways of sneaking into the stadium to observe Cal football from a much closer vantage point. As I look back, I am surprised we never got caught. It was rather challenging to scale the fence around the stadium or to steal past the ushers at appropriate times--thanks to adequate misdirected diversion, particularly after the game had begun.

The attraction of watching the Bears became so strong that, eventually, I decided to find a more legitimate, socially acceptable way of doing so. To obtain some monetary return for my efforts as well, I applied for and secured a position as a vendor of soft drinks, peanuts, popcorn, and the like. I could make what I considered at that time a considerable amount of money and still enjoy my favorite sport. I particularly recall, circa 1937, the Thunder Team with Johnnie "Jelly Belly" Meek, Vic Bottari, Sam Chapman, and all the outstanding players who went to the Rose Bowl after that memorable season. From then on, I thought the most fulfilling dream for me would be to play football for the University of California and, if possible, go to the Rose Bowl.

Meanwhile, in the 1940s, I attended Oakland High School. It soon became evident I would have to begin taking my studies quite seriously, so I could earn sufficiently acceptable grades to enter the university. I was a shot-putter, on the Oakland High track team and, in addition, played tackle for three years on the football team.

I was fortunate enough to become an all-city tackle in my final year in 1945. That fall I enrolled as a freshman at Berkeley and went out for football. The war was just ending, and there was no coach. However, Buck Shaw, who had been the head coach at the University of Santa Clara and taken that team to the Orange Bowl, had been named head coach of the new professional football team for San Francisco, eventually called the 49ers. But since the pro team could not begin until 1946, we were fortunate to have Shaw and his assistant, Al Ruffo, as our coaches at California. I was delighted to be a member of the varsity that year, and we had a quite respectable season. I cannot recall our win-loss record. (editor's note: it was 4-5-1)

The following year, 1946, Frank Wickhorst was recruited from the U.S. Navy to be our coach. Unfortunately, the team did not fare well and ended with a 2-7 season. As I look back, I feel what occurred was almost inevitable. Wickhorst had just returned from the Navy and tried to run the football team as a military operation. Most of the players, except for a few of us who were youngsters, were older and just out of the service themselves. They had seen enough time in the military that they rebelled against Wickhorst's strong disciplinary, almost militaristic coaching technique. Because of the unrest in the football team and the miserable season, Wickhorst was fired and his three-year contract was paid off. As a result, the University of California was characterized as a "coaches graveyard." The future did not look very favorable for the Golden Bears.

But in 1947, everything turned around: Lynn "Pappy" Waldorf was recruited from Northwestern to be our head coach. The team was delighted with his selection and became even more so once we got to know Pappy. He was like everyone's friend and yet everyone's father, rolled up in one. This big jolly man obviously knew football very well. He also made a point of learning all our names, even though more than 100 of us were competing to make the team. It soon became apparent how much he cared about each individual player. Even when you were down on the second, third, or fourth team--way across the field practicing--this bellowing voice would ring out "John, keep your head up when you're making a block." He knew who you were, no matter how low on the roster. You were important to him, to the University, and to the football team. What a difference from the previous season! It was not long before all of us would play our hearts out for this man whom we respected, admired, and above all, loved.

In 1947, the team was composed of many of the athletes who had played in 1946. The final roster was almost exactly the same. The only difference was a 9-1 season, rather than a 2-7 season! Our one loss was to our archrival, the USC Trojans. A better example of the influence a coach has on a team could never be found.

My football aspirations had grown up alongside my medical career goals. From the time I was 12 years old and almost died from a ruptured appendix (before the days of antibiotics), I had always wanted to be a doctor. I majored in pre-med at Cal, finishing my undergraduate training in 1948. One of my greatest satisfactions was being accepted into the only medical school that I had applied to, the University of California, San Francisco, School of Medicine. I shall never forget the day the acceptance letter came--the anxiety of opening it, the sheer and absolute joy over its brief comments. Only 72 students were accepted in the class, out of well over 5,000 applications. Many returning to college on the GI Bill had become pre-med or pre-engineering, so that competition was very stiff. My three years of forgoing parties and all the wonderful extracurricular activities that are so enjoyable in college, so that I could play football and still maintain my grades, had now paid off.

I began medical school in the fall of 1948. The first year was headquartered in the Life Science Building on the Berkeley campus. Since I had not officially taken my bachelor's degree yet, I had one more year of eligibility left, so I could play football my first year of medical school. What a dream to have your cake and eat it too--to be in medical school and at the same time to play football. Even better, I knew we were a winning team, under a coach who represented one of the greatest role models of my life.

Medical school turned out to be just as tough as I had thought it would be. The competition was intense and required diligent attention and study. Fortunately, in 1948, our football team began the two platoon system. Thus, I only had to learn the defensive plays and not any of the offense. I felt I could continue in football without jeopardizing my standing in medical school. But after about five or six games, I went into Pappy's office one day and regretfully told him I had to quit because I was getting too far behind in my studies. My fellow students were in laboratories all day, and would study all night. In contrast, I had to take time off in the afternoon to practice football and in the evening go to the training table. Then I had to try to study late into the night, and begin all over the following day. This grind became more difficult than I had anticipated. Pappy was kind enough to understand, and wished me well in my continuing pursuit of a medical career.

Before the Big Game, unfortunately, one of the tackles was injured and I was needed back on the squad. I will never forget when Pappy called me and asked me to come back and play in the last two games of the season. No way in the world could I turn down this icon, Pappy Waldorf, so I returned for the last two games. We ended with a 10-0 season.

As it turned out, the only team in the Pacific Coast Conference that we had not played was Oregon, and they were also undefeated in conference play. By Pacific Coast Conference vote we were selected to go to the 1949 Rose Bowl. Now I faced the biggest decision of my life. Since the 1930s, I had wanted to play for the University of California and to go to the Rose Bowl. I also had a very strong desire to become a doctor. As Christmas vacation approached, all my medical school peers would be studying for their finals in anatomy, histology, neuroanatomy, and other subjects. If I went to the Rose Bowl, I would be spending two weeks in Riverside practicing for the game. I thought about this for a long time, but eventually decided that I had wanted to go to the Rose Bowl long before I had wanted to be a doctor. This was an opportunity I just could not pass up. So I packed a suitcase filled with my anatomy, histology, neuroanatomy, and other medical books and took them to Riverside with me.

We had a wonderful time in Riverside. In addition to preparing for the Rose Bowl game, we were bused to Los Angeles and Hollywood for sightseeing, including tours of movie studios. Further, the Rose Bowl had just been expanded from 90,000 to 100,000 seats, and the game would be the first nationally-televised program of any sort, since they had just completed the co-axial cable from coast to coast.

We played Northwestern that year. Two very sad things happened. First, I never opened the suitcase filled with all my medical books that I had so carefully packed with every intention of preparing for my finals. Second, we lost the Rose Bowl game, 20 to 14. In actuality, we really won the game, yet the score does not reflect it. The next day, a *Los Angeles Times* article proclaimed "How to Win the Game Without the Ball." A picture taken by the *LA Times* photographer showed the fullback from Northwestern, Art Murakowski, carrying the ball toward the goal line. The picture clearly showed that a Cal player (I believe it was myself) had stripped the ball from the fullback: the ball was in the air, and he had not yet crossed the goal line. The official ruled that he *had* crossed the goal line *with* the ball, which the newspaper photographer's picture undeniably refuted. California had, in fact, recovered the ball in the end zone. The official's erroneous ruling gave Northwestern seven points, including the conversion, and the score became, 20 to 14. Had there been instant replay to show that the fullback did not have the ball when he crossed the goal line, we would have won the game, 14 to 13. Thus, the time for instant replay had come even 45 years ago.

However, my childhood goal had been reached: I started as a first-string defensive tackle in the Rose Bowl. I was able to play with my teammate all the way through high school and the last three years in college, my closest friend, Jackie Jensen. Incidentally, he was injured in the second half, which perhaps was one of the reasons we lost (although his backup, Frank Brunk, played an outstanding game that day). I will never forget Jackie and me sitting and talking in the locker room before the Rose Bowl. We thought back to our days at Oakland High School. As sophomores, we never thought we would be at the Rose Bowl, with 100,000 people in attendance and the entire nation able to watch on television. Jackie reached another of his goals, when he became an All-American. After that, in baseball, he was voted the Most Valuable Player in the American League and played with the New York Yankees, Washington Senators and the Boston Red Sox. I too, had reached one of my goals--playing in the Rose Bowl--and was on my way to becoming a doctor.

I learned a very important lesson that season: if you have something you want done, give it to a busy person. I have lived by that credo ever since. Because I had no time that fall to spare, I had to budget my time very carefully so that I could play football and still pay attention to my medical studies. In the fall, I ended up with A's in my courses and passed my finals without difficulty. But in the spring of that year--the second half of my first year in medical school--I had no extra responsibilities. I was no longer playing football, so I could put all my time into medical school. Yet I ended up with B's rather than A's because I did not have to budget my time, and could go to the occasional movie and have a night out with the boys for a beer.

I graduated from medical school in 1952, completed my surgical internship at the University of California Hospital in San Francisco, and spent two years in the service at Kirkland Air Force Base in Albuquerque as a Division Surgeon for the 34th Air Division. I then returned in 1955 to resume my surgical training.

During my surgical residency, I maintained my ties to the University of California by attending as many of the football games as my busy surgical schedule would allow. When the sun was shining and we still had grass in Memorial Stadium and the Cal band marched onto the field followed by the Cal football team--could there ever be a more wonderful way to spend a Saturday afternoon? As the beer commercial put it, "It never gets any better than this."

Still, I could not get enough of the Golden Bears, so I volunteered to be one of the camp doctors for the Lair of the Bear. Every summer we would spend two wonderful weeks at Pinecrest (Camp Gold). It was a great chance to make new friendships and renew old ones with Cal alumni and current Cal students. The memories of those days remain indelibly etched in my mind. The Lair also provided an opportunity for our very young sons to get a taste of the songs--the tradition and the spirit of the University of California. Mike Koll did something so unbelievably unique when he established those camps, the likes of which have never been successfully repeated elsewhere. Even after moving to Minnesota, I continued to return as camp doctor with my family for several years.

Following my residency, I spent three years in research, working first at the University of Pittsburgh in 1960, then at the Scripps Clinic and Research Foundation in La Jolla, California, from 1961 to 1963. I subsequently joined the staff at the University of California, San Francisco, in 1963 as an assistant professor, and began the first transplant program in California. In 1966 I was promoted from assistant professor to full professor, grade three, and made vice chairman of the Department of Surgery.

In the ensuing months, I was recruited by 13 different medical schools throughout the country to become chairman of their surgery department. But I turned them all down until the call came from the University of Minnesota, which I could not pass up. I eventually moved to Minneapolis in 1967 as professor and chairman of the Department of Surgery at the University of Minnesota, a position I have held ever since.

On my departure from California, the football team at Berkeley was kind enough to make me the 1967 Football Alumnus of the Year. I was honored as

Alumnus of the Year of the entire University of California, Berkeley, in 1974. And in 1977, I was named the Alumnus of the Year of the University of California, San Francisco, School of Medicine. Finally, in 1984, I was named the Distinguished Alumnus of the year of Oakland High School. Since that time, I have been very fortunate to receive many more honors, among them a Regents' Professorship (the University of Minnesota's highest honor) and the Jay Phillips Distinguished Chair in Surgery.

I have been privileged to direct one of the world's largest transplant programs, which has performed over 3,500 kidney transplants, as well as numerous heart, liver, pancreas, lung, and combined transplants. As chairman of the Department of Surgery, I have directed the Minnesota program into pioneering innovative, and difficult types of transplants. We have achieved unequalled success with diabetic, pediatric, and older patients. We have made many major research, clinical, and educational contributions to the field of surgery as well as transplantation. In addition, I have trained more than 60 transplant surgeons, who now direct transplant programs all over the United States and abroad and more than 200 other academic surgeons since coming to the University of Minnesota 28 years ago.

Internationally, I was admitted as an Honorary Fellow to the Royal College of Surgeons in England in 1987, a rare distinction shared by only a handful of surgeons throughout the world. I achieved the highest honor possible in the realm of American surgery, when I was elected 1989 President of the American Surgical Association.

Currently, I am the editor-in-chief of the journal, "*Clinical Transplantation*". I am also on the editorial board of 15 other medical journals. I have published more than 1,100 scientific articles and written several books in the field of surgery and transplantation. I was recently listed in the journals of *Science* and *Nature* as the world's 14th most prolific scientist (articles published) and ninth most cited (articles referred to by other authors) for the decade 1981-1990, according to the Institute for Scientific Information.

The numerous patients I have been able to help, either with transplants or with other surgical procedures, have given me some of the most gratifying experiences of my life. As I said in my presidential address to the American Surgical Association, I always have believed in "applying the golden rule to patients, along with the simple but absolutely essential act of touching them--the 'laying-on-of-hands.'"

On a more personal note, I am proud of our four sons, Jon, David, Paul, and Peter. Jon and David graduated from my wife's school, Gustavus Adolphus College, a liberal arts college in Minnesota. Paul graduated from my alma mater, the University of California, Berkeley. Peter graduated from the University of Minnesota. All four boys were linebackers, all four were Academic All-Americans. All played briefly in the professional ranks. Peter, who played for the Seattle Seahawks, the Minnesota Vikings, and the Tampa Bay Buccaneers, most recently played for the Sacramento Surge of the World League of American Football. Our oldest son, Jon, has his own company called Mercury Trading, on the Chicago Board of Options Exchange, which deals with trading stock options. David and Paul are running our Popeye's Chicken franchises. I must say that the way all four sons have turned out is largely, if not totally, due to my wife, their mother, Mignette. She has instilled in them the principles, honesty, integrity, and love of humanity that remind me so much of what I learned from Pappy Waldorf.

How proud I am to be one of "Pappy's Boys." I am grateful I listened to the long-ago call from Strawberry Canyon. The thrill of playing on the 1949 Rose Bowl team for the University of California has remained a singular highlight in my life.

PAX BEALE

⌘

The 1991 Mr. USA Bodybuilding contest at Zellerbach Auditorium at the University of Pennsylvania in Philadelphia was "just a contest" for men over 40. Well, in my case, I was 61, and had never touched a weight until I was 52. So, "**it was just a contest.**" Of course to prepare, you had to work out one and one-half hours on the way to work and one and one-half hours on the way home for one year.

How many people have the privilege of being the very best at something...anything? In the years of Pappy's Boys, I had my chance, and as a big raw-boned kid from Oakland, I should have really been a contributor to Pappy's teams. The fact is I wasn't. I blame my failure on the fact of a chronic bad back. I lost my scholarship after my sophomore season, and never finished either of my first two seasons. Maybe the blame should also have something to do with questionable athletic skills. Who knows? I do know it bothered me, because it is a joy to feel part of something that can be described by the word "excellence." I did benefit from being exposed to the greatest bunch of guys imaginable, but I only kid myself saying I was truly one of Pappy's Boys. I save that title for those who really deserve it like Bartlett, Karpe, Jensen, Richter and an army of others. They have my admiration. I had to wait 61 years for my chance at being the very best and, as I tackled that chance I finally utilized the lessons taught by Pappy Waldorf.

The sport of Bodybuilding is the ugly duckling of all sports. The ultimate Blue Collar Sport. I suddenly found I was good at it but, I also found out they don't just give away their prestigious titles, like "Mr. USA." So, I went for it as if experiencing the thrill and sacrifice of college football all over again. It was "Go Bears" one more time.

My thighs were too small in relation to my height. Thighs get priority. So, it's 600 pounds on the angled leg press, a God awful 30 times, then 700, 800, etc.--the eight set is 1,100 pounds, seven times. You've lifted 96,000 pounds for the first 8 sets. That is like lifting 24 Jaguar automobiles in 23 minutes.

The back is strong as hell, but I lacked width (lat spread). So, besides the 16 sets, it is special stretching exercises. Extensive muscle control practice to get the mind to spread out a back that after 61 years resists the spread with every inflexible muscle fiber, ligament and tendon. Back spread makes the waist look narrower, gives you the 'v' shape. You're fluid enough at 20 to learn the "art" of doing it. Now it is practice and more practice. Boom! One day the spread. A glorious feeling,. You wonder why it was so difficult. The mind has beaten the body. You find that it is mind control over the muscles, not muscle control.

Dieting is eating six small meals a day. Each meal with protein. Try stopping once you start eating. That is more mind discipline. Each meal has a predetermined amount of protein. Protein builds muscle. You augment with supplements, e.g.., vitamins, amino acids, and minerals close to the contest. Dieting does not mean strictly losing weight. It is losing fat and retaining the muscle...and it is a difficult discipline to lose only one pound per week. Not more, or goodbye muscle. No more dairy products or wheat. They bloat you. Stop fats. Acceptable cholesterol range is 140-200. I was already below normal at 123. The next two lab tests show an unheard of 99, lowest ever recorded by one of the biggest labs in the U.S.

One week to go before the contest. Stop all carbohydrates, your prime energy source, for three days and then load them back into your system, a little every hour (more discipline) to create an overload. The overloaded carbohydrated body holds more water in the muscle. This allows you to pump up back stage before the contest. Your muscles will be "fuller"; more massive.

Two days to go. Dieting now means flushing out the sodium salt and retaining potassium salt. The former holds water between the muscles, the latter does not. In the last week, no more toothpaste or tap water as they contain sodium salt. You carry your jug of distilled water everywhere you go.

It is physiologically impossible to lose weight, and have the loss be all fat. You lose muscle also. Will you look skinny? You never thought a 6'2", 226 pound guy could be "skinny", but put him against a 5'9", 209 pound fire plug and at best you look more like a big tight end on a football team, instead of maybe a bodybuilder. Nonetheless, you play the game with the hand you were dealt with. You now realize why diet is more important than lifting the "crummy" weights. And, all the time, you thought the sport was weight lifting.

In the last eight weeks, you run three miles every day, which supports your restricted diet to focus on losing fat rather than muscle or just burning off carbohydrates for energy. Weight lifting itself primarily burns carbohydrates. Fat is your enemy. How do you know if your diet is working? Well, if you are not one "grumpy son of a bitch" you are not dieting correctly. There is a more gratifying way., One day a fellow gym rat will tell you, "Hey, you are getting bigger!" You aren't. You are getting smaller, but the beginning of the "illusion" is being created. You are losing fat, and a little muscle. Actually your muscle definition is better, giving the illusion that you are getting bigger. A few days later someone else tells you the same thing--then another. You are on your way, baby! You now know you are doing it. You are on schedule. You are going to have muscle definition at contest time. Suddenly it is all worth it. You will have conquered your body. You begin to feel that surge of invincibility.

Tanning is mandatory, as is shaving off body hair--yeah right up into the crotch 'cause in the contest you are not exactly overdressed. Tanning in a machine is efficient, but the natural sun thins your skin better. Thin skin makes your muscles look better. You drive to Marin County from San Francisco mid-day to search for natural sun the last week. Now you are really blowing your entire day on preparation. Bodybuilding now dominates your life. Earning a living is passé. Question: When is a jockstrap not a jockstrap? Answer: When it is a pair of posing trunks for a bodybuilding contest. You were told the last time that your posing trunks didn't hang right and your color choice was not "you". You gotta be kidding! So long as the trunks don't climb up and get caught between your cheeks, what difference can it make? Nonetheless, you blow a Saturday and drive one hour each way to Richmond, to have special trunks made for guys with a big pelvis, and get color coordinated from a selection of 300 colors. Maybe clothes do make the man after all. On Saturday night, you are going to find out.

You have done everything bodybuilders everywhere do, be they in the professional Mr. Olympia, or a third Place finisher in some small contest in Walla Walla, Washington.

You choreograph your evening presentation to music, hoping you will be one of the top three who are the only ones allowed to present a posing routine in the evening. Otherwise, despite all your preparation, you only get introduced and, in some big contests, do not even qualify to be introduced!

You will be judged on the morning of the contest, over and over again. You will be "called out" and asked to do a mandatory pose next to two others. Then two of the three are sent back and two more are "called up". You hope you are not sent back! One by one you are assessed by seven of the most discerning judges to determine your place.

Mandatory poses and relaxed poses are demanded by the judges. The judges look at muscle mass (bigger the better), symmetry like pleasing broad shoulders and tapering back, and muscle definition which is how clearly each muscle stands out from the others. Good bodybuilders have each muscle set apart. Great descriptive terms are used to describe muscle definition: "Chiseled", "Cut", "Ripped", or "Razored"...they say it perfectly. Vascularity, while repugnant to inexperienced fans, nonetheless appeals to the judges. Some contestants sneak a few shots of alcohol back stage, or throw down excessive niacin tablets to increase vascularity.

Gimmicks and more gimmicks. You become paranoid and listen to every "gym expert" tell you the latest in preparation. And, if they can tell you, this is how Arnold did it, you do it without even challenging the concept. You are psychologically ready to grab any little thing to make you better for those few moments in the judges' eyes. Your goal is to look your best at that moment of competition. Not an hour before or afterwards. You've worked a year for that moment and to say you were "carrying too much water" (a bloated look" doesn't help. There is no excuse to compete and not be "chiseled". You just didn't get your mind to discipline your body. Albeit, in every contest, there are those who forsake muscle definition for muscle size, but bloated, bigger, smooth muscles invariably lose.

Bad symmetry can be blamed on your parents. However, the name of the game is to create an illusion and hide your bad genes. I never won a contest until I met a training partner who convinced me I could stretch and twist the "ole bod" to partially hide my genetic deficiencies. And, while he cannot make me 5'9" tall, it is truly amazing the art and science of creating an illusion to offset a bad body part. Perhaps this is the essence of bodybuilding. Taking your God-given genes and making the best you can of them. Some do it with oil paint, others with clay. The bodybuilder does it with the resistance of weight, diet, supplements, and most important, a 24-hours-a-day disciplined mind control.

If you qualify for the evening contest, your choreographed routine lasts one and one-half minutes. That's right, you have worked for a year to qualify to stand up for one-and-one-half minutes in a jock strap and not make an ass out of yourself. Hard to believe. But as I said, "**it's just a contest**."

Victory can be sweet and sour. Sweet in that I attained the top of my sport, albeit it took me 61 years. Sweet because seven days later I was invited to the Mr. Universe contest in London, which some guy named Arnold had won previously. Sour because I immediately had to commence training again, and I was exhausted and I hurt...even more than I admitted to myself in my pursuit of being the best. Sour because I fell off the aerobic equipment at the local gym and 72 hours later I had heart surgery, a six-way bypass! Was it worth it? Well, for the rest of my life I would always be "Mr. USA." Somehow I like the sound of that title.

LES RICHTER

⌘

When Lynn O. Waldorf arrived in California to take over the football program at the University of California, he brought with him a great deal more than just a high level of football technical knowledge.

He brought with him dedicated service to one of the greatest universities in the world.

First of all, he had a deep devotion to the highest ideals of teaching young men. For this he shall always be held in the highest esteem by all of those whose lives he touched.

Ingrained in his personality was an affection for others that attracted young and old alike to him. This affection, woven so naturally into his personality, is undoubtedly what gave birth to the apt nickname, "Pappy." This nickname was applied to him by Bert Ingwersen, his former line coach at Northwestern University. At a social gathering one evening, Waldorf was sitting cross-legged in a corner of the room with a drink in his hand and looking rather pensive when Bert said, "Why don't you get up and join the crowd. You're sitting there like an old Pappy."

Pappy always had a high regard for those who reached their optimum potential, whether it be in business, education, religion or in any other field. Pappy felt the fulfillment of an ambition represented the essence of accomplishment.

Another important element that Waldorf brought to California when he arrived in 1947 was a coaching style and a methodology that elevated collegiate football on the West Coast, and especially in the then Pacific Coast Conference, which included California, Stanford, USC, UCLA, Oregon, Oregon State, Washington, Washington State, Montana and Idaho.

I can remember back when coaches from everywhere swarmed to Berkeley during the off-season to see if they could acquire some of this magic formula that awakened "the Sleeping Giant," as Pappy referred to the dormant Cal football program. It wasn't "Magic" he always told his listeners. It was "organization." That organization, he would remark, started during spring football practice and included patience, attention to detail, and the delegation of responsibility and authority to his assistant coaches. The one clinic he staged every year, coordinated with spring practice at Cal, attracted standing-room-only crowds of high school and junior college coaches. Those sessions continued long into the night.

Pappy also liked to explore all areas and avenues of possibility. In a pre-spring practice announcement in the Daily Cal, he would welcome every able-bodied Cal man on campus to turn out. This drove his assistants and the Cal Athletic Department staff, including equipment men and trainers, out of their minds. Pappy felt that if one outstanding prospect emerged from this large group, the effort was worth it. At times there would be a turnout greater in numbers than the Athletic Department had uniforms.

Pappy remarked frequently how much it meant to him to observe, in retrospect, the success of his players in later life. Years after their graduation, the business and professional achievements of his players gave him the greatest rewards in life.

The Waldorfian principles also extended to the love of family--both his own and the families of his players. He called on former football captains and others who were leaders during their undergraduate days to keep him posted on the family and business life of those he had coached.

The game he loved so much brought great fame and distinction to this marvelous individual, something which he handled with modesty and with dignity. In physical appearance, he was the typical coach, if one could piece together such a character---portly, slightly disarranged in his dress, the ever-present cigar in his mouth and his white hair combed in backward fashion, and a baby clean, smooth rounded face with pinkish cheeks.

When Pappy entered a crowded noisy room, he commanded instant attention. All eyes turned toward this jolly, good-natured man and he would return the compliment with a gentle smile, a raising of hand to acknowledge the greeting and the acceptance of a foamy glass of beer, which someone would always place in his hand before too much time had elapsed.

Pappy touched the lives of countless players, friends and others, not only from the sporting world but from all walks of life. Somehow, he was destined to be a kind of "master"--one who commanded attention, respect, and admiration.

I saw this more and more in the years after I had graduated and spent more time around the "Wise Walrus," as he was affectionately called by the media. That effervescence and warmth permeated the campus. You could sense this in one of the yells that the rooting section would roar,"Keep Pappy Happy."

Beyond his rare coaching ability, Pappy had a unique personality, a charisma, a friendliness and a warmth that rubbed off on all of us. How fortunate we are that he influenced our lives in such a lasting and dramatic way.

JAMES (JIM) S. MARINOS

⌘

I was born in San Diego, California on September 5, 1929. I am a product of the very end of the "Roaring Twenties" and the very beginning of the "Great Depression". No wonder I have a variety of personality traits and perspectives. Both of my parents were born in Greece and were immigrants to the USA around the turn of the century. Neither parent was educated extensively either in Greece or this country, and both received minimal training to become American Citizens. My father, Sam Marinos, was in the wholesale produce business for more than 50 years, from around 1908 until 1959 in San Diego. My mother's oldest brother, Gregory, was in the ice cream business in San Diego and met my father as a young aspiring businessman and brought my mother, Marika, over from the old country in 1919 to meet my dad. He became not only Uncle Gregory but Uncle "Matchmaker". My parents were married shortly after they met. They produced four children: my brother , George, who is the oldest; my sister, Joyce (shortened from Euthemia); my sister, Athena, and finally me.

Although my parents were not educated to any extent they saw to it that my brother received a degree from USC. My two sisters attended but did not complete San Diego State University, and I was fortunate enough to attend Cal at Berkeley.

I grew up on the sandlots and dirt ball fields of San Diego. At every opportunity I was involved in playing pick-up baseball games, basketball and football games. We actually played tackle football in beautiful Balboa Park on weekends without any equipment or pads while I was in Junior High School. I was fortunate to attend San Diego High School where a wonderful head football coach, Bill Bailey, was responsible for developing a long succession of tremendous football powerhouses. He was assisted by Ron Maley, his ultimate successor, who was also a great coach out of USC. While at San Diego High School I was on both the football and basketball teams. I was too short to be much of a basketball player but was able to play a lot of football. In my senior year, I was honored to be elected as Student Body President of the Graduating Class of June, 1947. My grades were not all that great and I was only able to enter Cal in September of 1947 based on my principal's letter of recommendation. I completed my studies in the four years of undergraduate school while at Cal and graduated with my degree in Political Science in June of 1951. While at Cal I participated as a freshman in both football and baseball and played on the Ramblers in 1948 and 1949 and the Varsity Football Team in 1950. Although I was carried on the Varsity, I probably wouldn't have played at all had it not been for some of my comrades on the team. Two games into the season we were preparing for the battle in Los Angeles at the Coliseum against USC, and each week the players were allowed to elect a game Captain. Incredibly my colleagues came out of the conference room and announced that I had been elected Captain for the USC game. Not only was I astonished but Pappy Waldorf almost had a heart attack. I had been carried on the squad and had played a great deal of football as a Rambler as a Sophomore and a Junior, but 1950 was going to be a year of rebuilding with several young quarterbacks brought into the program. I was a Senior and was expendable. However, because my comrades and supporters on the team elected me Captain, when the coaches were revived and brought back to their senses, they actually let me start the USC game. We won the game and I was able to start every game thereafter, and we went undefeated. I am forever indebted to Dick LemMon and John Ralston for pressing to have me elected captain--from relative oblivion! Our only blemish that season was a 7-7 tie in the Big Game against Stanford. It was a titanic defensive game and resulted in a tie only because we missed one or two scoring opportunities that could have brought victory.

January 1, 1951 was our third Rose Bowl encounter in succession, and I was designated to start that game. Regrettably, like the two that preceded ours, we lost, 14-6, to a very versatile Michigan team that came off the deck to beat us in the second half. I was fortunate to throw a 49-yard touchdown pass in the first half to Bob Cummings which electrified all of the fans in the Bowl, our team and particularly my parents, brother and sisters. With that explosive start I was sure we would dominate that game and go on to win it. Regrettably, the momentum changed in the second half and we slowly lost the lead and were defeated in a real battle down to the last play.

I was able to scrape up enough credits and grade points to barely get into Boalt Hall School of Law at Berkeley and I attended there two years. However, before I took on the rigors of law school in September of 1951 I jumped on the first airplane to Anchorage, Alaska to join a traveling semi-pro baseball team and to witness the great frontier first hand. I was fortunate to get on a team captained by Ed Sanclemente, one of Cal's greatest third basemen. Ed played third base for the Bears with stellar athletes such as Jackie Jensen, Bobby Odell, Jim and John Fiscallini and many others who won the league championship. That was my first exposure to Alaska, and I have since returned approximately 25 times for hunting and fishing experiences beyond description.

After that great first summer in Alaska I started at Boalt Hall and the grind was on. After two grueling years at Boalt, I was worn out, fatigued and disenchanted. More than that, I was getting poor grades. I left law school disillusioned, bewildered and unsure of just what I would do in the future. Military duty was certain and mandatory; so I checked out a popular program available in the 1950s--joining the Marine reserves and playing football during a two-year tour of duty. I played football at the Marine Corp Recruit Depot, San Diego, in 1953 and then at Camp Pendleton in 1954. Just before I was released in the summer of 1955 I played and started in a military Pacific Coast All-Star football game against the Washington Redskins. That was my first and last mistake in connection with the NFL. I was lucky to get out of there alive.

After the Marine Corps I finished law school at a new fledgling school of law, the University of San Diego, which had its first class of seven students. Through a quirk in the rules I was able to take the bar examination in 1957 before I completed my final few courses. With even more amazing good fortune, I passed the bar exam while still in my last year of law school and I started practicing law in San Diego in June of 1957. I finished my classes and received my degree from USD School of Law in 1958, as the first person ever graduated by that law school to become a practicing attorney in the United States of America, let alone California.

I have had a continuing and vigorous law practice for 37 years and have also been involved in real estate, warehouse development, and various other businesses. I have been very fortunate to have a few more winners than losers and I find myself still very active and very involved in real estate management, business activities and primarily a civil litigation law practice.

Over the years, I have hunted and fished extensively in Alaska, and on several occasions I have enjoyed lengthy safaris into Africa on big game hunting expeditions. I have also had the thrill of catching major game fish not only in Alaska but in Mexico and Costa Rica.

Not inconsequentially, I have been the proud father of three fine daughters, the result of my first marriage. Incidentally, I remarried a beautiful young lady with six children and we ended up actually raising nine children between us. My three natural daughters, all well-educated, have adhered to the same work ethic I followed in helping bring them to maturity. My oldest daughter owns her own small ladies sportswear manufacturing company, along with her mother, and their partnership is succeeding very well. My second daughter is the chief buyer for the four Nordstrom's stores of San Diego County in the "Collectors" department, the ladies fashion wear. My youngest daughter is an administrative assistant at Beeba's International, a worldwide clothing manufacturing and production company. Obviously, all three of my kids love clothes.

In retrospect, I look back on what has been a most fascinating, sometimes thrilling and always challenging career. From the time I was a kid I received some powerful messages from my parents about dedication, loyalty, hard work and perseverance. Without those great educational lessons, I never would have been admitted to Berkeley, certainly would never have been admitted into Boalt Hall and I definitely would never have passed the bar examination. My experiences at Cal were monumental in terms of learning, and the competition on the football field was a major component of those experiences. The camaraderie with so many wonderful and marvelous athletes is beyond my ability to evaluate or quantify. My association with these great gentlemen has lasted so many decades that we still consider ourselves close and warm friends, even though we only see each other once or twice a year. The combination of my parental guidance and support, coupled with the faithfulness of my brother and sisters (who were my greatest cheer leaders), followed by my experiences at Cal and particularly on the football team gave me an advantage and put me well ahead of all of my peers.

THOMAS B. DUTTON

⌘

I was born and raised in Alhambra, California, and attended Alhambra High School where I was a student body officer and member of the football and track teams. In my senior year it was my good fortune to be selected for the football All Southern California C.I.F., first team, an honor which contributed to my recruitment to the Berkeley campus in 1950. The achievement in high school of which I was most proud was receiving both academic and athletic scholarships to U.C. Berkeley.

As the youngest of seven children, I had a rich and rewarding family life. I had gentle, kind and caring parents, whose personal values and optimistic philosophy of life not only were significant in my early development, but have continued to provide critical direction throughout my university, professional and personal life. Integrity, civility, tolerance, dedication and hard work were expected of me, and they provided a vital framework for my actions and decisions.

The most significant achievement in my life has been a strong and rewarding marriage of more than 40 years to my wife Eina. This relationship has been of immeasurable value personally and professionally and has provided a sense of fulfillment that otherwise would not have been possible. My children and grandchildren have also been a source of great pleasure and contentment.

I have had a rewarding career in higher education, serving for 36 years as a student personnel administrator. My survival in a field that is characterized by demanding expectations and high attrition was strongly influenced by the inspiration, encouragement and wisdom of individuals such as Pappy Waldorf and Clark Kerr. The quality of education on the Berkeley campus also was instrumental in my personal development and professional progress. The opportunity to combine achievement in academics and athletics in one of the finest institutions in the world was a great asset to me during both my academic and professional careers. As an undergraduate I was elected football captain, named an Academic All-American and appointed Commencement Speaker for the Class of 1954. I was graduated with highest honors. These were rewarding years.

In 1956, at age 24, I had the privilege of being appointed an Assistant Dean of Students at Berkeley after receiving my Master's degree. While serving full-term as a dean, I worked on my doctorate, completing the degree in 1961. My education and professional work at Berkeley contributed significantly to my appointment as Dean of Men at Ohio University in 1962 and Dean of Students in 1965 and later Vice Chancellor at Oakland University in Michigan. The reputation of the Berkeley campus was very high among educators in the Midwest and greatly enhanced my candidacy for these positions.

My most significant professional challenge was provided in 1970 when I came to Davis as Vice Chancellor for Student Affairs with responsibility for building a student affairs program in a rapidly developing institution. It was exciting and enjoyable to participate over a period of 22 years in the growth of a mid-sized campus of 13,000 students with a good reputation in higher education to a nationally acclaimed institution of 23,000 students with a budget of over $900 million and a distinguished record in research, instruction and campus life.

The challenge and reward came in transforming a decentralized, limited student affairs program into one of the most complex and highly regarded operations in the country. The program evolved in 1991 into a $120 million operation with a staff of 1,000. It was designed to assist students in their intellectual and personal development through high quality support services within a constructive campus environment. The program was unique in the United States because it not only consisted of all of the traditional student affairs services but of academic and general administrative functions as well.

Although the program received national recognition for its quality and diversity, what I valued most highly was the effect of the program on the growth and development of Davis students. In surveys conducted over several years, students and alumni expressed very positive feelings about their Davis campus experience. Another measure of the success of the program was the high level of student involvement in campus governance and decision-making, cultural and social activities, community service, athletic competition, and peer support services (advising, counseling and tutoring).

Recent evaluations by campus and external groups have cited the important contributions of the Student Affairs staff and services to student development as reflected in the character and quality of campus life. One reason for the program's recognized success was the long tradition of collaboration among Student Affairs staff, faculty and academic administrators. This partnership was based on the assumption that student learning can be improved by focusing on both intellectual and personal growth along with integrating developmental activities in and outside the formal classroom setting. An indication of the effectiveness of the integration approach to learning is the fact that UC Davis has had among the highest graduation rates in the UC system and that Davis alumni rate their campus experiences highly. Davis graduates are admitted to the best graduate programs and compete effectively for highly skilled and demanding jobs throughout the country.

Any program is only as good as its staff, and I was blessed with outstanding personnel over many years. Staff members were not only very competent professionally, but were highly committed to the educational mission and values of the campus. They ensured that high quality services were provided and that the vital interests of the campus were served, even in times of budgetary constraints.

The achievements of the program were also directly related to the philosophical and fiscal support of the campus administration, and the commitment and dedication of the faculty to excellence in teaching and to the general education of the students. Students, as clients, played an important role as well by articulating their needs, providing fresh ideas about how to improve service, and prompting, sometimes gently and sometimes very directly, those in authority to make necessary changes.

I take considerable pride in the progress the campus made in increasing the diversity of the student body. When I came to Davis in 1970 as a Vice Chancellor, relatively few minority students were enrolled. Now these students constitute over one-third of the student body. Over the years, a concerted effort was made by faculty, students and staff to expand the enrollment and graduation rates for these students, and their dedicated work achieved results. Although a stronger effort will be required in the future to attain student affirmative action goals, good progress was made and a foundation was established for greater success in the years ahead.

While serving as Vice Chancellor at UC Davis, I was elected President of the National Association of Student Personnel Administrators (NASPA), an important organization that represents student personnel staff nationwide. I was also appointed Director of Research and Publication of NASPA, which made it possible to complete several studies and publications of value to the student affairs field.

Finally, in 1976 I was the recipient of NASPA's Scott H. Goodnight award for outstanding performance as a student affairs administrator. My accomplishments and recognition in NASPA were particularly meaningful because they reflected the esteem of professional colleagues throughout the country.

As I look back on my years in higher education, I am well satisfied with my experiences and associations. Of greatest significance were the relationships with administrative colleagues, faculty and students and the opportunity to participate in the learning process in four institutions. The most important part of my work was in developing and administering programs and services that facilitated student learning and development, and it is my hope that these efforts ultimately enhanced the quality of students' lives.

JIM TURNER
as told to Judy Lowery

⌘

I was officially one of "Pappy's Boys" from 1947-1950, when I played tackle for the University of California football team. It was a privilege to play ball for a man who brought Cal into the public light. The publicity, experiences, victories, and losses too, were very influential in the years to come. But the relationship with Coach Pappy Waldorf has also had a lasting influence on my life.

As a student at Castlemont High in Oakland, I began playing football and made the All City team for two years. Basketball and track also absorbed my interest. But a pretty brunette named Madolyn Cochran caught my eye when I was a senior, and suddenly my interests changed! It was difficult getting her to go out with me because she hadn't forgotten the time I saw her crying in a movie theater (at a sad movie) and called her "cry-baby"! She tells me now that it was my letterman's jacket that changed her mind.

Maddie and I began dating. When I joined the U.S. Marine Corps Reserve in 1943, I was very glad to be sent to nearby College of the Pacific so that she and I could still see each other. During the next two years, I was able to play football through the Marine V-12 program. I earned four more letters to wear on my new jacket--two in football, and one in basketball and swimming. In 1944, I made the All-Coast team. I was hoping to impress Maddie, because I knew that a move to Quantico, Virginia, was next. She would have to choose between two boyfriends. I was hoping that the girl who was my first date would choose to become my wife.

I moved to Virginia for Officer Candidate School as expected. Maddie accepted my proposal of marriage and came out on the train. Our wedding was held on April 28, 1945, with Marine Corps buddies posing as best men, bridesmaids, and attendants. That evening, we just happened to look at the marriage license. The minister had given us the wrong one, accidentally switching our license with that of a couple married just before us. I was up before dawn, waiting on his doorstep to catch him before he left on a fishing trip. Now, officially man and wife, we once more said, "Good-bye," as I left for Japan.

While stationed in Pearl Harbor, I played with the Marine Corps All-Stars. There were 15 All Americans on the team. However, we lost every game! That should say something about the other teams. Navy had a line that averaged seven years per man of pro ball; Army boasted of players like Bill Dudley and George McAfee.

Coming back to the states and to my new bride was a fantastic experience. Since all of my football experience was in service ball, I still had four years of eligibility left. So, I enrolled as a freshman at U.C. Berkeley in September 1946. That year our team had a 2-7 record, under Coach Frank Wickhorst. I made the All-Coast team, now a 6'4" 220 pound tackle known as "Big Red" (for my bright red hair!). Marriage was agreeing with me.

The next season brought with it a new coach, Lynn "Pappy" Waldorf. Things started turning around for our team. Our record reversed to 9-1. I made the All-Coast team again, and Maddie gave birth to our team "mascot," Judy Lynn, who was born the night before the UCLA game.

Pappy's second season was even more successful--with a 10-0 record. Unfortunately, I missed half of it, due to a knee injury in the Washington game. I sat out the rest of the season until the Rose Bowl game against Northwestern. In spite of the injury, I was selected for All-Coast, All American honors.

After the Rose Bowl, I had major reconstructive surgery on the knee. Then, in June, 1948, tumors were discovered on two ribs. Another surgery was performed; but, three days later the doctor came in with the bad news: the wrong ribs had been removed! This was a real blow. I became so discouraged that I called Maddie and told her, "Goodbye," over the phone. Something in my heart told me not to give up--that I could make it. I called her right back and apologized. Everything would be all right. A few days later, two more ribs were removed, and I started back on the road to recovery. The scar went all the way around my body, from front to back on both sides. It made a good story for my swimmers at Bakersfield College. I told them a Samurai soldier came at me with his sword during the war and cut me right in two.

This was the most traumatic time of my life. I had to learn basic football all over again, due to a knee brace and protective rib gear. No more flying eagle tackles for this player. Maddie was a tremendous source of support and encouragement during this period. The old know-how started coming back. I was again selected for the All-Coast team, and made All American. My senior year ended with a second run at the Rose Bowl and the privilege of being team co-captain.

My three seasons of playing ball under Pappy were exciting ones, and they made my transition from player to coach easier. Maddie and I had two more children, Jim and Jan, while I was coaching the football team at Hayward High School, in Hayward, California. In 1950, we moved to Bakersfield where I became line coach and swimming coach at Bakersfield Junior College. My coaching was influenced by Pappy's strong values and good example.

Being a coach's wife was sometimes hard on Maddie, who put up with long periods of my absence. She raised our growing family, with my help in the off-season. The twins, Jack and Jill, were born in May, 1962, completing a family of five children...three girls and two boys, all with "J" first names (we had to name the pets after Maddie: Mopsy, Myrtle, etc.)

We were able to take the family on many outings--camping, fishing, and rock-hunting. We all loved the close, fun times we shared together. I was asked to be on the staff at a Fellowship of Christian Athletes conference one summer. The whole family was invited, so we drove to Ashland, Oregon for the first of many such conferences. The children got involved with the sports activities, Maddie worked with the coaches' wives and I had a group of high school athletes, from all over the West Coast.

For the first time in my life, I met Jesus Christ. I came away from the conference a changed man. As a successful athlete and coach, as a husband and father, I thought that I had everything I needed in life. But, I found out I was missing out on a fantastic relationship. Now, His plan started unfolding, as Maddie and I became volunteer staff members and began recruiting kids from our hometown to FCA camp.

My local Kiwanis group was able to give financial assistance to several athletes so that they could attend the summer conferences. I visited other clubs, asking them to raise money to send students from local high schools. Kids who had attended the conferences would come with me to Kiwanis meetings to share how their lives had been influenced by the FCA. Before long, we were getting calls to speak at Kiwanis Clubs throughout the state. Maddie and I began to anticipate retirement so that we could travel and represent FCA full-time.

Retirement came in 1988 after teaching and coaching for 39 years. Without shifting gears, we moved right into the volunteer phase of our lives, speaking at various Kiwanis clubs throughout the state and attending summer FCA conferences. Maddie became involved with the Nurses' Auxiliary at the hospital, working in the Emergency room. I taught swimming at the local arthritis center.

Life has been very fulfilling for me. I am thankful for the great coaches I was privileged to work with, for the experiences I had as a coach, for a wonderful wife and family. When the last quarter of this final great "Bowl" is over, I will know with satisfaction that the game was played well.

ERIC R. SCHULTZ

⌘

I was born on September 26, 1923, two weeks after my immigrant parents arrived in Middletown, Connecticut, from Germany. We lived in the German part of Middletown and, consequently, when I entered kindergarten most of my speaking ability was in German. This, of course, caused some heckling, but coming from a tough neighborhood, my friends and I were able to silence the hecklers whenever it became necessary.

Growing up during the Depression was an education in itself. Most of the time no one had two coins to rub together and whenever someone was fortunate enough to sell iron, brass, or aluminum to the junkman--he felt like he was sitting on top of the world. This type of life continued until I reached the age of 12. That summer, by lying about our ages, we were all able to go to work in the tobacco field picking Broad Leaf Tobacco, for which the Connecticut Valley was noted. We felt we had it made--working ten hours a day, six days a week for $2.10 per day. If you were big and strong enough and worked hard, you got moved up to a Basket-Hauler and then made $2.75 per day.

During this period, I can remember bringing my weekly pay envelope home containing all of $16.50 (nothing was taken out of your pay in those days). Still, I had earned more than my father, who worked as a weaver. I received $4.00 from my earnings and that made one feel like "you really had it made!" The rest went into the family coffers to help support our family of five, since I now had a sister and brother.

Also, during this period, athletics played a major role in my life. For recreation, all of us played every sport as a given season arrived. Like all youngsters, we all wanted to be around and with the "Big Guys." This proved to be the best athletic education we young ones could have earned. You had to learn to play tough in any sport, otherwise you became a spectator. This also gave us an edge when we entered high school. By knowing what had to be done athletically, most of those in our gang were fortunate enough to make varsity teams in football, baseball and basketball as freshmen.

As a sophomore, standing 6'2" and weighing 190 pounds I made the starting teams in football, baseball and basketball and was lucky enough to make All-State in all three sports for the years 1940, 1941 and 1942. In 1942 I was voted Baseball Captain and tied a school record by pitching 18 strikeouts in one game, a record which still stands.

In my freshman year, my father, who firmly believed everyone had to have a trade in life, forced me to go to trade school as well as high school. In 1939 and 1940, I went to trade school from 8 a.m. to noon, learning a machinist trade, and then to high school from 12:30 p.m. until 2:30 each day. This meant that I only had to take two courses each day in high school--English and History.

During the latter part of my sophomore year in high school, colleges began to take notice of my athletic ability. I can remember receiving letters from Tennessee, Fordham, Yale, Connecticut, Michigan and Georgia. Discussing this with my coach, Jacques Grenier, it became evident that there was no way I could accept a college scholarship by taking two classes a day in high school. If I wanted to go on to college, I would have to quit trade school. When I approached my father with the idea of quitting, I nearly started World War II early. After much hassling, Jacques Grenier, talked to my father and had other sports-minded people my father knew talk to him about my attending high school on a full time basis so that I could go on to college on an athletic scholarship. My father finally relented and I stopped going to trade school. Of course, he never let me forget the fact that I was making a big mistake by not following up with a trade.

Athletically, my junior and senior years were outstanding but from a scholastic standpoint, it was a bitter experience. I worked hard enough to graduate, but there was no way possible of going on to college, having taken only two full years of high school courses.

Then my life took a turn for the better, although I did not realize it at the time. Coach Grenier took me under his wing and became like a real father to me--spending money, allowing me the use of his car, etc. The best thing he did was to get me away from the crowd I was hanging around with. Some of the "old gang" ended up in reform school and the older ones in jail. In later years, I was always thankful for what he did for me.

World War II arrived and Coach Grenier was called back to active duty, so we lost contact with each other. I worked as a machinist in a defense plant and continued athletically by playing semi-pro baseball, football and basketball. The highlight was a pitching tryout with the old Brooklyn Dodgers at Ebbets Field. The Dodgers must have liked what they saw because I was offered a minor league contract for all of $600 per month. I turned this down, since I was already earning nearly three times that figure working as a machinist.

As the war came to a close, Coach Grenier was mustered out of the service in Santa Monica, California. Before he came back to Middletown in February of 1946, to finish out his high school contract, he applied for and got the football coaching job at St. Anthony High School in Long Beach, California. Our paths crossed again in May of that year. Coach Grenier thought that I was either playing pro ball, or away at school somewhere and when he learned that I was working as a machinist, he "blew his stack." He told me bluntly that he was leaving for California as soon as school was out in June and that he was going to set me up to go to school there. I figured that would be the last I would hear from him because of the grades I ended up with in high school. But, true to his word, he called me in July, and all he said was, "Be at my home in Long Beach by the middle of August, so you can begin pre-season football practice at Long Beach City College." Married by now, I discussed the situation with my wife, then sold everything we owned, paid off our bills and promptly left Ye Olde Middletown for Long Beach.

Things went well at Long Beach City College. All of my grades were made up and I was ready to attend one of four colleges on the coast. After visiting S.C., Loyola, UCLA, Stanford, Oregon and Washington, I met a Cal Alumnus, Gene Pickett. He arranged for me to take a trip to Berkeley and when I got off the train and saw the rolling hills of Berkeley, I knew that this was the school I would choose, because it reminded me of the rolling hills back home. This decision was made before I saw the school and met with Pappy Waldorf. Once I met Pappy, I knew I had made the right decision; I enrolled in the spring of 1948, in time for spring football practice.

My years at Cal were probably the most exciting and wonderful years of my life. When I arrived in Berkeley, my apartment was not ready, so I was asked by Pappy if I would "babysit" his home and daughter Caroline, for one month. The month ended up being four months and I really got to know Pappy, the man, and learned why he was loved by all who came in contact with him.

After spring practice in 1948, I came up with an idea that changed the recruiting procedure at Cal. At that time, Vic Schmidt, was Commissioner of the then Pacific Coast Conference, and he issued a directive stating that no coaches or alumni, of a given member school, could contact prospective athletes. One day during a "bull session" in Pappy's office, I asked him if Schmidt's ruling also prohibited a student from contacting prospective athletes whom alumni and coaches were interested in "rushing." Pappy called Attorney Herm Selvin, in Los Angeles to see what, if any, legal ramifications were involved.

Two days later, I was on a plane to Los Angeles to meet with the powers of the Southern Seas, namely: Frank Storment, Herm Selvin, Henry Frost and John Normandy. I outlined my plan and everyone agreed that it should work. Upon my return to Berkeley, Pappy and I sat down and went over the list of athletes that Cal Coaches were interested in seeing for football, baseball, basketball and track.

From that point on, my every weekend, or vacation, was spent flying all over the West Coast talking to high school and junior college athletes and making arrangements for those who wanted to come to Berkeley to visit the school. This was a very enlightening and enjoyable experience. Some of the names that still stand out in my memory are Matt Hazeltine, John Olszewski, Bill Mais, John Peterson, Dean O'Hare, Ray Willsey, Steve Turner, Bill Dutton, Tom Dutton, Steve Glick and Sammy Williams.

I continued working for the Southern Seas after graduation in 1950, through the Rose Bowl Game of January 1, 1951. At that point my procedures were outlined to Les Richter, who continued my work while he was still at Cal.

This was a fun and gratifying period. Talking to prospective athletes and Grid Clubs in various cities and meeting fabulous Alumni, having Pappy take me out to dinner after the 1951 Rose Bowl Game, with the "Powers that Be" of the Southern Seas, to thank me for what I had accomplished, will never be forgotten. Along this same vein, I have an autographed picture from Coach "Eggs" Manske, which I shall always treasure. His autograph reads: "To Eric--Pappy's Boys should be very proud of your contribution to the Waldorf Dynasty. I'm the one who remembers! Edgar "Eggs" Manske." A great period of my life.

In January of 1951, an Alumnus, Ken Verling, and two of his employees, Gene Pickett and John Graves (two of my fraternity brothers), convinced me to go to work for the Schmidt Lithograph Company in San Francisco and work out of their Los Angeles office. Unbeknownst to me, this must have been my calling in life, since things went exceptionally well, and in 1956, I was made the company's youngest Branch Manager in San Antonio, Texas, covering the states of Texas, New Mexico, Oklahoma, Arkansas, Louisiana, Alabama, Georgia and Florida. Again things went well, and in 1960 I was promoted to Assistant National Sales Manager and moved back to Los Angeles.

During my stay in San Antonio, I had two great experiences, one when Pappy Waldorf came through town on a recruiting trip for the San Francisco 49ers. This was on the same night that the San Antonio Grid Club was having its banquet. I took him to the cocktail party and introduced him to many of my friends. He made such an impression on them that they asked me to see if he would come to the banquet the next year as their main speaker. Pappy accepted. When I took him to the cocktail party that year, he proceeded to call all of the people he had met the year before by their first names, with no prompting from me. Some of my San Antonio friends still bring this up on occasion.

In 1961, I was divorced. I remarried in 1963. My second wife died of cancer in 1968. That same year, I organized the Marion K. Schultz Memorial Cancer Fund in Middletown, Connecticut, to help any needy person unable to afford radiation treatments or hospital charges. The Fund has helped numerous people over the years, and, in 1973, when a very dear friend, Steve Witkowski, passed away from cancer, we changed the Fund name to The Schultz-Witkowski Memorial Cancer Fund. Steve was the head trainer at Wesleyan University in Middletown and was the only man to be named as head trainer for two Olympic Games in a row. No one will ever again have this honor, since the Olympic rules have been changed so that no one can repeat as a head trainer.

In 1964, I realized that I had reached the pinnacle of my employment with the Schmidt Lithograph Company, so after 13 years I resigned and started Creative Merchandising Service, which was a printing brokerage. After a short period of time, I realized that this was something I should have done years earlier. During this time I got involved with harness racing. As both businesses grew, it reached the point where a corporation seemed to be in order, and in 1983 we incorporated and formed Eric R. Schultz Enterprises, Inc. The corporation is doing well and along with the printing business, we now have 13 horses in our stable.

In 1969, I married my lovely wife, Elizabeth, who has added a great deal to Creative Merchandising Service and to the corporation, as well as to my happiness for the past 26 years. From 1969 to 1987, we made at least four or five trips from Lakewood, California, to Middletown for visits. Finally, in 1987, we decided to move back to Connecticut permanently. We hired a man to run our office in Anaheim, California, and we semi-retired to Cromwell, Connecticut. We handle all of the billing for the corporation in Connecticut, as well as all of the harness horse business, since we mainly race at the Meadowlands in New Jersey.

Upon our return to Connecticut, I was honored to be asked to join the Middletown Hall of Fame & Museum, of which I am now treasurer, as well as the Cromwell Athletic Club. In addition to these clubs, I was asked to become a Trustee on the Board of Directors of The Independent Day School. This is a prestigious private school which educates students from preschool level through the eighth grade.

In closing, I can say that my years at Cal will never be forgotten. The lasting friendships that were made are priceless, and it is always a great pleasure to receive mail, or phone calls from some of the "Old Blues."

RICHARD STEVENS

⌘

I was raised in the Pasadena area, winding up at South Pasadena-San Marino High School where I played three years of football, first as a tackle and then as fullback. We won our league championship every year and placed third in the CIF the last two. I also was a sprinter, setting a 220-yard dash mark that lasted for more than 20 years. Recruited by Cal, I arrived at Berkeley with classmates Brent Ogden, John Boyle and Dan Ragatz, all of whom played on the 1948 freshman team. I pledged SAE and married in my sophomore year. I was also a member of the Cal Track team. I took a direct regular commission in the Army and started my military career coaching the Camp Polk football team. On my way to play football for the Army in Japan I was re-routed to Korea with the 40th Infantry Division. I was reassigned in 1953 to Japan and became Commanding Officer of the Yokohama Signal Depot. While there I coached and played on the Yokohama area football team.

Returning to the States in 1956 I resigned my commission and entered business, becoming vice president of a fledgling electronics company. In 1962 I stumbled across the Balboa Bay Club, in Newport Beach, where I had spent many happy summers and Easter weeks growing up. The club was deserted, and I vowed to become involved with it. After six months of chasing the elusive owner, Jack Wrather, I met him, and in twenty minutes convinced him I was the guy to turn the project around. I believed in the Southern California waterfront and in everyone's desire to live a recreational life style. Jack turned me loose and made me a "sweat-equity" deal for 20% of the company if I raised the money and did the job. Well, it took ten years to do it but we built apartments, boat slips, a spa and tennis club and then sold the property in 1972. In the meantime I became involved in the Wrather public company which had interests in the Disneyland Hotel, the Lassie programs, Muzak, real estate, and oil and gas. It was a great business education and evolved into a 22-year relationship with Jack Wrather, which ended upon his death. We really pioneered a lot of the resort club living life style in those years. I was then asked to duplicate this concept at the $80 million Marina City Club, a project of Hughes Aircraft Co., which I did over a four year span. Returning to the Wrather Organization in 1979, I set about to expand our hotel and real estate base. By accident I happened upon the Queen Mary and conceived of the idea of a major development to be constructed on the adjoining property.

While in the midst of that negotiation the famed Spruce Goose became available. I thought the idea of displaying the world's largest airplane with the world's largest ship had appeal, and thanks to our relationship with the Hughes family I was able to put this deal together in a matter of weeks. The thrill of becoming deeply involved with the genius of Howard Hughes and the people who helped him create this marvelous aircraft has to be the highlight of my business career. Having the responsibility of moving the huge airplane out of its hangar where it had been kept in secret since 1947 was awesome. No one knew whether it would ever float after all those years. The move, played out before the International Press, took 70 hours and a million dollars. What a day! Then we had to figure out how to exhibit it, culminating in our construction of the world's largest Geodesic Dome. We had no idea whether the public would share our enthusiasm, but over 1.5 million people visited the attraction in its first year on display. With Jack

Wrather's health failing, those of us who had been together a long time realized that the company would soon have a different work environment. Fortune smiled on me when Peter Ueberroth and Harry Usher asked me to join the LAOOC as Vice President of Marketing and Commissioner of the Modern Pentathlon for the 1984 games. The organization and execution of this particular Olympics is well recorded, and I can only share the feeling we all had that we were part of a once-in-a-lifetime experience.

The opportunity to be involved with International athletics of the highest order and with perhaps the best-organized event since D-Day cannot be reduced to a few words. Peter and Harry were magnificent in orchestrating every facet of what turned out to be a hugely successful Olympics in every dimension. I learned more about massive organizations during those years than I ever thought possible.

The letdown after the Games was predictable, and Harry Usher, then Commissioner of the ill-fated USFL, called me and asked me if I would like to "babysit" the Los Angeles Express as chairman of the board. This enabled me to fulfill every guy's dream of "owning" a major sports franchise without having to risk a penny. What a blast! Sometimes we had more people in the owner's box than there were in the stadium but the quality of football was great.

In 1977, my then new bride, Joan, and I decided that we needed a balance to our high-charged social life. So we bought the 495,000 acre Cabin Bar Ranch in the Owens Valley and set about raising cattle and selling water. Over the years we found out why cowboys ride off into the sunset--raising cattle is a tough and risky business. Ten years later, we were fortunate enough to sell the ranch to Anheuser Busch, which used copious amounts of our spring water as a back-up for their LA beer operations. In the intervening years, we enjoyed the John Wayne lifestyle and could honestly say we owned everything as far as we could see (subject of course to bank debt).

Returning, thereafter, to my first love, recreational development, I bought the famous Jockey Club in Miami. I thought this would be great fun and I could supervise things from California. No such luck, and we had to relocate there. I loved the water, boating, fishing and beaches of Florida and hated living there. We were fortunate enough to sell out in 1988 and return home to San Diego. Since then I have been busy developing my consulting business specializing in--what else?--recreational land development and hospitality operations.

My project in Monterey, California, the 3000-acre Monterra Ranch, one Gladstone's fish restaurant and a new addition, Westworld in Scottsdale, all serve to keep the juices flowing. However, we're always looking for new challenges and new ideas. Having been in the "people business" for 30 years, I have been blessed with meeting the great, the near great, and the would-be great. Sharing their dreams of helping to make life more enjoyable has served me as full satisfaction for the work involved. I wouldn't trade any of it. In fact, I hope for a little bit more of it. Blessed with a great marriage and good friends, I can't wait to see what tomorrow brings.

FRANK "BUD" VAN DEREN

⌘

I was born in Boston, Mass., in 1924 to Frank and Helene Van Deren. My parents were very good to me, although, at times, I didn't know it. My dad attended MIT after his discharge from the Navy (WWI). He got a job as a mechanical engineer at Oliver Filters in Oakland, and we lived in San Leandro. Two of my closest friends were Harry and Norbert Pieper, both Cal graduates. Norb became a fine architect, and Harry was the starting center for the Bears in 1942, and 1946-47.

My dad attended Cal before WWI, and was an avid Cal football fan. Two or three times a year (in the '30s), he would take me to home games at Berkeley. My heroes were Bill Archer, Arliegh Williams, Vic Bottari, Bob Herwig, Sam Chapman and Bob Reinhard, to name a few.

I did not attempt to enter Cal after graduating from high school in 1942. I knew I didn't have the grades; besides the competition was awesome. I was 17 years old as a senior and an average football player. Santa Rosa Junior College seemed an alternative. I played football there one season and then joined the Navy in November. The J.C. team that season was composed exclusively of 4f's and 17 - 18 year olds. Our coaches were Floyd Terry (WSC) and Dick Blewett, a Cal player in the '20s. We played some J.C. teams twice, and also had games with St. Mary's Pre Flight and San Francisco State. It seemed as if each week the roster was reduced because of the draft or enlistments.

My service career was no big deal. Boot camp at Farragut, Idaho; radio school at the University of Wisconsin and duty at the small craft training center on Terminal Island. I was assigned to the USS Sentry (AM 299), a minesweeper. We left Seattle in June of 1944 and returned to the states at Galveston, Texas, in February, 1946. The Sentry swept close to 500 mines, participated in 13 invasions, starting with Leyte, and shot down one enemy plane. Actually the plane was a kamikaze and would have crashed anyway.

Santa Rosa J.C. again attracted me in the spring of 1946 (so did Erma Loder). The maturity gained during three years of service awakened me academically. After playing one season of football and studying hard to qualify for admission to Cal, I enrolled at Berkeley in the fall of 1947. Erma and I were married the previous June.

My friend, Harry Pieper, helped me get acclimated to the big campus, helping with registration, advisors, and other such routines. In fact Harry made out my first class schedule which was immediately discarded by Dr. Henry (PE).

Lynn Waldorf was the new football coach. On my way home from Santa Rosa in the spring of 1947, I stopped by Memorial Stadium and watched spring practice. I almost had second thoughts seeing Eggs Manske put the ends through their drills. There were so many, and all so big, like John Cunningham and Herb Poddig. I was also considering St. Mary's, Santa Clara and Stanford just because they showed interest. But Cal was my hope and dream, so I became a "walk on" with no spring practice. What a break to have Lynn Waldorf as the head coach.

Up until this time my life had been very average. Millions of guys played football, were in the service during WWII, got married, and voted for the first time. I feel very fortunate to have attended Cal and graduated, and to have been a part of such a great football era--the Waldorf early years. The football staff was outstanding: Wes Fry, Bob Tessier, and Eggs Manske. As an end I was associated more with Eggs. He was a great coach. Ends are sort of castoffs--too small to play tackle (except

Cunningham), and with not quite the speed and athletic ability to be a running back (like Jensen or Swaner). If we were good, it was because of the coaching and the system--the great emphasis on fundamentals.

I played two seasons, 1947 and 1948, the most eventful years of my life excluding those spent raising a family. Nineteen wins and two losses. It was hard to believe. What great crowds, filling Memorial Stadium time and again. The most negative experience was on the kickoff of the Big Game in 1948 when Don Campbell of Stanford and I met knee-to-chin and he suffered a concussion. Our team physician, Dr. Harkness, performed a tracheotomy on the spot. I visited Don in Cowell hospital the next day. He was okay, but this experience upset me no end.

The last game I participated in as a player was the Celeri-LeBaron game at Lodi in February of 1950, a 22,000-fan sell out. Playing just defense was a real change. We had a lot of fun, and received $500 and a cold beer for our efforts. Ted Kenfield was one of the organizers along with Bob Celeri and Eddie LeBaron of COP.

Aside from the university experience, the associations and friendships I acquired during this time will be forever treasured. Many of our close friends today are those teammates of 1947 and '48.

Erma and I have three children. Sandra Lin, born 1949, and married to Andy Westfall (their children are Loren, Graham and Rosemary); Douglas, born 1952, and married to Diane (their children are Justin and Danielle) and Steven, born 1954.

My football coaching career lasted 37 years. Although eventful at times, it was hardly extraordinary, except, possibly, for its longevity. Twenty-eight of those years were as a head coach--Oakdale High School, Yuba College, and Humboldt State University. During those years, I had great teams, average teams, and lousy teams. I never coached a dynasty and I was always in a non-scholarship situation.

When reminiscing about teams and players, we tend to talk about winners and great athletes. But I always treated both good and bad players the same, as long as they performed at their best--this I learned from Pappy.

I would like to mention three teams of mine that were champions, and four players who were outstanding at their level. My first head coaching job was at Oakdale High School. My assistant, good friend, and a Cal graduate was Jack Walker. In 1955 ours was the first championship team in the school's history. Our "great" player was G.W. Wingo, a farm boy from Waterford, who was a running back and state champion wrestler. He eventually became a teacher at Oakdale H. S. This team earned me the job of coaching, along with Chuck Hughes of Downey H.S. in the North-South All Star Game at Lodi. With a few Oakdale boys on the team we were able to beat the favorites from Sacramento.

The Yuba College team of 1958 was outstanding, winning the Golden Valley championship, and beating a strong Olympia J.C. (Washington) team in the Lumber Bowl in Redding. Jack Greb, from Eagle Point, Oregon, was an outstanding running back and defensive back. He wanted to attend Oregon so Len Casanova, an old friend, sent him to Yuba to qualify (and hide him). He is now a dairy farmer in Eagle Point. Incidentally, in three of my six years at Yuba, Jim Hanifan was an assistant. He worked in town and volunteered. Jim was an outstanding end at Cal, and is now coaching in the NFL.

The Humboldt State team of 1968 was--and still is-- the most successful football team in the University's 91-year history, a winner over Fresno State in the Camellia Bowl, the only team in its conference to win an NCAA championship (college division). We did it primarily with locals--mill workers and a stevedore. Our tailback was John Burman, the finest athlete and football player I have ever coached. Actually I didn't coach him much after he got the hand-off. He is now doing well as a stevedore in Eureka. And, I might add, during my 20-year stay at Humboldt, I was fortunate to have two fine assistants in Fred Siler and Scott Nelson, both former players of mine.

As the offensive line coach at Cal in 1964 and '65 (Ray Willsey was the head coach and Jim Cullom, my office partner) one lineman stands out: John Garamendi, an All Coast guard, Pacific Coast wrestling champion and an "A" student. He has since been a California State Senator and is now the State Insurance Commissioner. He is one of the many fine young men Cal attracts.

Erma and I moved several times because of job opportunities--Berkeley to Santa Rosa, to Oakdale, to Marysville, to Arcata, to Concord (Cal job), to Arcata, to Redding,, and finally to retirement in Fortuna.

Two of our kids graduated from college. Sandra attended Humboldt State one year and transferred to Cal. During this time she met another Cal student, Andy Westfall, a football and rugby player from Eureka. They were married in 1970.

Douglas attended College of the Redwoods and Humboldt State. His major was primarily football and baseball. He was an outstanding athlete, making the "all" teams in both sports at both schools. He was also named Athlete of the Year in Humboldt County. He spent three years playing for California Angels' farm teams.

As a family, we enjoyed summer camping in our small house trailer. When the boys were old enough we backpacked in the Marble Mountains and Trinity Alps.

In 1970, we built a houseboat which we enjoyed on Trinity Lake for several summers. During the drought of the mid-'70s our boat was stuck on the beach for four years. In the meantime, we built a cabin just north of Trinity Center. The houseboat is gone, but we still enjoy the cabin. Occasionally "Old Blues" will drop in: Rod and Lois Franz, Harry and Lenny Pieper, Doug and Betty Clayton, Jack and Elaine Walker, Jack and Sandy Dalton, Dick and Sue LemMon, Ray and Jean DeJong. After a few belts we all sing "Hail to California."

My most important accomplishment was, I suppose, coaching the 1968 football team which put Humboldt State on the map for a brief period.

As for impact on my profession, that might be keeping the Humboldt football program alive during severe budget restraints and student government apathy. Our budget was so sick the coaching staff had to raise funds for equipment and other things you'd think a University would provide.

On a more positive note my 22 years (two years as an assistant under Phil Sarboe) at Humboldt were rewarding. I attained the rank of full professor, and I was never under pressure (other than self inflicted) to win "x" number of games or get fired. It was a good job and I've had a good retirement.

FRANK E. HUMPERT, JR.

⌘

I was born in Napa, California, on January 26, 1926, the younger brother of Robert Humpert and the second child of Roberta and Frank E. Humpert, Sr. The 1920's and '30's were the quiet, small-town days of Napa before the wines of our valley achieved national and international acclaim. As a youngster, I often accompanied my father, who was the local manager of the telephone company, on a tour up-valley as he emptied the coin boxes of pay telephones. He identified the ten or so wineries established at that time. Today there are probably more than 250.

In our quiet neighborhood I began to play football at an early age in a vacant lot especially designated as our playground. There was a variety of regulars, both male and female, and my lifelong love of the sport rapidly developed. I wasn't a speedy runner so my future as a linebacker was forecast early.

My father died when I was 13. He was a sports enthusiast, and I have always wished he could have cheered me on from the stands at Napa High School and at U.C. Berkeley. Even today, as I applaud the efforts of our grandchildren in T-ball or baseball or soccer I often think of him and add an extra cheer.

I entered Napa High School in January of 1940, and, of course, signed up for football at the first opportunity. At the time, most freshmen and sophomores played on the lightweight teams for players weighing 140 pounds or less. By my junior year, I weighed 170 and moved up to the varsity level as a tackle. We won the North Bay League Championship in 1942 and 1943, playing against teams from Vallejo, San Rafael and Santa Rosa.

My high school coaches, Herm Meister, Glenn Du Bose, John Colledge and Hal Buffa were all very special people and certainly superior coaches. The skills and attitudes I learned from them increased my love of the game and would later prove a positive influence when I returned to Napa as a football coach. In 1990, the coaches and football players at NHS gave me a plaque commemorating 50 years as a player, coach, administrator and trainer. It was a thrilling and touching presentation.

In May 1944, I joined the Merchant Marine Cadet Corps and found myself at sea on the S.S. Cape Domingo by August. We visited and unloaded cargo at virtually every inhabited island in the Pacific. The war became a vivid reality near Babelthrop when our ship narrowly missed being hit, and possibly sunk, by a U.S. submarine that received mixed-up signals.

The following June of 1945 I was sent to Kings Point, New York, to continue my cadet training. I promptly signed up for football as a tackle, weighing about 172 pounds. The coach, Lt. Chuck Gladchuck, USNR, told me I made the team because he thought my techniques in blocking and tackling were much better than others who were larger and heavier. Bill Montagne (later to be a teammate at Cal) and I became acquainted there, played together, sustained similar knee injuries and were sent home. By then, Japan had surrendered, so it was time to resume our civilian lives. I enrolled in Napa Junior College and played football in the seasons of 1946 and 1947, first as a tackle and then as an end. I was named to the second team of the All Northern California Junior College Team.

In January of 1948 I was offered the possibility of a scholarship to Stanford. I was on my way to Palo Alto to discuss details when I stopped in Berkeley to visit my brother, Robert. He urged me to stay long enough to visit Coach Waldorf. My future was decided. Pappy promptly inquired if I was a "back" and what was my time in the

"40". He accepted the fact that I was a tackle at 175 pounds, with an interest in being an end. He introduced me to Paul Christopulos, who helped locate employment and lodging. Needless to say, I did not resume my trip to The Farm. Instead, I enrolled at Cal two weeks late and worked part-time at the True Blue Cafeteria. My salary was the huge sum of 90 cents per hour but also included whatever meal was being served during my shift.

When spring practice concluded, I was the fifth end and eagerly awaited the arrival of the fall semester. That summer I worked for Pacific Gas and Electric and made marriage plans. My wife, Analee, and I were married on August 22, and football practice began one week later.

On the first day of practice, the end coach, Eggs Manske, called out seven strings and didn't mention my name. I inquired about my assignment and was sent to the seventh string as an extra. I became a Rambler, and we played three games, against Mather Field, Chico State University and a Navy team known as DESPAC. We defeated DESPAC by a lop-sided score of 37-0, and their team went on to defeat BYU later in the season. I also suited up for varsity games and had some limited playing time. During our daily practices I was a defensive end. It was my task to hit pulling guards such as Rod Franz, Jon Baker, Forrest Klein, Bobby Dodds, and Ray De Jong, all formidable players. On Tuesdays, I was part of the upcoming opponent's defense. On Wednesdays, I became the opponent's offense. Upon arriving home each night, I was covered with bruises over most of my 175-pound body. The fact that I learned to play college football was the saving grace.

An interesting incident occurred one day when I tackled a player. Somehow my little finger became entangled in the laces of his pants and I was dragged several steps. My released finger had a new shape--slightly crooked. Eggs reacted by telling me to put it in an unnatural place to keep it warm! Williamson, the trainer, made an adjustment and applied adhesive tape. I returned to practice.

Every day except Friday, the ends "went to war" with the tackles. Coach Manske would lead us over to the tackle arena. To this day I have a vivid recollection of getting in my stance and gazing at Gene Frassetto, John Najarian, Herb Schmalenberger, Jim Turner and Hank Borghi, all in line waiting to pulverize an end. In the background I could hear Coach Manske calling , "set - hike," as I directed my head under and into the mid-section of one of those behemoths. Then I would hear, "come up - come up." More times than not, I arrived first and won the battle. In 1971 I had two vertebrae fused in my neck as a direct result of those confrontations. In my opinion, it was well worth it.

When 1949 arrived, I decided there was little future for me as an end so I became a center in spring practice. That period was fruitful for me because I learned new skills. On defense, I was a linebacker and found that position and center more suited to me. By then, my weight had skyrocketed to 180 pounds.

That fall my competition at center included George Stathakis, Charlie Harris, Dick Groger and Les Richter. Now instead of hitting tackles we launched ourselves at guards and fellow centers. I felt I was making excellent progress, and so did Coach Bob Tessier. One day, as we practiced one on one, my opponent was Les Richter. I came up on signal, drove underneath him, put my hands down and felt a 'pop' in my right wrist. I shook off the tingling sensation and moved against Les again. This time my hand gave way: I had broken the small novicula bone in the wrist.

After practice, I talked to the trainer, and he sent me to Cowell Hospital. X-rays confirmed the broken bone, and a fiberglass cast was fitted on the arm, which allowed me to shower. The next day I was back on the field. Since it was rather difficult to center the ball, I concentrated on being a linebacker. In our first three games, I played with the cast on. Then we met the University of Wisconsin, and the officials ruled the cast must be removed so I played with tape and padding prepared by Jack Williamson. It proved to be even more comfortable than the cast, and I played in that manner for the rest of the season. The only problem was, I could be easily spotted in the game movies.

The 1949 Cal football team was a superb group of young men. There were WWII veterans as well as 18-year-olds just out of high school. Mutual respect was obvious. I can't recall any bickering or personality conflicts. We weren't a team of stars. Rather, our object was to function as a unit with a common goal of winning games and eventually going to the Rose Bowl. After defeating Santa Clara in our first game of the season, we sang "Nine more rivers to cross." Each successive victory meant one less river to cross until that exciting afternoon when we defeated Stanford, 33-14, and knew we were headed for Pasadena.

Pappy Waldorf was not a coach who gave impassioned pep talks. Instead, he was calm and factual. He always stressed that we represented the University of California, the State of California, our team and ourselves, and that we should do so with pride and skill. The Rose Bowl loss to Ohio State was a bitter blow for our team, but the coaches showed their class in accepting the defeat. There was no blame nor were there any recriminations.

In retrospect, my football experience at Cal made me a much stronger, more mature person. I learned to handle defeat and emerge with a clearer image of what was needed to succeed the next time. I became aware also of the importance of having capable assistants (whether in sports or elsewhere) such as those Pappy had chosen. I have tried to emulate Pappy's coaching style by encouraging players to do their best, while implementing firm guidelines for performance and behavior.

At the end of the semester in January 1950, I graduated from Cal with a BA in History. My former principal at Napa High School, Dr. Harry MacPherson, had become the superintendent of the Napa school district and encouraged me to return in the fall as a teacher and football coach. As an additional incentive he offered my wife an elementary school position, using an emergency credential since she had not yet graduated from college. The prospect was exciting and challenging. One semester, one summer session, and a post-session later, I completed all the requirements for a credential on a Friday and began teaching the following Monday at Napa Junior High. My assignment included two seventh grade classes in English, two in Social Studies and two eighth grade math classes. After a long day in the classroom, it was indeed a pleasure to head for the high school gym and the football team. I was joined daily by Fremont Klein, who taught science at the Junior High and was also an assistant coach. That season we defeated Tamalpais High School where Matt Hazeltine and Billy Hildebrant were players.

My first year of teaching ended early, as my Air Force Reserve unit located at Hamilton Field was activated in April, 1951, and I reported for duty as a corporal. In September, my wife and I departed for San Antonio, Texas, where I entered Officer Candidate School. I was commissioned a second lieutenant the following March. As a Distinguished Graduate I was offered a commission in the regular Air Force. I declined because I was eager to return to teaching once my commitment was met. After a few months at Mountain Home AFB in Idaho I was assigned to Wheelus AFB in Tripoli, pre-Khadafi Libya. Ten sandy, fly-infested months later, my wife and year-old daughter, Sheri, got the good news that we would leave shortly for Rhein Main AFB in Germany. I had learned that an Intelligence Officer was needed there at the 60th Troop Carrier Group. There was also a football team there. I felt a strong sense of deja-vu as I joined a team of young officers and recent high school graduates. For two years we played at various Air Force bases in Germany and England. My lessons learned under Pappy Waldorf served me well as I coached and played again with 18- and 19-year-olds. We lost the European championship in the final game at Ramstein AFB where the quarterback was a West Point graduate, Lt. Charles Gabriel, who later became Chief of Staff of the Air Force.

In 1955, my family and I returned to the United States where I had been given an ROTC assignment at the Montana School of Mines in Butte. Of course the football coach gratefully accepted my voluntary services. Another challenging season unfolded, with snow frequently a factor. One game at nearby Carroll College was played on a snow-covered field where the line markers were outlined with coal dust. Victories were few and far between for the School of Mines. Our biggest challenge was to keep morale up, and I feel we succeeded in that respect, for the team spirit never faltered.

A year later, I returned to civilian life in Napa, teaching at Ridgeview Junior High (the community was growing) and coaching at the Junior College. In 1957, I was transferred to Napa High as a US History teacher and assistant football coach under my good friend Bob Covey, with whom I had played ball in high school and junior college. We won the North Bay League championship that year, and again I savored the memory of "days at Cal and Roses."

A third junior high school was scheduled to open in 1958, and I became the Dean of Boys at Silverado Junior High. In our school district, administrators could not be paid for coaching, so I became a volunteer at Napa High. After eight or nine hours on Silverado's campus I rushed across town to assist the football team. This continued until 1965 when I was chosen to be the principal of Silverado, and the demands on my time became even greater. I decided to concentrate on taping, padding and applying some of the "psychic balm" I had learned at Cal from Jack Williamson. This gave me the chance to be actively involved with football, and I frequently applied "Pappy's Principles" to the coaching staff as well.

During those busy educator/trainer days, I was also a member of the Air Force Reserve at Hamilton AFB. Our unit was briefly activated during the Cuban Missile Crisis, and when the USS Pueblo was attacked in 1968, we began a 21-month period of active duty. I managed to be the Friday night trainer for the football season of '68, largely because I was an administrative officer, not a pilot. Later I spent several months in Da Nang, Vietnam, and experienced for the first time exploding rockets and gunfire aimed at me. It really wasn't much worse than facing those intense tackles at Cal.

In 1972, I was granted a sabbatical from Napa Valley Unified School District to attend a year-long Air Force school for senior officers in Montgomery, Alabama. Our son, Frank, III, was enrolled at Jefferson Davis High School and decided to try football southern style. That was my opening. I volunteered my services as trainer and enjoyed the late afternoon practices until the day my right Achilles tendon ruptured. I didn't miss a Friday night game, maneuvering my thigh-high cast and crutches wherever I was needed. On a rainy, muddy night in Huntsville, the crutches faltered momentarily, while I crossed a river of mud. I discovered a "new kind" of intensity in high school football played southern style, but found the competition exhilarating.

When we returned to Napa the following summer, I had completed the Air Force school, earned a Master's Degree in Counseling and Pupil Personnel at Troy

State University, and had been promoted to full colonel in the Reserve. Our son attended the new high school in town, Vintage High, and I followed as trainer there for five years. During that time I was also placed in a Brigadier General's position at Lowry AFB in Denver and promoted to the one-star rank.

In 1978, I became the principal at Napa High School, the first graduate to return in that capacity, and I resumed my football training schedule there. At the same time, my Reserve assignment took me to the US Air Force Academy where I was the mobilization counterpart of the Superintendent. Extra-curricular activities in high school occur approximately 75% of the 180 days school's in session, and my goal was to attend all of them, if possible. After two years, I asked to be re-assigned as counselor because my energy level was being seriously depleted. "Burning the candle at both ends" on a year-round basis had become too much for me at age 54.

Counseling allowed more time to work with students, both academically and on the athletic fields. Regular attendance and consistent endeavor is essential for success in each arena. "Pappy's Principles" were still being applied and emphasized. At the Air Force Academy I worked with the cadets and their training officers when I visited there. It was inspiring to witness the concerted efforts of 4,000 of our brightest and most able young people.

In 1983, I retired as a Major General, ending a Reserve/Active Duty career of 34 years that began during my undergraduate days at Cal. Three years later, I retired from "the school business" after 36 years, which included credit for military active duty.

Since leaving Cal 45 years ago, I have tried to distill and implement the knowledge and skills I learned there from coaches and teachers alike. It is vital to take whatever you are given and work to mold it into a winning combination through cooperation, understanding and guidance. This applies equally in the classroom, on the football field and in school administration. Very seldom are we given a team of stars in any of these endeavors, so we must do the very best we can with what we have.

In 1952, Pappy wrote a book, "The Game of Football," in which he devoted two paragraphs to me. Of all the accolades I have received in my military career and as a coach, teacher and administrator, I treasure those comments from Pappy the most. I have worked and served with many special, talented people, but Pappy Waldorf was truly inspiring.

CARL J. VAN HEUIT

⌘

I was born August 13, 1927 in Alameda, California. Within three years, my parents moved from Alameda to Curtis St. in Berkeley. We lived four houses away from the house where my mother was born. That house was built by my grandfather around 1907. My grandparents and three uncles still lived there.

I had a normal childhood growing up in Berkeley and going to Berkeley public schools, except for one traumatic event. My father died from pneumonia after a routine hernia operation, leaving my mother a widow with four children, ages nine, eight, five and three months. Some of the relatives wanted to split up the family but my mother was determined to keep us together. She did so with a Veteran's pension (my father had been in the Army in WWI) and part-time employment. Two years later, when we were old enough, my brother Babe and I both secured part-time jobs. From that time, I always had employment until I retired from the Traveler's Insurance Company on October 1, 1985.

During those years, my brother Babe and I were introduced to athletics by our uncles. My Uncle Bill was the most prominent influence, having played varsity football and baseball at Humboldt State University. I learned later that his football coach had been Charlie Erb, Boots Erb's dad.

Another person who coached me in sports early in my life was Bill Tully. He was a student at Cal at the time and was the playground director for Burbank Junior High School. He taught me to never give up and that when things are down, to try all the harder. He later went on to be an outstanding teacher, principal and superintendent of schools in Ukiah.

I competed at Berkeley High School in football as a quarterback in the single-wing formation as well as at safety on defense. I was also the second baseman on the baseball team and a miler in track. I had an average high school football career, playing mostly defense. Coach Fred Moffet noticed then that I had a natural ability as a pass defender.

In my senior year in high school, I was elected president of the Block B Society and sat on the student Board of Control.

In the spring of 1945, upon graduation, I had a major decision to make. At age 17, one could enlist and choose a service. Alternatively, one could wait until age 18, be drafted and assigned to any service without choice. My Uncle Bill had served in the United States Marine Corps in the South Pacific throughout WWII. I decided to enlist, and naturally I chose the Marine Corps.

Boot camp was a shock: going from Big Man on Campus to the lowest being on earth, a Marine recruit. It was a tremendous feeling of accomplishment when I graduated from boot camp and was declared a Marine. The other wonderful thing that happened was that I was in the best physical shape I had ever been in my whole life, but I still weighed the same as in high school, 148 pounds. World War II was soon over so that my duty stations were stateside: the Naval Ammunition Depot, Bremerton, Washington; Personnel Classification School and Permanent Personnel, Parris Island, South Carolina; U.S. Shipyard, Bremerton, Washington; and lastly, Treasure Island, San Francisco Bay Area.

In each of these locations, I continued my training program, consisting of calisthenics and long distance jogging. Toward the end of my tour of duty at Treasure Island, and just prior to my honorable discharge in the fall of 1946, I became acquainted with Jack LaLanne at his Oakland Gym. He enrolled me in his workout program with the goals of gaining strength and weight. I ballooned up to 162 pounds (which was my playing weight during my Cal athletic career).

Just before the Big Game of 1946, my brother Babe and I were invited by Assistant Coach Vic Bottari to visit the Cal campus and attend the game. Frankly, I believe the one they wanted to recruit was my brother. He went on to attend St. Mary's College and was an outstanding athlete in both football and baseball.

For me, my choice had always been Cal from the early days, when my heroes were the very same Vic Bottari (unfortunately fired after the '46 season), Bob Herwig, and, later, Jack McQuary and the Herrero brothers, George and Jack. So, I enrolled at California for the spring semester, planning to be a walk-on for the freshman team in the fall of 1947.

I turned out for the initial freshman football practice to discover a unique pre-evaluation format: Coach Hal Grant had the first team in Gold jerseys, the second team in Red jerseys and the third team, as well as the remaining unassigned squad members, in Blue jerseys. I was in a Blue jersey.

The second day, I was called aside by Coach Grant and advised that I was ineligible. I had taken a minimum number of units because I needed a chemistry course given by Cal Extension as a prerequisite for my P.E. major. The university would not count the four units of Cal Extension chemistry and therefore my class load was not enough for me to be eligible to play. I was allowed to practice and be involved in everything except Saturday's games. Ray Solari, guard-linebacker, was also ineligible, as was Mike Dakais.

The members of the Gold team whom I can remember included Chris Markey at quarterback, Pete Schabarum and Jim Monachino at running back, Bob Minahen at end and Bob Witter at tackle. The only person on the Red team I can remember is Quarterback Al Huber. He, unfortunately, became ill in his sophomore year and never played. The other members of the Blue team included Halfback Dick LemMon, End Bob Cummings, and Quarterback Jim Marinos. This Blue team formed a very potent scout team and gave the starting team all it could handle whether it was an offensive or defensive scrimmage.

Coach Hal Grant, at the end of fall of '47 and prior to spring practice in '48, wrote an individual evaluation of each person on the Freshman squad. He must have given me a pretty good score card. I found I was getting individual attention, as were several other of my fellow Blue team members, in the ensuing spring practice. At the end of spring practice, I was part of the fourth or fifth team as a halfback.

From my high school days, I had had employment on a part-time basis with the Berkeley Recreation Department. Arno Gustafson, Director of Recreation, and his executive assistant, Ms. Alta Huber, liked to hire athletes for their temporary or part-time school playground director jobs. They offered, and I accepted, a job for the summer of 1948 as a playground director at Berkeley High School. As work did not start until mid-morning, I took two 8 o'clock courses at the University Summer session in order to get units ahead and eliminate any future ineligibility.

Fall of 1948 was my first experience with two-a-day practice sessions. I soon got back into top shape. By the end of pre-season practice I was first team Rambler at left halfback and looking forward as a sophomore to the 10-game Rambler schedule. The first game was against a powerful Sea-Pac Navy team from San Diego, that we beat by three touchdowns. Our second game was against Mather Field in Sacramento and we beat this Air Force team about 56-0. All other teams on our schedule immediately canceled except for the Chico State Varsity. We were to meet them in a preliminary game the week before the Big Game. The Rambler team was always scheduled for these preliminary games in the morning before the Varsity played. During our season's first two games I had scored five touchdowns and thought of myself as a running back. Added to that was a touchdown in the 21-13 victory over Chico State with a pass reception from the flanker position. This made me think of myself as a receiver.

The main function of the Ramblers was to provide offensive and defensive scout teams for the Varsity. I thoroughly enjoyed this assignment and because of my enthusiasm found myself wearing the jersey and number of our weekly coming opponent's star back. This continued weekly up to and including our pre-Rose Bowl practices in Riverside. Those were particularly rugged and grueling practices but I was rewarded when Coach Waldorf, much to my surprise, told me that I was suiting up for the "Big Show". This was the first Varsity game that I had suited up for during that season.

I was deeply honored at a team awards banquet when the varsity players voted me the Ken Cotton Award for the most courageous player on the team. This, to my knowledge, was the first and only time that a non-Varsity Rambler player was given this award.

Early in 1949, I was recruited by Coach Miles "Doc" Hudson to play rugby. He taught me the basics of the game and immediately established me as a starting scrum half. Coach Waldorf had encouraged his football players, who were not engaged in other sports, to turn out for rugby as a conditioner for spring practice. It was also great fun. Pappy and Doc coordinated their schedules so that spring practice began immediately after the rugby season was completed.

Although I thought of myself as a running back, as I reflect back, I was utilized more on defense in the 1949 spring practice. The 1949 football season had a major rule change that would have an impact on me and my career. Before that year, there were limited substitution rules, but that changed to free substitution. This meant there were separate offensive and defensive teams. Another major happening was that Billy Main, the starting left halfback and safety for the 1948 team, was ruled to have completed his college eligibility. Whereas most of the positions were filled by returning lettermen, the starting safety position was open. I was one of several candidates being considered for that place on the squad. By the time the fall practice was over, I was the tentative starter, but did not start the opening game against Santa Clara. Coach Waldorf did this to take some of the pressure off. When I did get in the ballgame, I had an average day, with only one mistake: I let a receiver get deep in my zone. Fortunately, the Santa Clara quarterback overthrew him.

Defensive backfield coach Nibs Price, I subsequently learned, pleaded my case in the next week's staff meeting and convinced Pappy that I should get a chance to start the next game against St. Mary's. During that week's practice, Nibs worked with me, re-emphasizing deep coverage on the zone defense. That was what we played on every down except goal line defense when we switched to man-for-man. The basic defense on a roll-out or sprint-out was complete rotation by the safety to cover the deep outside. I promised Coach Price that no one would get deep or catch a touchdown pass ever again in my zone. They never did.

I had a good day against St. Mary's, and on a sprint-out pass, in covering the deep outside, I intercepted the ball. That solidified my position and I started every game at safety for the rest of the season. My brother, Babe, played only one year of football and after two years of baseball at St. Mary's signed with the Cincinnati Reds organization. Therefore, we never played against each other. It was during the St.

Mary's game that the coaches allowed me to return my first punt. We played two deep punt returners so that I did not return every punt. My total for the year , for 18 punt returns was a 12.7 average. I led the team and did not fumble a single punt.

Generally a safety can do well if he returns punts, blocks for punt returns, plays pass defense, including pass interceptions, and makes open field tackles. In our 5-3-3 defense, the successful pass defense meant you were stopping the opponent. If you were having a good day making open field tackles, the other team was probably moving the ball on you by getting through the line and linebackers.

The Washington game of 1949 was one of the five that I considered my best in the two years I played Varsity football at Cal. During that game I intercepted three passes, including a halfback pass thrown by the great Hugh McElhenny, on the goal line. At the end of the season, my five interceptions led the team.

Our Rose Bowl opponent that year was Ohio State. Starting at safety, I had what I believe to be the second of my five outstanding games. This was based on rushing defense and open field tackling. I had no punt returns and no pass interceptions. Ohio State won the ball game, 17-14. In my opinion, this was the best team of the three that we played in the Rose Bowl. My teammates voted me the Vard Stockton Award for defensive play in the game. At the banquet following the Bowl game, Les Richter announced, at our request, the good news of the engagement of Eileen Jumper to Carl Van Heuit.

The next year, 1950, began as a downer when I broke my jaw in a varsity rugby game against the University Club. Coach Waldorf excused me from spring practice and assured me that my position would be waiting for me in the fall.

On June 25th, two days after her 20th birthday, Eileen and I were married at St. Mark's Episcopal Church across from the University practice field. The year had taken an upswing.

Nineteen-fifty was a rebuilding year for Cal football. We had lost a great many of our starting players via graduation, including All American Guard Rod Franz, All American Tackle Jim Turner, All American Linebacker Forrest Klein, All Conference Tackle Jim Cullom and our two Quarterbacks, All American Bob Celeri and "Boots" Erb. The coaches later confided they were not sure we would be contenders, let alone go to the Rose Bowl, that year.

We opened against Santa Clara with four sophomore tackles on offense and defense, a patchwork offensive line and no idea who would be Quarterback. We beat Santa Clara 27-9, led by probably the best trio of running backs in the country, Pete Schabarum, Jim Monachino, and sophomore John Olszewski. I had one of my better games with my longest punt return of 48 yards setting up the first touchdown. Three pass interceptions in that game were made by defensive back Dick LemMon, linebacker John Ralston and yours truly.

As the undefeated regular season progressed, we realized we had an excellent defensive team and an offensive team that could move the ball on the ground. The defensive team gave up an average of only eight points per game, the best of the three Rose Bowl teams. Before the USC game in Los Angeles, the coaches finally settled on Jim Marinos as quarterback. Marinos was a very steady, competitive quarterback for the rest of the season.

The key game of the year was the University of Washington game in Seattle. Les Richter was outstanding on offense and defense. He later was named a consensus All American, and rightfully so. My contribution to this game was two open field tackles on Hugh McElhenny, and five punt returns in the misty rain.

In the game before the Big Game, against USF, I suffered a bruised liver injury on a punt return. It was the result of a "cheap shot" late hit by Gino Marchetti, later of the Baltimore Colts. Coach Waldorf was quoted in the book, "The Big Game," by John Sullivan as saying, Van Heuit "is the best safety man in college football."

The Rose Bowl game that year was against Michigan. In my opinion, we had personnel superior to Northwestern, not as good as Ohio State and equal to Michigan. Pete Schabarum, Jim Monachino and Bob Minahen from the freshman Gold shirts started for Cal. The Blue shirts were well represented with starting quarterback Jim Marinos, who threw a touchdown pass to Bob Cummings for our only score. Other Blue shirt starters on defense were Ray Solari, linebacker; Dick LemMon, defensive back, and yours truly. My contributions, again, were several tackles and one pass interception. In probably the most disheartening loss of my athletic career, Michigan won, 14-6. I was honored to be selected once more for the Vard Stockton Award, and also for a second time, the Ken Cotton Award.

Once again, I led the team with 20 punt returns for a 9.7 average. A rule change was a one-year-only elimination of the fair catch. I was instructed by the coaches to catch any ball I could reach. I led the team in pass interceptions for the season with four and I finished in the top ten Cal career totals with nine interceptions. My 38 punt returns for an 11.1 average is third on the all-time list, without a single fumble.

While I was selected for a couple of All American teams and several All Coast teams, my proudest achievement was being named to the All Conference First team along with my teammates, Ed Bartlett, Bob Karpe, Bob Minahen, Jim Monachino, Les Richter and Pete Schabarum. The conference coaches select the official All Conference team.

I'm looking forward to showing my grandchildren, when they're of age, Pappy's comments about me when I was a player many years ago. In his book, "The Game of Football," Pappy wrote of me: "His courage under fire and his ability to analyze and anticipate opponents' moves and to direct our defense, far outweighed any lack of speed or height....Football will cease to be football on the day it has no place for a boy like Carl Van Heuit, who is by any measurable standard too short, too slow and too light to make a college football player."

After informal inquiry indicated that the Conference would not grant me another year's eligibility, I opted to graduate in February of 1951. Those six units of summer session in 1948 provided enough units for graduation. Subsequently, I was chosen, based on scholarship, campus activities as well as athletic endeavors, to be the 1951 male Commencement Speaker.

In spring of 1951 I had an offer of employment from the Group Department of the Traveler's Insurance Company. I had been referred to them by a Cal alum who was a member of the San Francisco Grid Club. At the same time, I had an offer to be a "student assistant" for the 1951 season by Coach Waldorf. I was not drafted by the National Football League. Francis Powers who was a principal selector for the East/West Game was also a West Coast scout for the Chicago Bears. He offered me a free agent contract. There was no bonus and there were no guarantees. I had a major decision to make. I decided to accept the Traveler's offer, which included an agreement to allow me sufficient time to coach football. They not only agreed but encouraged me. The company even gave me additional time as needed because of the public relations engendered. Thus began my coaching career at Cal.

I would like to acknowledge the coaches who taught me the game of football. First Nibs Price on playing safety as a pass defender and how to use proper pursuit angles. The second person is Coach Wes Fry who taught me the proper way to catch punts in a punt return. Coach Eggs Manske drilled into me the proper way to be a hitter and, lastly, I want to acknowledge Pappy Waldorf for being a great head coach.

Before the opening of fall practice in 1951, Coach Waldorf had staff meetings to go over the entire Cal Football program. I discovered several things that I had not fully comprehended before that time. The first was how little I knew about the Cal offense. The second was that Pappy's philosophy of football as head coach was one of delegating and evaluating. The third, of which I had had some inkling as a player, was that he was a perfectionist. (We all remember Thursday night practices when Pappy checked the new part of the offense for that week, and his statement, "Let's do it one more time." It was sometimes pitch dark when he finally said, "All right gentlemen, take it on in." Or "The hay is in the barn.")

As a "student assistant", I was assigned to help Wes Fry with the offensive backs, and to assist Nibs Price with the defensive backs. The other "student assistants" were Augie Mara, who worked with Herm Meister on the offensive and defensive line and Ray Solari, again assisting Coach Meister with the offensive line and linebackers. Two other people, who had not played football for Cal, participated as observers in preparation for going into coaching. They were Will Sullivan, who played college ball for St. Mary's and Jim Bush, who was a track letterman at the University. Bush became quite well known as the successful head track coach at UCLA.

Wes Fry, that year and in ensuing years, taught me the basics of coaching offensive backs. He did not, however, delegate any responsibility, as that was not his nature. I acted more as a "go-fer" as the price of learning. Practice was organized so that offensive and defensive emphasis came at different times. Progress was made on a part-whole teaching method. We went from individual work to group work to team work.

Coach Price undertook teaching me to be a defensive backfield coach by giving me considerable responsibility right from the beginning. He would outline what he wanted me to accomplish and have me conduct the drills. A great deal of the instruction came from lessons learned from him, such as reading the quarterback's (tailback's) eyes and teaching defensive backs to communicate with each other on crossing receivers, pursuit angles and other drills. As the years went by, Nibs gave me more and more responsibility up to 1956, when he retired as defensive backfield coach but continued as a scout. Continuing in this assignment, I also helped Augie Mara with the Freshman and JV teams for a couple of years.

In 1954, I was named Rambler coach, and continued in that role for the 1955 season. This was in addition to my other duties. Pappy reorganized his staff for the 1956 season and hired Rod Franz as Freshman coach and John Ralston as Rambler coach. I became the defensive backfield coach. My contract with the ASUC was for employment during the fall football season and spring practice only. I had no formal responsibility for recruiting, although I assisted occasionally.

During the 1956 season, an interesting thing happened: my brother, Bob, competed as an offensive guard in his last year of eligibility. Weighing 195 lbs., he was on the small size for that position, but he was a tough, hard-nosed player. My brother, Babe, who had been in the Army in the Far East during the Korean War, enrolled at Cal. He served as an assistant freshman coach under Rod Franz. Babe served as freshman baseball coach for the next two years under George Wolfman. He graduated in 1958, as did brother Bob. (Our sister, Marilyn, graduated from Cal in 1954 along with my wife Eileen.)

As the 1956 season progressed, it became evident that while we had some good veteran players, most of our better players were younger and inexperienced. It was a re-building year. Several of the sophomores, such as Joe Kapp and Jack Hart, were the nucleus for the Rose Bowl team in 1958 when they were seniors. Pappy decided to retire after the 1956 season. He subsequently became Director of Player Personnel for the San Francisco 49ers. The week before the Big Game, he made the announcement to the squad.

The Stanford team in 1956 was quarterbacked by senior John Brodie, and featured a running back named Lou Valli. We were determined that Brodie's passing would not beat us, and set up our defense accordingly, encouraging Stanford to run the ball. On offense, Wes Fry had noticed when studying a Stanford film that the Indians' defensive linemen would split out with the offensive linemen and their linebackers were keying and reacting to offensive guards. He established an offensive game plan featuring line splits that enabled us to run inside with both the halfback and the fullback. The most significant change was having Joe Kapp running the quarterback sneak in which the Bear guard gave Stanford false keys. Kapp completely outplayed Brodie, rushing for over 100 yards. Herb Jackson and Jim Cherry ran well at fullback with Jack Hart blocking and Hart, himself, scored one of the touchdowns. Cal caught Stanford off guard. We managed to gain a halftime lead and then held on in the second half. John Brodie had a very average day passing, but Lou Valli set a new record for rushing in the Big Game. The game was decided late in the fourth quarter when defensive right halfback, Hart, intercepted a pass deep in California territory. Cal won 20-18.

Because this was Pappy's last game, he wanted very deeply for his team to win. Coach Waldorf, I had observed during these years, had great control over his emotions. The first time I had ever seen him with tears in his eyes was after the game.

Pete Elliott was hired as head football coach for the 1957 season. He interviewed the younger staff members from the 1956 season. He employed Rod Franz and John Ralston for continuity in recruiting and because they were outstanding coaches. He had offered Billy Taylor, who was on his staff in Nebraska, a position. If Billy Taylor declined, Coach Elliott said that I was next on the list to be offered a full-time job. The remaining members of his staff he brought from Nebraska. Taylor accepted the job. We agreed that I would help John Ralston with the Freshman team and scouting for the 1957 season on a part time basis.

Rod Franz retired from coaching at the end of the 1957 season. Coach Elliott, true to his word, offered me a full-time coaching job. I was in a quandary because my business career at Travelers was moving ahead rapidly. I made the decision to respectfully decline Pete's offer. He agreed that I should continue assisting with the Freshman squad and thus began my 20 years as a volunteer assistant football coach at Cal.

I did not coach in Mike White's last year as coach, 1977. But, I was invited out to assist in pre-season and fall practice as an "Alumnus Observer" by Coach Roger Theder in 1978, and I served in this capacity until Roger's last year, 1981.

At Travelers I became, first, Manager in Oakland, then, Manager in San Francisco. In 1967, I was appointed Regional Officer in charge of the San Francisco Region. I was appointed Regional Vice President in charge of the consolidated San Francisco and LA Regions in 1982.

During my 15 years as Regional Officer in charge of the San Francisco Region, I used the management philosophy taught to me by Coach Waldorf: delegate and evaluate, but be available for assistance if needed. This resulted in successful years, and the field staff in the region received national recognition within the company. In 1982, the consolidated Western Region placed second in the National Sales Contest. In 1983, we tied for first with Dallas.

Our banner year was 1984 when we swept all three of the "Oscars". The statuettes were awarded to the members of the Western Region for winning the National Sales Contest. San Francisco was named the National Office of the Year based on its performance, and Ernie Garcia, a young man in our San Diego office, was awarded his statuette as National Salesman of the Year.

In December of 1984, an early retirement package was offered to all members of the Group Department, aged 50 and over. Having developed a disability, Parkinson's Syndrome, and after the stellar performance of 1984, I decided to accept retirement. The company persuaded me to stay on to help select and indoctrinate my successor. We selected Robert Brook, whom I had employed out of the University of California in 1960. Bob was a member of the Big C Society, having been captain of the Crew.

Thus, at retirement on October 1, 1985, I was without a job or major activity for the first time since I was a youngster. Fortunately, the Baseball Head Coach, Bob Milano, contacted me and, together with Margo Schmeil of the Bear Backer office, persuaded me to be chairman/coordinator of the Capital Fund Raising Campaign to build the Jackie Jensen Memorial Press Box. Although I had admired Jack as an athlete, I did not really get to know him until we began playing tennis together when he was head baseball coach at Cal during the early 1970s. Fine guy, and I readily accepted the challenge. Working with Dick Larner in Southern California, Mike Noakes in Central California and Glen DuFour in Northern California, together with the very creative Margo, we were successful. There was enough money raised also to replace all of the seating.

This was followed by an appointment by Bob Milano to co-chair with Stuart Gordon the Evans Diamond Improvement Fund. The monies raised in this campaign were used to re-do the entire field with underground drainage and a sprinkler system. Sufficient monies were also raised to modify the dugouts and install restrooms and a new refreshment stand. We now have a baseball facility comparable to any in the Pac-10.

At the dedication ceremony in May of 1992 Stu Gordon had the first base dugout dedicated to him and a plaque in his name affixed thereon. The third base dugout was dedicated to me. The U.C. Berkeley Foundation recognized my volunteer efforts in awarding me the Trustee Citation in 1991. Recently I received a letter from the Athletic Department advising me that I had been selected to the California Athletic Hall of Fame. This is the ultimate in honors and I voice my appreciation.

At times like this, I wish I had the eloquence of Professor Garff Wilson to express my feelings. Growing up in Berkeley, I had a dream of attending the University and playing in Memorial Stadium. Coach Pappy Waldorf gave me the opportunity to play football and I shall be eternally grateful to him. The same is true of my rugby coach, Dr. Miles Hudson.

Another Outstanding coach at Cal, Andy Smith, once said,

"We do not want men who will lie down bravely to
die but men who will fight valiantly to live"

This is engraved on the Cal bench at Memorial Stadium. For those of us who have had the joy of competition, the camaraderie of teammates, the achievement and recognition of success, we have an obligation. That obligation is to give back to the University in time, talent and resources the assurance that the young men and young women of today will have the same opportunity to compete and to carry on the athletic tradition of the University of California.

I have tried to be a giver rather than a taker in a situation or relationship. Beneath the plaque in the foyer at the Berkeley Community Theater honoring me as a member of the Berkeley High School Hall of Fame are the words, "All American humanitarian." I would add to that, caring husband, good parent, and United States Marine. I have not always been successful in my goals, but I have reached a new level of maturity in the past few years.

We have three adult, mature children and I have become less judgmental and more respectful of their individuality. A wise man once said, "To be happy in retirement you must have three things: someone to care about who cares about you; something to do each day when you get up in the morning, and lastly, something to look forward to in the future." I am a happy man.

BOB KARPE

⌘

I am possibly the only person ever, at the same time, to be president of the "Big C" and Beta Gamma Sigma, the business administration honor society at Cal. And in 1968, I became the youngest president, before or since, of the California Association of Realtors. Then, in early 1971, I was going about my real estate business in my Bakersfield office when I got a surprising telephone call. It was the Governor's office asking if I would be interested in being the State Real Estate Commissioner. I said, "If you want the answer right now, it is, No." The caller said, "Do you want to think about it?" I said, "O.K., how long?" He said, "a couple of weeks." I said that if I decided the answer was yes, I wanted to be sure the job would be mine, that I didn't want to be just standing in line.

So I thought about it, discussed it with my office and members of my family and in a week-and-a-half gave my answer. A few weeks later, I was the Real Estate Commissioner. There was nothing grand or pompous about my swearing-in, which was by a notary public in Bakersfield. Later, however, when I became president of the Government National Mortgage Association ("Ginnie Mae")' I received the full treatment.

After my first week as Real Estate Commissioner in '71, I was heading home for the weekend to be with my family and was paged in the San Francisco Airport. It was Governor Reagan telling me to be in his office at 10 a.m. Tuesday morning with my goals on one side of one piece of paper. You can imagine my busy, rather nervous weekend.

The goals I showed to him were:

1) To protect the land and the competitive free enterprise system.

Result - This was a tightrope walk because at that time, hundreds of thousands of acres of California land were being cut into lots and sold, not for homes but for speculation. Bad -- but one of the great American freedoms is privately owning land and that includes doing what you want with it. This is being eroded today. We mitigated the problem by being very tough with regulations directed at the promoters and by starting an "undivided interest" concept, i.e., private parks which would not cut up the land.

2) A color blind real estate industry.

Result - The Realtors (White) and the Realtists (Black) were at each others throats. We got them together in a long range flexible plan for merger. They have not been at each other's throats since then.

3) Professionalize the real estate industry.

Result - There are now strong educational requirements.

4) Keep costs down.

Results - When Reagan took office there were 350 employees in the Department of Real Estate and they were having a tough time making payroll. When I left, there were 228 employees. There were enough reserves for a full year's budget and I was the only Commissioner ever to reduce licensing and subdivision fees.

In the meeting with Reagan (he was not a man to waste time), he said "O.K. I approve. You run the Department of Real Estate. I don't scratch where I don't itch." -- and he never did interfere in the affairs of the Department of Real Estate. We met at monthly meetings. I sent in regular reports through channels. Thank Heaven, he never itched.

Before I left Reagan in Sacramento, I would like to mention one thing, not widely known, that perhaps helped him become a great man. At a monthly department head meeting, there was a break, and we were all kind of just chatting and the old saying came up, "The buck stops at the Governor's desk", and Reagan said "That's not entirely true. It is true I can look behind me and there is no one there, but I can look up and He is always there."

I was with Ronald Reagan at Kansas City when he lost the Presidential nomination by a very small margin to Gerald Ford. The morning before the final vote Reagan made it very clear he would not accept the Vice Presidency. In a letter he wrote:

To my friends in the California delegation:

I have learned of your concern about whether I would or would not accept the nomination for V.P. on the Ford ticket if he should be the nominee for Pres.

I thought I had made this clear--evidently I hadn't. Here is my reply as plainly as I can say it.

There is no circumstance whatsoever under which I would accept the nomination of V.P. That is absolutely final.

Ronald Reagan.

The morning after the final vote, I would guess there were 3000 people at the Ford meeting. I was one of about 65 at the Reagan meeting. People don't gather around a loser.

Reagan told us:

"We are beaten, but not slain. We shall lay us down and bleed a bit and then get up again."

Winners always get up again, I thought.

That statement was true 28 years earlier with another great man. I can remember Pappy would have the whole team, sometimes more than a hundred people, doing a drill. It seemed to me that thousands of times we had to fall down and then get up as quickly as we could, find out where the ball would appear and get to the ball. And Pappy told us about life--he said, "Everyone gets knocked down, but winners get up again and rally to the ball."

My direction at "Ginnie Mae" led to lowering the cost of home ownership to millions of Americans through opening of overseas investment markets for

G.N.M.A. securities sales and resulted in increased sales opportunities through more readily available real estate financing.

When I first met G.N.M.A's regular Wall Street people and suggested we go international, the reception was very cool. I backed off. After some months of thought with my staff, we decided the brokers we had talked to were brokers who did business only nationally and didn't want more international competition. We also learned that the German Pension funds were the lenders of the European investment market and that they had a regulation that said they could not buy investments at a price higher than the latest listed price, nor sell lower than the latest listed price. They couldn't buy G.N.M.A.'s because we weren't listed. We talked about the idea and exposed it to several Wall Street firms. First Boston agreed to pay for a listing on the Luxembourg Stock Exchange and an original selling trip through Europe. That was an expense that would have taken months or years to get through government. We met with the Luxembourg people after much preparation, had an official listing, then sold in Frankfurt and various places in Switzerland and Paris and London. That started the ball rolling and the international business grew. G.N.M.A. was later listed in Singapore. Maybe this was an example of my getting up again, after first being told it was a lousy idea.

I stopped the G.N.M.A. tandem program which was costing the government one billion dollars a year.

I was President designate of the Solar Bank, a potentially costly lending program which Congress wanted but Reagan did not. We successfully got new legislation to stop it before it got into full scale operation.

What was the Solar Bank? During the energy crunch, Congress passed a law for a nationwide lending agency that would make small loans or large ones to people who wanted to save energy. Imagine the bonanza this would have been for insulation people, siding people, people wanting to try solar heating, etc. Shortly thereafter, Reagan was sworn in as President and he refused to carry out the legislation. The Congress sued him in '81 and in late '82 the court decided in favor of Congress.

Shortly after this, a White House representative came into my office and asked if I wanted to be President of the new Solar Bank. I said no. I came here to be President of G.N.M.A. Then he said you can do both. I said, "I know, but the Solar Bank is explosive politically and I think it will hurt G.N.M.A" A couple of days later, I was asked to visit the White House. When I came back I was President designate of the Solar Bank. I hired a person who was an expert on energy, an executive director, who actually ran the day-to-day business while I stayed mostly with G.N.M.A., a brilliant young computer and financial person, a capable assistant to the executive vice president and a secretary-receptionist. We had a staff of five instead of 500 or 5000. We decided, while attempting to get legislation to put us out of our jobs, that we would make a proposal to the States that if they wanted a lending program we would participate. This cut our chances of loans dramatically. Approximately $30 million was spent before the program was stopped, instead of billions.

While in Washington D.C., I lived with my daughter. My reputation at G.N.M.A. and in other Washington circles was enhanced by the fact that I was a personal friend of Nick Veliotes, (an end on my freshman football team.) Nick was in charge of the MidEast desk, (all Middle Eastern countries) reporting directly to the Secretary of State. I attended a banquet with my daughter given by the Lebanese Embassy with perhaps five other Mid-Eastern countries represented. What became obvious throughout the evening was that despite sometimes severe differences between themselves they all respected the quiet, polite and brilliant American Ambassador, Nick (he was neither quiet, polite or even completely law-abiding when he was in school). Nick was kind enough to invite my daughter and me to his family Thanksgiving dinner. During the meal, General Alexander Haig called Nick personally asking that he come down to the department. General Haig said he needed Nick to solve a very important problem. Nick never mentioned what the problem was.

President Reagan liked to be introduced by his own people who also knew the people to whom he was going to speak, so on rare occasions, I was asked to introduce him. On one such occasion, in the middle of his tight schedule, I was asked to introduce him to a group of about 4000 people and I knew that Reagan was going to tell them he was not for a major program of theirs. I appropriately had checked out everything the day before, and was standing on the sidewalk when his entourage brought him in. I took him by the most direct route to the stage door, and gave the appropriate signal. Then the unbelievable happened -- The man in charge of the meeting said "We are running late. You will have to wait about five minutes." That was the longest five minutes of my life. You could see Reagan was dead tired. I said nothing. I was nervous and you don't talk to someone who is going to make a speech shortly anyway. Then the signal came and the champion qualities of Reagan came out. He stood up straight, put a great big smile on his face, said, "Here we go Bob", put his arm in the air like a cheerleader and said "Ra ta ta ta ta ta!"

He then walked so fast into the meeting that I could hardly keep up. He told them why he was against their program, why they should support his other programs, and left to a standing ovation.

I am presently chairman of the board of Karpe Real Estate Center in Bakersfield. We are involved in sales, financing, escrow, appraisal, investment and development -- the complete real estate package. I also manage several partnerships, including CALSC Co., which consists of Les Richter and me from Cal and Frank Gifford from USC. Our company has returned its original investment nine times, is currently returning approximately that much annually and has a present value more than 30 times its original investments.

WILLARD H. (BILL) RUSH

⌘

If the world is a better place because of me, it could well be because of my work in the savings and loan business, my involvement with the Santa Rosa Junior College Board of Trustees and my service with the Peace Corps in Costa Rica.

I was connected with the Santa Rosa Savings and Loan Association from 1952 to 1968. Hired initially as a real estate appraiser (obtaining Class IV) I worked in all phases of the business--real estate lending, construction, and commercial and residential development. The Association grew from an $8 million business in 1952, my first year, to $125 million in 1968, when Santa Rosa Savings joined, via merger, Great Western Savings (now Great Western Bank, a subsidiary of Great Western Financial Corporation.)

From 1968 to 1969, I was in charge of the Loan Service Division of Great Western in Northern California. Our total loan portfolio at that time was $2.5 billion. From 1969 to 1975, I was a regional vice president. At that time, regional administration included both savings and lending functions. From 1975 to 1983, I was regional vice president for retail banking. Charges varied between the 12 to 15 savings branch facilities, portfolios varying as regional realignments were made. Portfolios were between $800 million and a billion dollars. I took early retirement at age 57 in 1983.

Great Western Savings was asked by the Federal Home Loan Bank and Federal Savings and Loan Insurance Corporation to assume operation of Centennial Savings in Santa Rosa, which had been placed in receivership and had been taken over by federal authorities. Great Western was asked to form a management team to reorganize Centennial and ready it for sale to a qualified buyer. I was asked to be executive vice president and chief operating officer of the management team. Besides the Savings Association, Centennial included several other corporations, and I held various positions in all of them: president of Piombo Construction Company, vice president of Santa Rosa Mortgage Company and vice president of Centennial Real Estate Company. I was also a member of the boards of directors of each of these companies.

The Great Western management team successfully liquidated Centennial. It was one of the few receivership companies that actually made a profit. Upon liquidation of most assets and the sale of savings accounts and facilities to another savings and loan company, Centennial's need of a management team ended, so I once again retired to devote myself more to community activities.

I found my terms as a member of the Board of Trustees at Santa Rosa Junior College and my work with mentally-impaired people were the most satisfying in terms of truly repaying something to a college and an area that had been very good to me and my family. Serving as a college trustee in the 1960's was a rare challenge and opportunity. To be involved in the give-and-take of this meaningful position was both rewarding and eye-opening. It offered me a chance to work with all segments of the college--students, administrators, teachers, and the public--in some very significant areas. To be given a chance to repay your alma mater for all that it did for you is not often granted to a former student.

I served as a director of the Sonoma County Mental Health Clinic during my working career. However, after my second retirement from the savings and loan arena, I had a wonderful opportunity to do what I considered to be more meaningful work with the Creative Living Group of the Sonoma County Mental Health Department. I served as a van driver, picking up mentally-impaired people of all ages and transporting them to and from their live-in home to various creative living activities. This was usually their only "outside-of-a-care-home" activity--their one bright ray of sun for the week.

Later I expanded my activities with this group and became a teacher's aide and helped conduct various activities for a few of the group's clubs, such as field trips, movies, and camp-outs. To be a helpful friend and a sympathetic ear for members of this group was very meaningful for me.

When the Peace Corps was first started by the Kennedy administration, both Shirley and I felt it was a truly rewarding and genuine activity for our country to offer to underdeveloped nations. At that time, and for several years following, we were unable to participate because we were raising our children and moving upward in our own chosen careers. When we retired, we were able to give freely of ourselves to help others. Because both of us have a strong sense of social consciousness, our admiration for the work being done by the Peace Corps since its inception never waned. We were enthusiastic and felt privileged, indeed, to be allowed to follow other Peace Corps volunteers.

We entered training on February 9, 1989 and completed an intensive 12-week course. We were sworn into the Peace Corps on February 1, 1990 and completed service on January 15, 1992. We were stationed in Hatillo, San Jose, Costa Rica, in the integrated community development program. We worked with Costa Ricans and, when we left, a Costa Rican was trained and in charge of each project we undertook. We made good friends with the Costa Ricans and have exchanged letters with them now that we have returned. Some of the activities we became involved with were providing exercise, supplying free Costa Rican National Symphony tickets to a group of seniors, and also providing them with free vegetable and flower seeds, and teaching marketing, accounting and selling skills to a women's group which made handcrafts. We also built a solar oven out of inexpensive materials and taught 161 people to build and cook with it.

Also, I built a solar water purifier that could purify five to ten gallons of water a day and passed the project on to another volunteer. We gave English-as-a-second-language classes in our home and also in the Hatillo Elementary School on Saturdays for two years. We escorted the high school English speaking group to the University of Costa Rica for a campus tour and on another day to an English language movie. We cooperated with the local government and the Lions Club to plan what to do before, during and after natural disasters such as cholera epidemics, earthquakes, and tornadoes.

We worked with people of two squatters' villages, helping to raise $1,500 by making dolls and selling them in the U.S., and kept the financial records for the project. The money was for materials to make a recreation building where "latch key" children could have recreation and homework tables. Also, we gave a three-day workshop for teenagers on how to paint interiors. I taught members of two small businesses we helped start how to keep books.

My wife and I and four others co-chaired the annual Thanksgiving feast for all Costa Rica Peace Corps volunteers. We coordinated the Peace Corps volunteers season ticket symphony project and submitted articles to the monthly volunteer magazine "La Cadena."

These are only some of the activities my wife and I took part in with the Peace Corps in Costa Rica, but they provided us with great satisfaction. Next to being married to Shirley, our tour with the Peace Corps had to be at the very top of my life's meaningful adventures. There simply is nothing so rewarding as being able to work with and help people who are less advantaged. Without really knowing it, Shirley and I spent a lifetime getting ready to be good Peace Corps volunteers. Our education, friendships, family activities and achievements all went toward preparing us for one of life's most rewarding experiences. To be able to repay the very big debt of a very good life by helping others is a very, very special reward indeed.

PAUL C. KECKLEY

⌘

I was born January 10, 1924 in Topeka, Kansas; however, my family moved to California when I was one-year-old. I grew up in Pomona in a family of four children and had a wonderful childhood. My parents were very loving and supportive of me while growing up. All through school I was active in many sports and student activities.

My coach in high school, Archie Nisbet, was not only a fine coach, but a wonderful man, and an inspiration to all boys who knew him. He encouraged me to go to U.C., where he had played on the "Wonder Team" in the 1920's. So after high school graduation in 1942, I went to Cal and dreamed of playing baseball and football, but with World War II going on at that time, everything was very unsettled. Instead of being drafted, I joined the Navy. While in training to become a pilot, I played football for the Navy at William Jewell College and at Iowa State. I was also on the track team for the Navy at Iowa University. I received my wings in Corpus Christi, Texas. I had operational training in Florida, and while there I married my high school sweetheart, Peggy Todd, on July 14, 1945. She was attending Stanford at the time. We then went to Glenview, Ill. and I finished training as a carrier-based torpedo bomber pilot.

After the war, I returned to Cal and played football on the losing team of 1946. When "Pappy" arrived at Cal in the spring of 1947 and had his first meeting with the team, I was impressed with his enthusiasm and with his confidence that we would have an outstanding team. There were a lot of wonderful and dedicated boys on those teams and I know every single one of them admired Pappy and would do all in his power to please him. Football was a lot of fun in those days and I've been proud to be known as one of "Pappy's Boys." He instilled confidence in me which proved valuable in later life. College life was a real mixed bag in those days. I was one of 19 players who were married, and we had our first daughter in 1947 and second daughter in 1948. I had several jobs besides playing football. Life wasn't easy, but it was a wonderful time in our lives and we have many fond memories.

My most memorable play was in the Big Game of '47. (I think probably everyone is tired of hearing about it.) I had been out of practice for two weeks with a shoulder injury, and it was doubtful that I would be able to play against Stanford. The game was almost over, time was running out on the clock, and we had several boys out injured. The score--Stanford 18 to 14 Cal. I asked Pappy to let me play, but he said my shoulder still wasn't healed enough. I said it would be okay. He told me to get my helmet and be ready. I sat on the sideline with my helmet on and when he looked in my direction, I took it as a nod for me to go into the game. (Later there was a question about that!) Three minutes left and Cal was on its own 20-yard line. When I went into the game, I told Dick Erickson, the quarterback, I had a good play in mind and he said he had a better one "Pass 31-X", which surprised me as that play involved me. Jensen threw a short cross field pass, which I fortunately caught and went the distance for a touchdown with the help of several key blocks and some good luck. I have always been given credit for winning the Big Game of '47, but it always takes a lot of team effort to win any game. If Jim Cullom hadn't made all the conversions we wouldn't have won. The final score: Cal 21-Stanford 18.

Probably the most horrifying, and yet humorous thing that happened to me while playing football, was when I was responsible for the cover picture on LIFE

Magazine. The cover on LIFE magazine showed a picture of Cal's rooting section. The horrified, dejected and sick look on the faces of all the students in the rooting section was one of complete despair. On page two, where LIFE always explained the cover picture, it was said that the downcast look of the cheering section was caused by Cal's left halfback dropping a certain touchdown pass on the goal-line. That left halfback was me! I am probably the only Cal player who can take credit for the front page picture on LIFE magazine.

After graduating from Cal in '49, I went to Stanford for my Physical Therapy training. Peggy had graduated from Stanford in the meantime as a Physical Therapist and had worked at Herrick Memorial Hospital in Berkeley. We had our third daughter in 1950 and moved to Redwood City that year to open our first Physical Therapy office. We soon had the Physical Therapy Department in Sequoia Hospital. Besides raising a family, Peggy taught expectant mothers classes for years. Our son arrived in 1953, which completed our family. We resided in Redwood City for 41 years, during which time I practiced Physical Therapy and ran the Rehabilitation Department at the hospital. We were also very active in our church and youth activities, plus community work. I have been fortunate in having a very rewarding life, and I feel I have helped many individuals and contributed to the life of my community.

Our families and grandchildren have been the light of our lives and now that we are retired, we can even enjoy them more. In 1991 we moved to our property in the country, which we purchased in 1980, and that has become the family gathering place. We are truly enjoying the peace and beauty of country life, and the wonderful wildlife that is in abundance, such as deer, wild turkeys, all kinds of birds, foxes,--- and our small herd of black angus cattle. We are blessed with eight grandchildren, and they and their parents visit often.

This has been a different life style for us, but we are adjusting. I've given up my plane for a Kubota tractor. We miss our many friends in the Bay Area; however, we have had lots of company and our guest rooms are constantly being used.

JACK D. SWANER

⌘

Being raised in the San Joaquin Valley is something I look back on with great pleasure. While I was born in Taft, February 17, 1925, my family moved to Coalinga early on and most of my growing up was done there.

As a youngster I learned to camp out and fish and hunt, getting my first buck at age 12, but in my senior year in high school, war broke out. The principal immediately felt he had several boys who could qualify for the Navy's V12 or V5 program. Fortunately I was one of them and we were put into an accelerated course at the local Junior College in January of 1943, and in June 1943 I was in the Navy Air Corps. We were sent to the University of Texas for two semesters, then became regular members of the Corps. By the time I finished my training, the war was over and I returned home in October of 1945 in time to help my family move from Coalinga to Napa. In January of 1946 I entered Cal and immediately began to enjoy a number of sports. I had played football in high school and the Navy so, of course, that was first. I also enjoyed three years of track as a shot-putter.

A knee injury early in the season of 1949 kept me out until the eighth game, but I did get to play in both the 1949 and 1950 Rose Bowl Games. I had married Betty Barnum in February of 1949, and the announcement of our first daughter's birth was made from the field during the 1950 Rose Bowl Game. In January of 1950 I graduated with a degree in Forestry and left immediately for my first job with the Union Lumber Company at Fort Bragg, California.

In June of 1950 we moved to Eureka, where I went to work for my father-in-law in the timber business. There I oversaw the logging operations as well as the purchase and sale of standing timber. Three more daughters were born during our ten-year stay in Eureka. At that time I became active in the Rotary Club and was one of the founding members of the Baywood Golf and Country Club.

In 1953, I left the family business and formed a real estate company dealing primarily in timber lands. Shortly thereafter, I was appointed sole State Inheritance Tax Appraiser for the County of Humboldt by Robert Kirkwood, Controller of the State of California. I was the youngest appointee in the State. During this time I volunteered as an official at Humboldt State football games and selected high school games and really enjoyed being involved with sports again.

In late 1957 the timber business began to slow, and being a sole proprietor had a limited life, it seemed to me. As a Tax Appraiser I had a close and busy exposure to the legal profession in Humboldt County and it interested me greatly. In 1959 I moved my family of wife and four daughters and one "on the way" to San Francisco and enrolled as a full time law student at the University of San Francisco--obtaining a degree in June of 1962. I was admitted to the California bar in January of 1963. I was able to form a partnership with a fellow already practicing and so the firm of McNeal and Swaner began in 1963. I was very proud and happy that my peers in the legal profession gave me the highest legal rating --A.V.--you can have in Martindale-Hubbel.

My career in law was a busy one from 1963 until I retired in 1987. During that time I served as a Director for the San Francisco Parking Authority and on the board of and then president of the Presidio Society of San Francisco. This was very gratifying, as we sought to preserve the Presidio as an Army facility and avoid commercial development of it. For many years we were able to achieve this. I also served on many law committees during those years as well as on the board of the "Big C" Society.

My practice began in taxation, which evolved into representing many local state and federal chartered banks as well as savings and loan associations. Besides this, I maintained a general business practice.

In 1975 my wife and I were divorced, and in September of 1982 I married Pat, my present wife. Together with her daughter and two sons and my five daughters we have a large family. There are currently ten grandchildren.

As I reflect back over my college days as one of Pappy's Boys, I can see it was certainly a wonderful time. My knee injury in my last year was probably a blessing in disguise as I had been drafted by both the Philadelphia Eagles and the Chicago Rockets and if I had been able to respond, I'm sure my life would have been quite different.

In 1987 my wife and I sold our home, retired and moved to Black Butte Ranch in Central Oregon. We have two beautiful 18-hole golf courses on the property and I play at least three times a week during the season. Until last year when the knee required surgery, I skied at least two days a week in the winter.

We stay busy here on the ranch. I serve as an elected director and treasurer of the Black Butte Ranch Rural Fire Protection District. I'm active as Vice Chair of the Architectural Review Committee. I belong to a fishing and hunting group and get to South East Oregon for those activities.

Our beautiful Black Butte Ranch sits in the midst of a ponderosa forest in the lovely Cascade Mountains, and this is now our home.

DAVE HIRSCHLER

⌘

I was born October 21, 1924 in San Jose. My family moved to So. Pasadena in mid 1932 where I attended South Pasadena High School. I played B football in 1939 and varsity football in 1940 and '41, and as a senior I made the All San Gabriel Valley League team. I entered Cal in 1942 and played first string on the frosh team under Clint Evans. I left Cal at the end of my freshman year to go to Navy boot camp in San Diego. I became an Aviation Radioman and was picked out of the fleet to return to Cal for officer training in 1944. I went out for football for the '44 season and played end for Stub Allison in his last season at Cal. Out of a possible 600 minutes (10 games) I played 532 including six 60 minute games. As far as I know, this could be a Cal record. I was named second string All Coast on two news services and first on another. After the 1944 season I went to Columbia midshipman's school and then to the South Pacific as a gunnery officer on an aircraft carrier. After the war I returned to Cal to play for Frank Wickhorst on the 1946 team. I missed the Big Game that year because of a knee injury received in the game before. I sat in the stands to watch the Big Game and was nearly rolled trying to get to my seat. When the game was over the students tore up the seats and sent them down on the field. It was more dangerous in the rooting section than on the field.

Nineteen-forty-seven saw the beginning of the Waldorf era, and the first game was against Santa Clara. This was the highlight game for me personally. Santa Clara took an early lead but we won going away. I caught a deep pass from Bob Celeri and raced to the end zone. Later in the game I recovered a fumble for a touchdown and made some key plays. The next morning the San Francisco Call-Bulletin gave me the Tommy Thompson Topper for Bay Area Player of the Week. I received a medal and a $15 merchandise order to buy my own hat. During the summer of 1947 at a fraternity picnic at Stanford a small argument ensued between me and three Stanford fraternity brothers (who were also members of the Stanford team) on the outcome of the Big Game. I made a bet of $10 and my football pants with Dick Flatland (Stanford center), $10 and my helmet with Pete August and $20 and my jersey with George Quist (Stanford captain and fullback). The loser was to pay off after the game at the 50-yard line. I was in the game thinking about how I would look in a jock strap at the 50-yard line when the play was called for Jensen to throw the pass to Keckley. My pattern was deep to clear out for Keckley. Bobby Dodds made a great downfield block. I came back and took out Dick Flatland. When the game was over I headed for the 50-yard line but nobody showed up. I went into the Stanford dressing room and collected my loot.

Later, on George Quist's 50th birthday, I gave him his jersey as a present. Monday after the game when Pappy reviewed the pictures he played the Jensen to Keckley pass many times and made a special comment about my block on Flatland. He said that without Bobby Dodds' and my block, Keckley would not have scored. After the semester ended, I stayed out of school for six months to earn money so I could get married and then returned for the fall practice of 1948. I broke my hand two days before the first game and missed the first three games. I played sparingly but earned my letter. It was my fifth letter playing football at Cal which is a record (one year as a freshman and four on the varsity). I believe Hank Borghi also did the same. During my time at Cal I was president of the Big C (1947). I was elected to the Winged Helmet, Skull and Keys and Golden Bear honor societies.

I graduated from Cal with a degree in physical education. I had always wanted to be a football coach, but Eggs Manske suggested I pursue a business career instead because he didn't think I would be happy with the compensation of a coach. My dad died the week before the '48 Big Game so after the Rose Bowl game I moved to South Pasadena and took over my dad's laundry and dry cleaning business. When he died he had 10 employees. In 1949 when I headed home to take over my dad's business I had no idea what the dry cleaning and laundry business was about. For the next ten years I worked an average 80-hour week to learn all I could about the business. I learned every job from operating the machines to ironing the shirts, delivering to the customer and doing the books. At night I attended school, taking accounting, business and industrial engineering courses. As I learned, the company grew. As Eggs taught me, I did it until I got it right. My dad's original plant was in South Pasadena, and when I sold the business 18 years later I had 200 employees and five separate plants with 16 delivery trucks and a store. If I could attribute my success in the business world to anyone I would have to give credit to my Dad, my high school coach and to "Eggs". All three taught me that planning, hard work and setting goals were the keys to success.

After 18 years in the business, I sold the company and retired. At the time of the sale the company was probably the largest retail dry cleaning and laundry business in the state. I did some consulting work and played a lot of golf. In 1971 I divorced and moved to Emerald Bay in Laguna Beach. I remarried in 1975 and came out of retirement, and in 1977 began a career as a residential real estate broker. I chose residential real estate because I thought I was in a growing market in Orange County and I felt my business background would give me an advantage in dealing with successful people. Twice I was named top agent for the company and have now sold about $100 million in residential real estate. I have concentrated the last 10 years on the communities of Emerald Bay (where I live) and Irvine Cove where the average sale exceeds $1,000,000.

I had four daughters during my first marriage. The two oldest graduated from USC and have two children each. The next two daughters graduated from San Diego State and have two children each. My hobby is collecting Frank Sinatra records and traveling and spending as much time as possible at the beach and with my grandchildren. I have four stepchildren, one of whom graduated from Cal. I also have a hobby of reading and studying Ayn Rand and her philosophy of objectivism, which I believe to be the only philosophy that can return the United States to a political philosophy of capitalism. Capitalism is a social system based on the recognition of individual rights, including property rights, in which all property is privately owned. Since the late 19th century, capitalism has progressed towards socialism, with the state controlling more of our lives every day. Capitalism cannot survive in a culture dominated by altruism. Altruism is now taught in almost all colleges and universities in the United States, particularly at Harvard, Stanford and Cal.

RICHARD OSORIO

⌘

How is it that a Golden Bear ends up graduating from UCLA?

Well, I'd like to blame it on just plain having a good time with a bunch of great guys in my fraternity, not the least of whom included that unforgettable Augie Marra, John Miksits and the Hibbs brothers.

I had played on the Hal Grant Frosh team that had Les Richter on it and then on one of Zeb Chaney's junior varsity teams before I was activated as a U.S. Marine during the Korean conflict. Upon returning from this stint, I never really settled down, and it got so bad that the Dean called me in one day to remind me that it was November and I hadn't taken one midterm exam. He gave me one of two choices--either I could try to salvage what I could of the semester or he would wipe the entire slate clean with the proviso that I couldn't return to any UC campus for one year. I opted for the second choice and decided on UCLA as I didn't think it would be as congenial a situation, especially in view of the fact that my fraternity had no chapter on that campus. So, off I went in the fall of 1953.

While I was an undergraduate at UCLA I started "moving" with a group of actors and actresses and, for a time, I lived in a theatrical boarding house. It didn't take me long to realize how much I enjoyed their company. There were several reasons for this. For one, I was taken by their great enthusiasm for their work. That's all they talked about and, little by little, their world became mine. For another, I was fascinated with their knowledge of plays and classic books. I had never really been exposed to literature in any deep sense. Finally, I felt very comfortable with them as they were poor and so was I. Often we would "pool" our monies for a gallon of gasoline to go see a "triple" movie bill; and if the fellas couldn't come up with enough funds, the ladies did their part.

Well, simultaneously I was living in another world. I was attending UCLA majoring in business administration and after I graduated I moved to Boston to attend the Harvard Graduate School of Business. Once there, though, I realized that I had left an important part of my world behind in Los Angeles. Clearly, I had made a mistake.

So, at the Thanksgiving "break" I traveled to New York to have dinner with some of my friends who happened to be in New York. I asked one of them, a successful playwright, how to get started in the professional theatre. He suggested that I submit resumés to most of the listed theatrical producers, which I did, and, to my surprise, I got lots of replies. While it's true not many contained offers of employment, many came with advice and a willingness to meet with me. One of the classic letters I received was from Howard Lindsay who, with Russel Crouse, adapted Clarence Day's book, Life With Father, for the stage. He was pretty candid. He urged me not to consider his profession because, as he said, 20 years from now it wouldn't matter what profession I was in as long as I was successful. Well, I can only speak for myself when I say that he was wrong because I wouldn't trade any of my experiences in that marvelous field for anything.

My first job was at a summer theatre in upstate New York and my second was as an assistant to a theatre manager at the Anta Theatre in New York, and as I moved along I became a company manager, which eventually took me to the David Merrick Organization. My first assignment with Mr. Merrick was company manager of his show, "Don't Drink The Water." Later I was his manager for "Rosencrantz and Guildenstern Are Dead." At that time, all of his managers operated out of one central office and our major contact was not with Mr. Merrick but rather with his general manager, the late Jack Schlissel. If we saw Mr. Merrick at all it was at an opening night or during one of his occasional visits backstage. Eventually, though, this was to change insofar as I was concerned because of a number of things that were happening to me at that time, principally my involvement with the Broadway production of "Hair", for which I was the general manager. When this show became the raging success of New York I started to have more contact with Mr. Merrick, for whom I was still working on "Rosencrantz and Guildenstern Are Dead." In one instance, when I was a petitioning member of the Broadway Producers League (I think that was the name of the organization) for "Hair" to be considered eligible for the Tony Awards, Mr. Merrick asked me point blank at that session the following question: "Whom do you represent today, Mr. Osorio?" Being the good lawyer he was he knew how to undermine my presentation, which he did.

The last time I saw him was in his office in 1972 when I was involved in a musical presentation which we were trying to "mount". This was a show written by one of the authors of "Hair" and at this traditional audition, our author accompanied himself as he sang his score. It was not a successful presentation because as one of Mr. Merrick's main assistants pointed out, we really didn't have a libretto. Oddly enough, this same assistant had written me an extremely thoughtful note in reply to one of my resumés that I had sent some 16 years previously.

"Hair" was my last involvement on Broadway and after that I did one off-Broadway show, toured with a Native American Theatrical troop and completed my theatrical career with El Teatro Campesino. Overall, it was truly a great adventure and I wouldn't have had it any other way.

Presently I am involved in a library setting working with children and it has proven to be an exhilarating experience in its own right. You might say that I have had my cake and eaten it.

JIM "TRUCK" CULLOM

⌘

Like most of my teammates, I met Pappy in the spring of '47. Miles "Doc" Hudson had treated Pappy for a severe dental ailment when he arrived to interview Brutus Hamilton for the open football coaching job. After he had accepted the offer and had come to Berkeley to stay, he came to a rugby match as a courtesy to "Doc".

Rugby in '47 was pretty informal, and "Doc" pulled me out of the game to meet the new coach. Now, ask yourself, what does a freshman, sweating, muddy and wearing shorts, do when he meets the unknown, but exalted figure he hopes to play for, for the next three years? Honestly, I don't remember what he, or I, said, but I know after the meeting I had good feelings about the future.

I can't recall Pappy that spring without including his staff. I'd played for Zeb and Nibs on the Ramblers in '46, and didn't really get to know Hal Grant until I became a student assistant coach in the spring of '50. That left Wes Fry, Bob Tessier, and Eggs Manske.

I started as a fullback (which I'd played in high school,) and worked under Wes for two or three weeks. Then came the group break-up after team calisthenics, when Pappy called out, "All the linemen to the South End, all the ends to the West Side, and all the backs to the North End for group work.--Not so fast Cullom, Wes wants to talk to you."

Thus began my close association with Bob Tessier, who, with Pappy, became one great role model.

I used to ask Jon Baker, another rugger/fullback: "How'r ya doin, Jon?" His response was invariably "I'm twelfth string--but still a fullback." He later became an All Coast guard and an All NFL linebacker for the NY Giants.

What I remember most about that spring was that I was learning just how much I didn't know about football. It was then that my real education began, and while we worked long and hard, I think most of us enjoyed the work. It's currently heresy to admit you enjoy spring football.

The final day of spring practice was, as became a tradition, a marathon scrimmage. The date is lost to me, but it was also the day of the Fresno Relays. My brother lived in Fresno and I had a date for the Relays, so I was concerned that the scrimmage might never end. End it did, and I raced without lunch or dinner to my date and the Relays. After the meet we went to a party at her family's house. Gin and Tonics and Tom Collins were the drinks of choice, but I drank only beer. After an hour or so, and a half case of beer, two gentlemen arrived at the party, Pappy and Jeff Cravath, the USC coach, who was a college friend of my date's father. I was, for once in my life, speechless. I didn't know what to say (I was perfectly willing to lie, but couldn't think of a good one,) but Pappy saved me from making a bigger ass of myself. He glanced around the room, seeing all the tall frosty glasses, the one beer, and the half case of empties. He said, "The least you could have done, Cullom, is save me a few." Right then, on the brink of blowing it all, I recalled my first good feelings after our first meeting and doubled them.

The next three years were a blur, they went so fast. They were great years, filled with unforgettable friendships, experiences, emotions--high and low--and a gradual growth in knowledge and maturity. I think most graduates look back on college with similar feelings, but I feel that my teammates and I were extraordinarily fortunate to have spent these years with each other and with a group of leaders like

Pappy and his staff. Trite as it sounds, there was a chemistry there. I don't know if the catalyst was Pappy or Bob Sproul, the University, or Hirohito, but whatever or whoever it was created a family that maintains its ties to this day.

We went our separate ways on graduation; I had a short stint in the NFL before being called into the Marine Corps. I had served three years before coming to Cal and intended making a career in the Corps. An injury in Korea cut that career short.

Eventually, I worked my way back to Cal and worked for some great coaches, one of whom was Pappy. The others, while achieving success in the coaching profession, lacked something I only found in Lynn Waldorf. He was always helpful and supportive to all Cal Coaches. He was a great man. If I knew exactly what made him great, I'd bottle it and make a fortune. Many of us tried to emulate him, without success. We're all better for trying.

I've heard a lot of philosophers say that the greatest accomplishment is "to have made a difference." Pappy touched us all, and made a helluva good difference.

WILL LOTTER

⌘

Pappy had a profound influence on me, not only in terms of my technical knowledge as a football coach, but perhaps more importantly in teaching me a sense of fair play and the value of giving every individual, regardless of ability, the opportunity to participate in athletics. In my 41 years of coaching and teaching, at both the high school and university levels, I tried to practice this philosophy, not only in coaching football but in other sports such as soccer and tennis as well. Under Pappy, the Ramblers made an important contribution to the success of the football program and also gave each of us who played Ramblers the feeling that the program was open, and that with hard work there was a chance to eventually work up to the varsity. I've always been proud of the fact that I came up from the Ramblers and finally made the varsity in my senior year. Had it not been for Pappy's philosophy that players could be developed in the Rambler program, I feel I probably never would have played varsity. This experience and philosophy stuck with me throughout my coaching, and I tried to apply it in every sport I coached.

Another important thing I learned from Pappy was that you don't have to hate your opponent or take cheap shots on the field to have a successful program. I can't recall Pappy ever saying anything disrespectful about an opponent or ever condoning illegal or unsportsmanlike play. This, too, made a deep impression on me which I tried to carry into my coaching.

As for what Jane and I have been doing in our "other lives" when not attending games or going on road trips, in 1965 we took our four boys and went to Malawi, Africa, where I was on the Peace Corps staff. This experience of living two-and-a-half years in an African culture changed our lives and the way we viewed the world, and it gave us an understanding of the U.S. role in the Third World. When we returned to Davis, we got involved in the civil rights movement, and other social justice issues. Since 1982 we have been working in the Sanctuary program, which supports refugees from Guatemala and El Salvador who have had to flee their countries due to the military death squads and government repression. As a result of this involvement, a young Guatemalan refugee has been living with us for four years. He saw his father tortured and murdered by the Guatemalan military and then escaped to Mexico on foot at the age of ten where he lived on his own until he was 14.

Our work with refugees has taken us to Central America more than 15 times in the last ten years, and we recently spent ten weeks in Guatemala and El Salvador.

As for our four sons, they are all in their late 30's or early 40's, living in Northern California and so far have been staying out of any serious trouble, at least as far as we know. Only one is married. We have two grandchildren.

After 41 years teaching and coaching at UC Davis, I officially retired January 1, 1993.

DWIGHT ELY

⌘

When Pappy came to Cal I was a junior in high school. As everyone knows, his success was instantaneous. My three trips to the Rose Bowl put my relationship with Pappy into perspective. My first trip was as a high school senior who took an all-night bus from San Rafael to Pasadena to work as an usher on one of the aisles in the stadium--an end-zone aisle at that. During the next Rose Bowl, I was a freshman sitting in the rooting section with a terrible hangover. For the third Rose Bowl, thanks to Pappy, I was an 18-year-old actually playing in the game. As far as I was concerned, Pappy was a god and I was in awe of him. This feeling never really came to an end.

One incident I remember may be best described as my greatest moment in football--almost. In my junior year in practice before the Oregon State game, I believe, Pappy decided to put in a tackle eligible pass play. As it turned out, I was the only dumb tackle who could catch the ball. On game day, late in the second half, when we were safely ahead, Pappy called me over and told me to go in and call the tackle eligible play. Instant dreams of glory raced through my head. I charged out onto the field. About half way to the huddle I heard Pappy scream, "No, don't call the play." For the rest of my life I shall kick myself for admitting that I heard him. Had I claimed deafness, I might have had my moment of glory!

While in the Army, I decided to go to law school (it would get me out a month early). My qualifications were marginal and I am convinced to this day that football helped. There were three rabid fans on the faculty: Professors Kragen, Keeler and Kagel, and I believe they helped get me into Boalt Hall.

After graduation and passing the bar in 1958, I went to work for a law firm in Vallejo. We did general practice. I became a partner after about three years and worked in the same office for 21 years. During that time---1968 to be exact---I was elected to the Vallejo City Unified School District Board. I was Chairman one of the four years I was on the Board.

In 1980, as a Republican, I was appointed a Superior Court Judge for Solano County by Democrat Governor, Jerry Brown. To date, I have been Presiding Judge for two separate one-year terms. During the 15 years I have been on the bench, I have done every assignment we have, including criminal law, civil law, family law and juvenile court. I have handled just about every kind of trial there is from high publicity criminal cases to small claims appeals.

I was married for 37 wonderful years before my wife, Patricia, died. I have four grown children, all working and healthy, and two grandsons.

ROBERT "BOBBY" DODDS

⌘

A native Californian, I was born in Berkeley and raised in San Francisco. As I grew older I wanted to follow in my brother's footsteps. Johnny was an All City Football player at Polytechnic and played two years at the University of California under coach Stub Allison. He was a great athlete and an inspiration to me. Unfortunately his career and life were cut short in 1945 when his B-24 bomber crashed, and he and his crew were killed. I wanted to carry on his legacy and was determined to go to Cal. After a two-year period as a pilot trainee in the Army Air Corps, I entered Cal in February 1946 and graduated with the class of 1950. My degree in criminology enabled me to work for the U.S. Navy Department as a Special Agent and later with the Department of Defense. I retired from government service in 1976 and spent the next 14 years operating transit buses and light rail vehicles until my retirement in 1992.

In 1948 I met my future wife, Lua, who was a Cal student from San Diego. I have three wonderful boys born from this marriage, all of whom are employed and living on the Peninsula. My son, John, has given me two grandchildren.

Speaking of world class athletes, I want to recognize 13 players who played with Pappy's Boys, all from San Francisco. I think it is great that so many of us wanted to go on to Cal and to carry on the tradition of coming from San Francisco. They are: Jon Baker, Dan Begovich, Clayton Calender, Richard Calender, George Fong, Rod Franz, Gene Frassetto, Dick Groger, Forest Klein, Ronald Sockolov, Ray Solari, Glenn Stern, and Staten Webster.

It's a long road from college days--football, dating, excitement, fun, laughter, tears and a full head of hair--to retirement. It's also a long road from cramming for exams to watching "Cheers". Along that road I was proud to have had the opportunity to work for the Navy Department and Department of Defense for 26 years. I consider that a part of my education. In fact, in December 1968, I had the honor of being a part of the debriefing team that interviewed the officers and crew of the ill-fated USS Pueblo upon their release from capture and return to San Diego. There were several other government agencies involved in the process and I spent a large part of my time listening to the crew's harrowing reports of the past year of captivity. I was very enlightened and honored to be chosen. I am proud to have a book authored by Commander Lloyd Bucher, USN retired, the skipper of the Pueblo, which he personally autographed for me.

Some people grow up wanting to be policemen, firemen or pilots, but I always wanted to drive a bus. The transition from government service to transportation was easy, and when the opportunity arose I took it. After one and a half years of driving a school bus in Cupertino, CA, I spent 15 interesting and challenging years with the Santa Clara County Transportation District. Working for county transit has given me many pleasant memories of being in the hub of life. It was fun to get acquainted with people who do not walk the same path as I do. It also gave me the chance to listen to their stories and hear their problems. It made life very interesting for me. I achieved my goal in 1992 when the National Safety Council honored me as a member of the "Million Mile Club" for twelve years of safe driving in public transportation.

To get back to the beginning of the long walk, football gave me the moral fiber I have passed on to my family. It taught me that good healthy habits and nutrition are essential to a good life. I think football has made me a caring person who loves people and tries to help them. THANKS PAPPY. It was also great to have had the background to be able to support my sons in sports, little league, soccer, etc. It gives me much satisfaction to watch my grandchildren grow and excel in their own fields.

Retirement is a full time job and is turning out to be exactly what it is supposed to be. I enjoy and look forward each month to attending a luncheon with my associates and buddies, all retired from government service. I thoroughly enjoy once a year attending a Poly High Grid Club party where I get a chance to see and talk with all the friends I played with back in the 1940's. My wife and I recently returned from a trip to the East Coast visiting friends of her family and, all-in-all, having a wonderful time. And I find myself fully occupied in my yard.

And finally as to my greatest achievement, I believe that if a man, with his wife, can raise his children with love, compassion, decency and honor, it can be said of him, "well done." I asked each of my sons to comment on the positive impact their father had upon their lives and this is what they said:

John Dodds

When asked by my father to write a little bit for this chapter, I remembered the Cal Bears in the '91 season as they started their run for a Bowl bid. I felt a sense of pride just as I had many years before as I learned of my father's years as a lineman with the Rose Bowl Cal Bears of '49 and '50. I also felt that sense of pride being a native of the Bay Area and of being born in Berkeley on April 30, 1950 when my parents were still students and had their entire adult life ahead.

I also remember feeling a sense of pride while watching a video of an old USC game film in which I could actually see number 65 make diving tackles and key blocks along with his teammates opposite the Trojan line. And how as an adult, I appreciate the complexities of putting together such a team effort and carrying off a game plan. The lessons learned in these efforts can be carried with us throughout life.

I feel that Pappy Waldorf has always been an influence on my life because of his influence on my father's life. In some ways Pappy Waldorf seems like a grandfather I never knew, like my two grandfathers and father's brother who died before I was old enough to know them.

I also feel that this sense of pride is being passed on to my two children, Kelly and Noel, as they grow up and get to know their grandfather and his accomplishments and especially of his being a part of one of the nation's greatest teams. I'm glad they have his life and its memories to take them into adulthood, and with them a little part of Lynn Waldorf.

Edwin Dodds

I can recall a time when my folks took me to see dad play with Pappy's Boys at the alumni game at Cal. At age seven, everything seemed larger than life, even the gash dad got on his hand from a cleat. That same evening we all had dinner in town. Even though I was just seven years old, I felt I belonged because I was Bobby Dodds' son.

One of Dad's accomplishments, which stands out in my mind, was how he helped establish the Los Altos Hills Little League for which my older brother, John, and I played. Dad coached our team to first place one year.

As a coach, father, and friend my dad gave me what Pappy gave his boys: a level head and a strong positive attitude.

Richard Dodds

Growing up the son of one of Pappy's Boys has filled me with a sense of pride and a feeling of excitement. Pride comes from knowing that my father is a part of one of college football's most prominent eras. Excitement comes from the stories of the many glorious moments in my father's career at Cal. My favorite memory of the era is that my father played in not one, but two Rose Bowls. That must be the crowning glory in any college player's career. I'm sure my father is most proud of that achievement. I believe that it was because of Pappy Waldorf's coaching that they were able to achieve that pinnacle of success. So thanks Pappy for giving my father the chance to succeed and for giving his sons something to be proud of.

NICHOLAS A. VELIOTES

⌘

From 1955 to 1986 I served as a Foreign Service Officer of the United States. In carrying out my responsibilities, I was an active participant in the decades-long, unique exercise in collective security that led to the end of the Cold War and, ultimately, to the end of the Soviet Union. This is a source of general satisfaction.

If pressed, I would cite the following specific examples where I believe my personal role had an important positive impact on people and policy.

> In the early 1960's, I led a reorganization of the International Educational and Cultural Programs of the Department of State which revitalized these important tools of communicating American values abroad. Tens of thousands of people, foreign and American, have participated in and benefitted from these activities.
>
> In the early 1980's, as Assistant Secretary of State, I was responsible for ensuring the implementation of the Egyptian-Israeli Treaty which was negotiated in 1978 and 1979. In April 1982 the treaty was implemented and has been the bedrock of other peace efforts in the Middle East.
>
> In the fall of 1985, as Ambassador to Egypt, I was responsible for implementing our policy of "no negotiations and no deals" with terrorists in the context of the hijacking of the "Achille Lauro". We stood firm, the hostages were released and the terrorists were subsequently imprisoned in Italy.

Looking back, I can't say the world is a better place because of me, but I am certain I did not make it worse -- and maybe that is not a bad epitaph!

RICHARD RIGBY

⌘

Life in general has been very gratifying and our rewards have been great through the good Lord's gift to us of having had four very healthy children at this particular time and giving us six fine, healthy grandchildren. We had the good fortune of putting four children through college at the same time and somehow (I can't remember) getting through the process in one piece.

Have I had a beneficial impact on my business or profession? I believe the organization of the Bank of Fresno was a tremendous and enjoyable personal experience. It now offers the community a financial institution of substance and an entity which cares for local survival and future growth. I feel a great part of that foundation.

A group of prominent local businessmen decided they needed a bank that could be responsive to community economic needs and could project and present a philosophy which would lend itself to helping smaller businesses. I was approached by this group to create the loan policy, formulate marketing strategies, and actively serve as Senior Loan Officer. We capitalized with $1,250,000.00 and opened our doors on July 20, 1973. I was appointed President of the organization in 1975 and remained with the bank through the formulating years until 1979.

Today, Bank of Fresno is the dominant independent bank in the Central Valley and ranked among the top five in the state. The bank is well represented with branches serving Merced, Madera, Fresno, Sanger and Kingsburg to the south. It is also purchasing a large independent bank in Bakersfield which will give it complete coverage of the San Joaquin Valley. Today, Bank of Fresno is one of the largest (total assets), independent banks in the state. It has had a tremendous impact on the markets it serves. As a local bank, it has responded more efficiently to local investors and, in general has given credibility and reliability to the local economy.

I don't know that the world is a better place because of me but I do know I have enjoyed every minute of my time on this earth and can sincerely say that my years at the University of California provided me with one of the greatest experiences of my life. I believe all of us then were winners for having had the benefit of Pappy Waldorf's philosophy and guidance. That time prepared us to face the world and, we hope, to pass on a better society to our children and grandchildren. (I sometimes wonder what the hell is happening out there in this world today, but we can't give up).

Memorial Stadium at Full Capacity - 83,000

SURE, I ADMIT MY FIRST STRING IS PRETTY GOOD—
PRESS
COACH
—BUT LOOK WHAT'S LEFT WHEN WE HAVE INJURIES !!
COACH
GUESS HE'S IN FOR A ROUGH YEAR.
YEA.— HE CERTAINLY DOESN'T HAVE THE DEPTH FOR THE TWO PLATOON SYSTEM.
PRESS
PRIVATE
KEEP OUT
DEEP FREEZE
OKAY, BOYS— BACK TO FUNDAMENTALS !
LEE SUSMAN

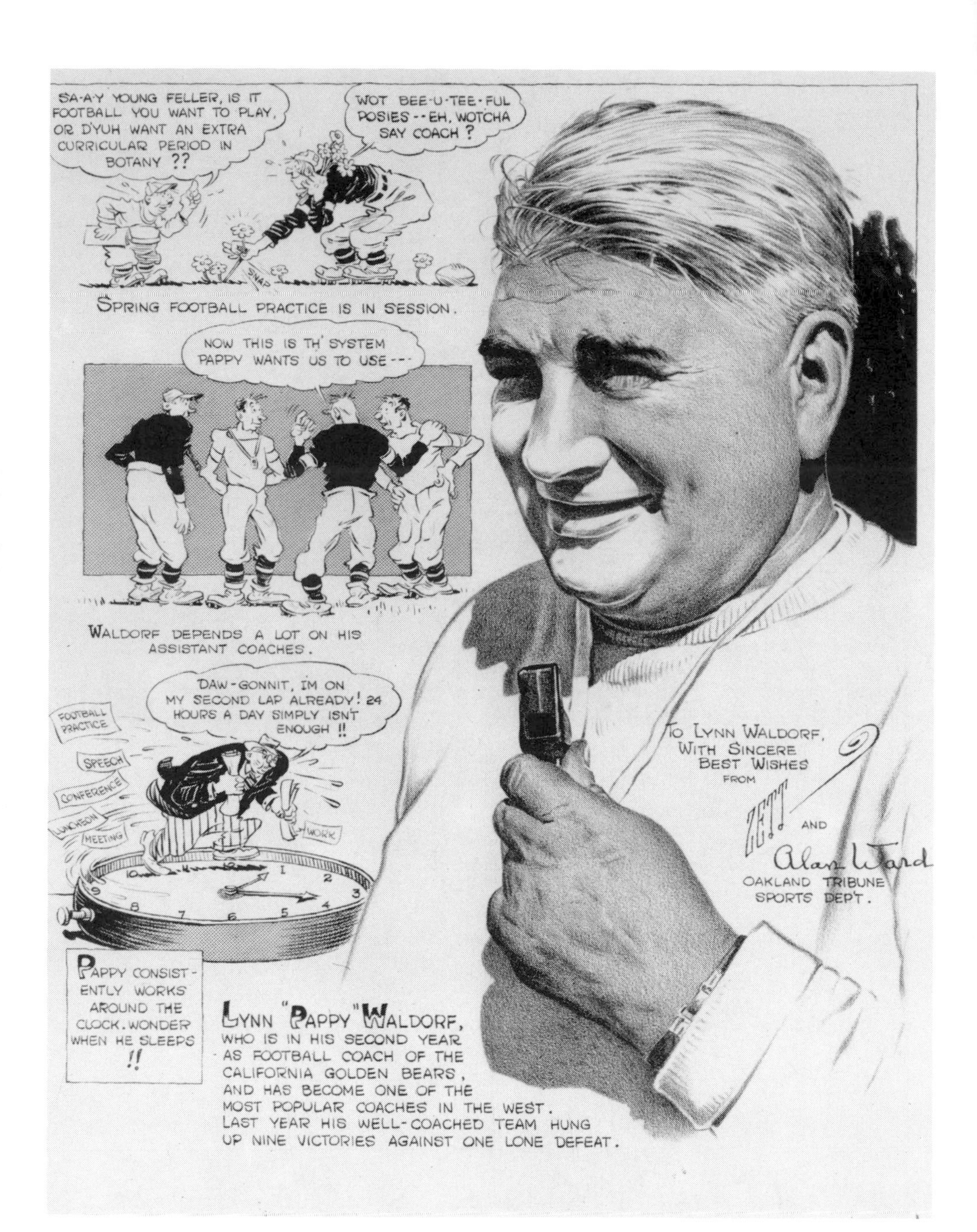
SA-A-Y YOUNG FELLER, IS IT FOOTBALL YOU WANT TO PLAY, OR D'YUH WANT AN EXTRA CURRICULAR PERIOD IN BOTANY ??
WOT BEE-U-TEE-FUL POSIES--EH, WOTCHA SAY COACH ?
SNAP
SPRING FOOTBALL PRACTICE IS IN SESSION.
NOW THIS IS TH' SYSTEM PAPPY WANTS US TO USE---
WALDORF DEPENDS A LOT ON HIS ASSISTANT COACHES.
DAW-GONNIT, I'M ON MY SECOND LAP ALREADY! 24 HOURS A DAY SIMPLY ISN'T ENOUGH !!
FOOTBALL PRACTICE
SPEECH
CONFERENCE
LUNCHEON
MEETING
WORK
PAPPY CONSISTENTLY WORKS AROUND THE CLOCK. WONDER WHEN HE SLEEPS !!
LYNN "PAPPY" WALDORF,
WHO IS IN HIS SECOND YEAR AS FOOTBALL COACH OF THE CALIFORNIA GOLDEN BEARS, AND HAS BECOME ONE OF THE MOST POPULAR COACHES IN THE WEST. LAST YEAR HIS WELL-COACHED TEAM HUNG UP NINE VICTORIES AGAINST ONE LONE DEFEAT.
TO LYNN WALDORF, WITH SINCERE BEST WISHES FROM
ZETT AND Alan Ward
OAKLAND TRIBUNE SPORTS DEP'T.

1948 TEAM

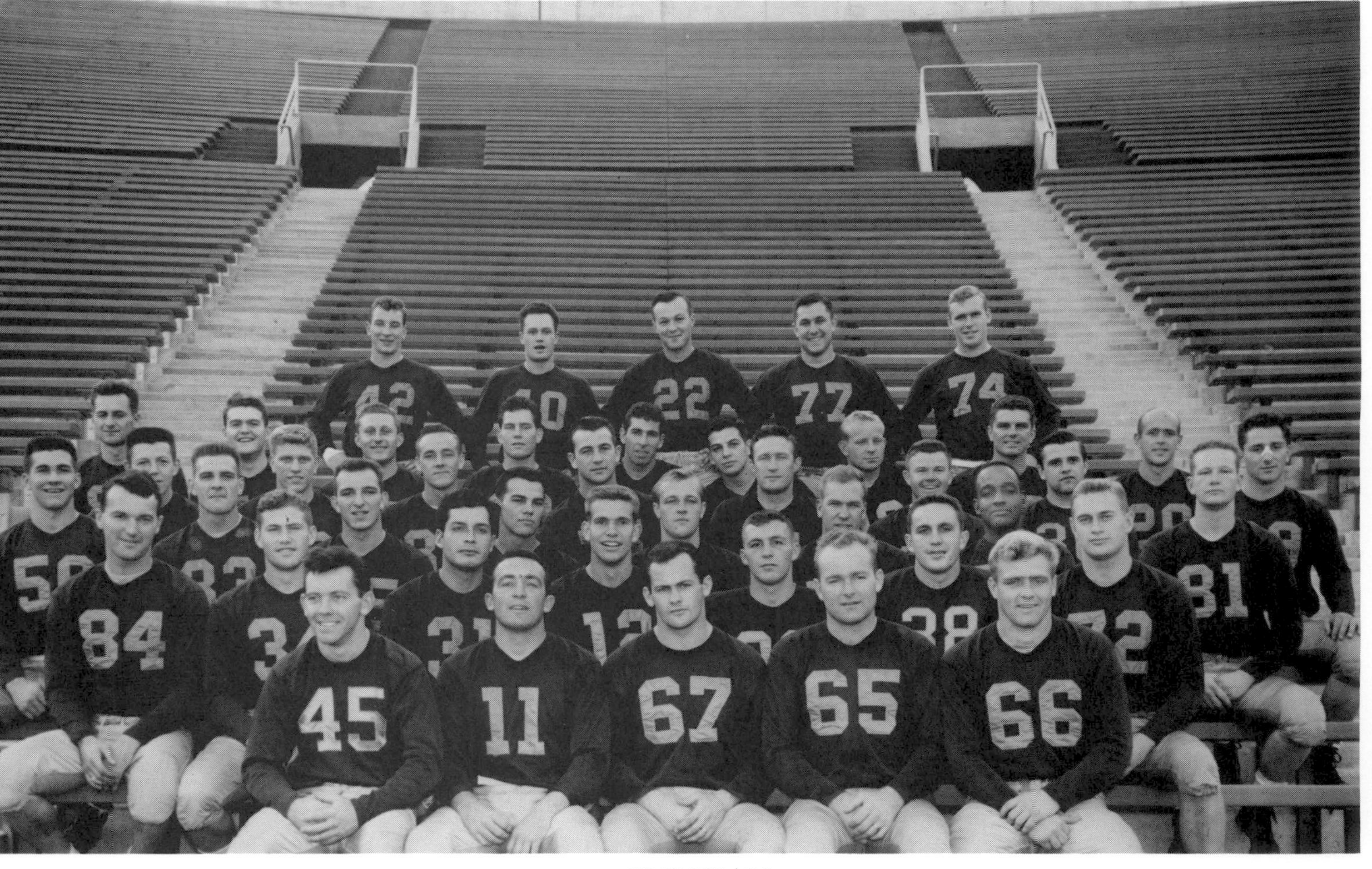

1949 TEAM

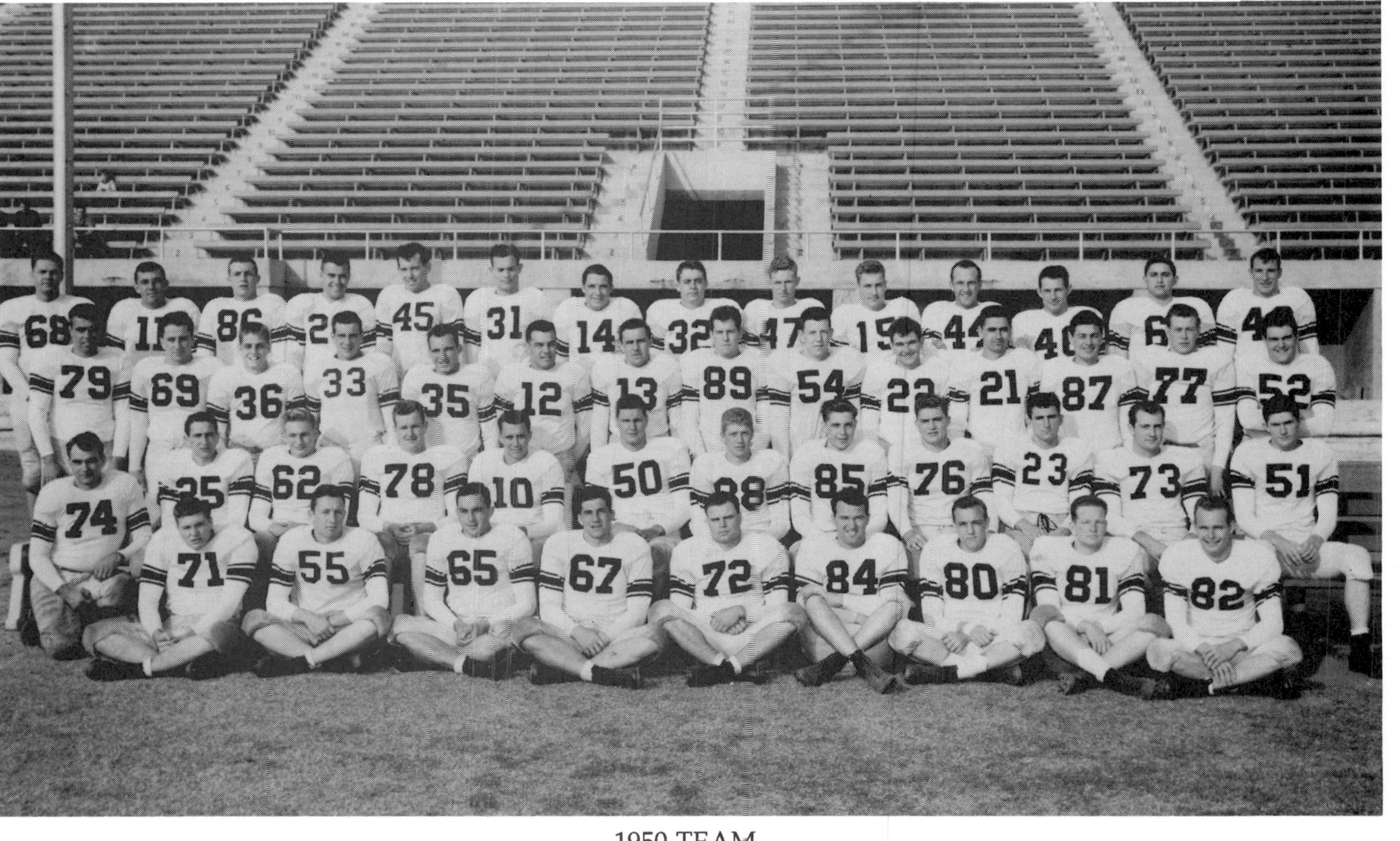

1950 TEAM

Rose Bowl Coaches 1948 and 1949
Top: Eggs Manske, Pappy Waldorf, Zeb Chaney, Hal Grant
Kneeling: Wes Fry, Bob Tessier, Nibs Price

1950 Rose Bowl Coaches
Top: Hal Grant, Eggs Manske, Zeb Chaney, Herm Meister, Wes Fry, Nibs Price
Kneeling: Pappy Waldorf

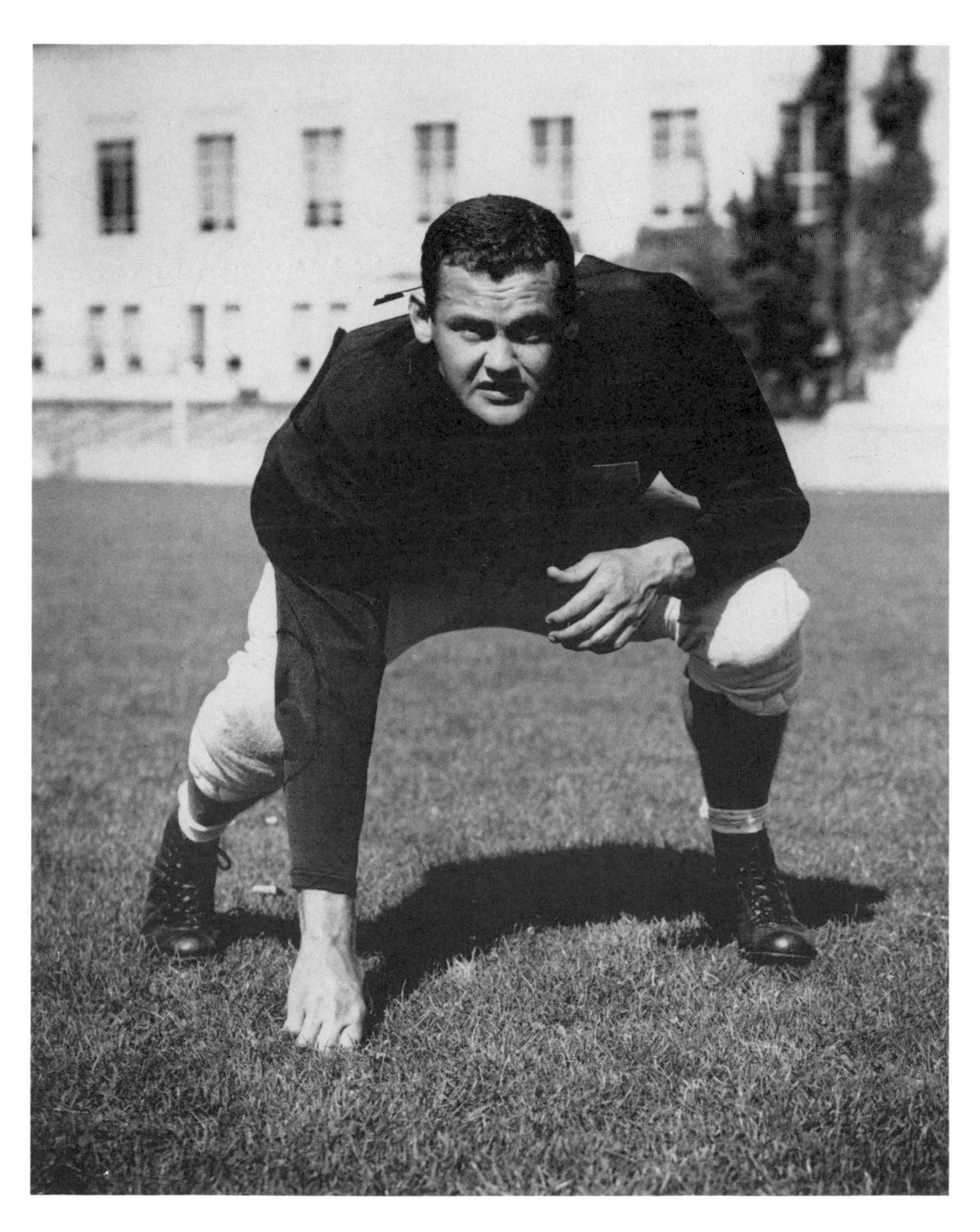

Rod Franz - Three Time All American

Jack Jensen - All American

Jim Turner - All American

Bob Celeri - All American

Forrest Klein - All American

Carl Van Heuit - All American

Les Richter - Two Time All American

Jim Monachino - All American

John Olszewski - All American

One of Pappy's Famous Balcony Appearances

Gene Frassetto - Team Captain 1948

Waldorf Statue - Faculty Glade

1949 - Frank Brunk 102 Yard Kickoff Return vs. USC

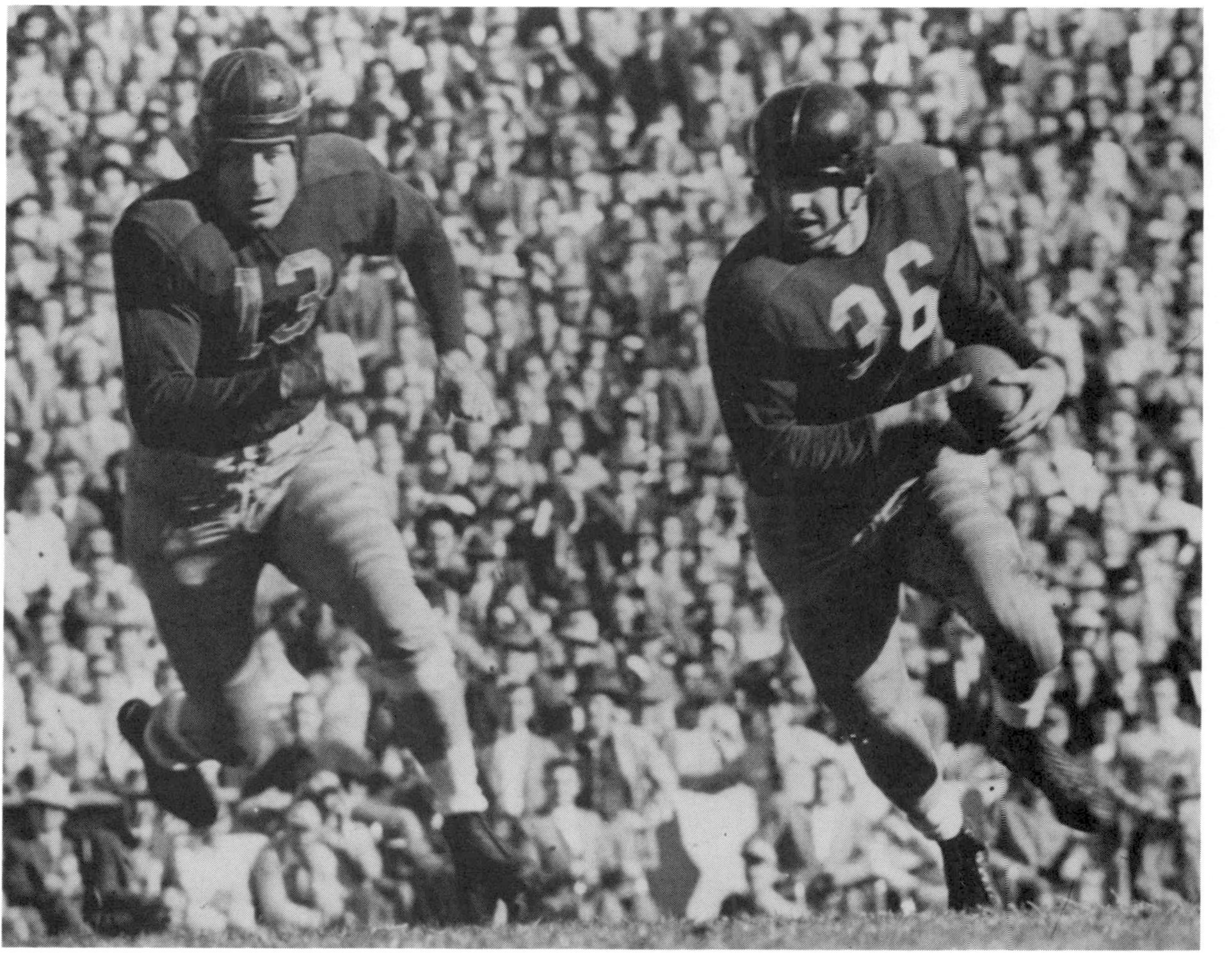

1948 - Swaner Runs Interference for Jensen

1948 - Jensen Runs Interference for Swaner

1948 - Erickson Scores

1948 - Keckley Carries Against Wisconsin

1949 - Dan Begovich TD Catch vs. Oregon

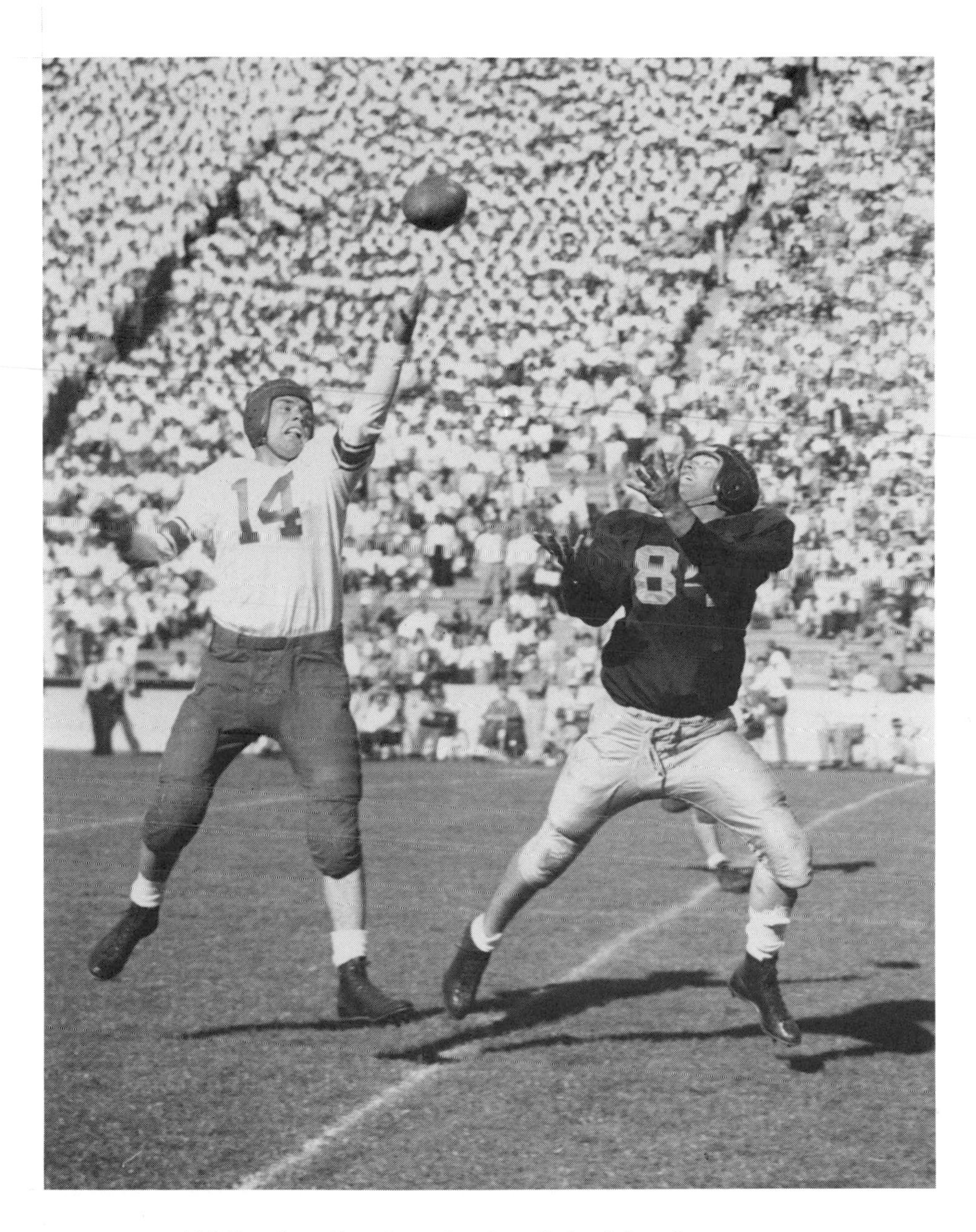

Ed Bartlett Catches Against Saint Mary's

Bob Minahen Catches Against Santa Clara

1950 - UCLA - John Olszewski Scores Again

1950 - Santa Clara - Bill Powell Leads Harry West Around End

Richter Returns Reception

1951 - Cal 20 - Stanford 7 - Robison Carries, Richter Leads Interference

1951 Rose Bowl - Pete Schabarum Blocks for Jim Monachino

RAY DEJONG

⌘

My family has been the most important thing in my life: my wife, son and daughter and for the last few years, my grandson. Outside of my family the most important thing to me has been the game of football. It has been my privilege and pleasure to have been involved in the game as a player and coach for 45 years. It seems every major and a lot of minor decisions I've made in my life revolved around football.

I was born in South Dakota, lived with my folks on a farm and cattle ranch, 15 miles from a small town. I attended a rural one-room school for my first six years. Total enrollment for the eight grades ranged from seven to twelve, depending on the number of families and students in the area. From this beginning I have often marvelled that I graduated from such a big and prestigious institution as U.C. Berkeley.

In 1938, before my seventh year in school, my family moved to Enumelaw, Washington. There my father became a dairy farmer, and I had the privilege of helping milk the cows, by hand, morning and night. I saw my first football games. I was not very impressed, as I did not understand the game or know the rules, and the practices looked like a lot of hard work.

My eighth grade science teacher, who was an assistant football coach at the high school, turned my life around. Before school was out that spring, he asked me if I was going to play football in the fall. I answered no. He said he thought I should because he thought I'd be good at it. With this encouragement, I decided I wanted to play the game. I had to convince my folks that I would not get hurt and that I would continue to do my farm chores. Thank God, they gave their permission.

With my high school success, I started dreaming about going to college to play football, but because of World War II, I enlisted in the Navy V-12 Officer Training program. In July 1944, I was sent to Gonzaga University, where to my disappointment, there was no football team. Still, I was able to complete a year of college work. I arrived at St. Mary's (Moraga) Navy Pre-Flight School in July 1945. They had a football team, which I joined. When the war was over, most of the cadets on the team took the option of getting out of the service. Because it was during the football season, I elected to stay in. I wanted to finish the season. We played Cal that year as well as USC and UCLA, plus other service teams at Kezar Stadium. Many of my teammates that year became members of the original 49er team in 1946. Frankie Albert was our quarterback, and Len Eshmont was one of our running backs. Emil Sitko, who became famous at Notre Dame, and later played for the 49ers, was another of our running backs.

After being in the service for one and a half years, I still wanted to fly an airplane, so I went down to Corpus Christi, Texas. I got to fly and I also got to play another year of service football on the Corpus Christi Naval Air Base team. I was elected Captain of the team. We played a post-season game for the Southwest Service Championship. The Captain of the opposing team was Doak Walker, who later became famous at S.M.U. and with the Detroit Lions.

In 1947, I came to Berkeley because I had met my future wife (Jean) while at St. Mary's Pre-Flight and wanted to be close to her and play college football. Playing in the Rose Bowl had been a dream since I started playing the game. To play in two Rose Bowls was double sweetness. In my nine years of playing football, I had six different head coaches. Without question, my three years under Pappy had the most influence on my life.

After playing in the Rose Bowl on January 1, 1950, I coached my first football team at South San Francisco High School. I was hired there because of Pappy's success at Cal. I continued to use Pappy's system and methods with only minor adjustments for all the years I coached. In 1950 my won-loss record on the Frosh-Soph team was 6-1. I do not know my record on the Frosh-Soph from 1950-85, but guess it was about 50% or slightly better.

Worth it? Gosh, yes. Football has been the most important thing in my life besides my family. Football has given me many emotional highs and lows. Certainly winning the right to play in the Rose Bowl was a real high. Losing those two games was a real low. But I will always be thankful I was able to be actively involved with football for 45 years. My three years at Cal gave me the stepping stones to my future success.

I also had another dream for many years. When I was a sophomore in high school (1941), Enumelaw went over the mountains to play Yakima High School. We played the game and stayed overnight in a hotel, the first time in my life I had not slept in my parents' home. Since starting coaching at South San Francisco High School in 1950, I had dreamed about taking my team on an overnight trip. Finally in 1977, I was able to take my players to Hawaii for a game. We stayed for five days and four nights; won the game and had a ball.

BILL MAIS

⌘

St. Anthony's is a Catholic parish in downtown Long Beach which includes a school with grades one-through-twelve. The school was started in 1921. It was the most unlikely Southern California high school to ever be in a championship. The pastor, Monsignor Bernard P. Dolan, who ran the parish and the grammar/high school, was not the least bit athletically inclined. Athletics, and specifically football, were not a priority item. Facilities and equipment were poor to non-existent.

In 1944, just prior to practice, the team formed a line to walk the hard dirt field and strip it of broken glass and debris. The next year practice moved to a bowl which was used during the winter as a rain-runoff holding pond. The dirt was as fine as flour. Every play created a veritable dust storm. The Montana Land Company, which was developing the 'city of tomorrow' at Lakewood, donated land to St. Anthony, designated specifically for athletics and recreation. While it represented a giant step forward, the field did have problems in terms of time and distance, since it was ten miles from the school. A big truck with a canvas top was purchased for transportation. What a scene: the St. Anthony Saints, headed to the world famous Rose Bowl to play a Catholic League rival, riding in the back of a truck with players' legs dangling above the street. The "truck" was famous in St. Anthony lore as it was used for every sport and was in active use right up to the first CIF playoff game when it was temporarily garaged and replaced by a bus.

Was it possible, in anyone's wildest imagination, that five years later four players from this small rag-tag band would arrive at the same Rose Bowl gate in luxurious buses with a police escort? Or that 104,000 fans, including dignitaries from every level of government, business and entertainment would watch them along with a nationwide TV audience?

St. Anthony's new football field was dedicated in 1946. Along with the field came a new coach, Jacques Grenier. Coach Grenier was originally from Connecticut, but the war had brought him to Southern California where he had helped coach some of the great college players then playing on the military teams.

Whether it was by fate, luck, destiny, God or whatever, it certainly was not by design that Coach Grenier should end up coaching this small band of talented, tough and intelligent boys.

The chemistry between the coach with the heavy French accent and his players was perfect. The boys had come primarily from St. Anthony's grammar school and St. Matthews, another grammar school nearby. From the third grade on, these two schools competed against each other in every sport, not in any organized way but merely at recess and lunchtime, usually at the suggestion of someone saying, "Let's play St. Matthews!" These boys came together in the ninth grade now as teammates.

Coach Grenier was a communicator. While his French accent was not always understandable, the players knew exactly what he meant. He was ingenious at devising a system that fit his players and in instilling within them enthusiasm, desire and confidence. He saw a newsreel of a Notre Dame game and dreamed up a play in detail that night that became our Notre Dame 38. It produced many touchdowns for Johnny Olszewski. The coach officiated a COP game and observed Eddie LeBaron's double spin. It became a key offensive weapon for Billy Mais. Before the semi-final CIF playoff game with Chaffey, Coach Grenier, at breakfast with

Cal Coach Wes Fry, established a link which in retrospect very subtly started us on the way to Berkeley. Wes diagrammed the play that Jackie Jensen had used so successfully. Coach Grenier installed the play and appropriately named it the Cal 36, just in time for the semi-final CIF game. In the Saints' first play from scrimmage against Chaffey, Johnny O ran the Cal 36, 72 yards for a touchdown. He ran a second Cal 36 for 64 yards, and in all scored four touchdowns to lead the Saints to a 28-20 victory.

St. Anthony overnight had become the Cinderella team in Southern California. In the first-round playoff game held in Long Beach, San Diego High thought so little of the Saints that they elected to leave the school band at home, saving it for the next round. The Saints' victory was the first major upset. Here was a school with only 77 boys in the senior class and a total squad of just 32. The opposition out-enrolled them by four to six times. Monsignor Dolan by now had become a full convert. He bought the Saints new uniforms for the first time in years, including for the first time capes, and now they arrived by bus.

The final CIF championship game in the L.A. Coliseum was with Santa Barbara High which was led by Punky Bowman, who reputedly had a bright future in baseball, and Eddie Matthews who in fact did (Baseball Hall of Fame). The Saints were without the services of Johnny Olszewski, the all-city, all-CIF, High School All American and Southern California Player of the Year, who had been injured in the previous game. The Saints again were heavy underdogs, but with the Monsignor and even the Cardinal in attendance and groups of nuns praying for a victory, the absolutely impossible happened: the Saints were victorious. It was truly a rags-to-riches, Horatio Alger, David and Goliath story.

The Saints were feted, honored and entertained, but mostly recruited. Eastern schools, Notre Dame, the service academies, and all the western colleges vigorously pursued them. One school offered scholarships for the entire first team offense and defense, which numbered about 15 different players. USC, UCLA and Stanford were prime candidates along with Cal.

Continuing to play in front of the home folks was a major theme of UCLA and USC recruiters and it had a strong appeal. Sunny Southern California and the beach environment were also strong reasons for the boys to stay home. Cal actively promoted its educational excellence and the opportunity for the Saints to move away from "home" but not so far that they couldn't return for weekends, vacations between semesters and the summer. The Southern Seas with Frank Storment, Henry Frost, Herm Selvin, Judge Stan Barnes, Bill Rawn and others worked hard to convince them that Cal was best for them. Johnny Graves and Stan Morketter, the swimmer, had a beach apartment in Long Beach where the Saints were always welcome to stop by and shoot the breeze and, inevitably, hear stories about the virtues of Cal. John Graves' ability to expand his chest and balance two Coke bottles on it as if it were a shelf was not lost on these athletes. They were impressed. Eric Schultz, who had played high school ball for Coach Grenier in Connecticut and had moved to Long Beach, played for Long Beach City College and then Cal, was influential in recruiting the Saints.

Once the decision had been made to stay on the West Coast, the boys and their parents continuously evaluated the big four: Cal, UCLA, USC and Stanford. UCLA had a Red Sanders single wing team which was not overly appealing. Coach Sanders pressed hard on Dean O'Hare by, in effect, promising him captaincy of the team and All-American status. This tactic seemed a bit much to this high school linebacker who incidentally was a lifetime California Scholarship Federation winner. The meetings with Stanford Recruiters also revealed that school's attitude of superiority.

With UCLA and Stanford fading, the choice narrowed down to Cal and USC. In the end there was really only one choice: 'Pappy' Waldorf and the Cal Bears. It was 'Pappy's' magnificent stature as a man and as a Coach that spelled the difference. The entire backfield of Bill Mais, John Olszewski, Dean O'Hare and John Peterson, along with tackle Jim Blanchard, guard Bob Parkin and back George Hainley, all entered as freshmen and played for Coach Hal Grant.

The picture of 'Pappy'---the rotund one, the 'Whale', he of the silver hair, the deep commanding voice and the sense of humor--adjusting his pants and telling us we were good in spots but the spots were too far apart, will be with us forever. He was obviously a very bright man who was well-organized, in-charge and well-educated. A knowledge of the humanities, a sense of humility and a caring and fair approach were all Pappy attributes.

The privilege of playing for Pappy and a great university like Cal was immediately evident to these boys. The transition from a highly-structured Catholic school to the Berkeley campus was indeed an eye opener. The opportunity to fail was everywhere. From fraternity life, to the local watering holes, to San Francisco, the temptations, at times, were overwhelming. Of course, this test was all a part of growing from boyhood to manhood. The father figure of Pappy loomed large whenever these distractions became strong.

The memories abound---

...Ray Solari winning 17 straight Blackjack hands at the Arrowhead Springs Hotel prior to the Rose Bowl---and he was a lineman.

...Dick LemMon being injured in a game and, as he was escorted off the field, a concerned Pappy asking him, "How are you, Dick?" and LemMon replying, "Fine, and how are you?"

...Pete Schabarum in a huddle during a crucial drive: "Nice crowd we have today."

...Pappy asking Earl Rose to rerun that play again with a hundred feet or so of film wrapped around his arms and legs every Monday night without fail.

...Eggs Manske describing the next team we were going to play as a combination of the Chicago Bears and New York Giants. He had long ago mastered the overstatement.

...Toots Carlton making sure we were taking the right classes, her magical ability to cut through the bureaucracy.

...Paul Christopulos' friendly smile, especially when we had shown him a passing grade in a course.

...Augie Mara being struck on the head by the tailgate of a dump truck and spraining his ankle.

...Dr. Malm, history professor, standing on his tiptoes at the rail of Golden Gate Fields watching his loser cross the finish line.

...Dr. Hines, Geology I professor, leading the Cal songs every Friday in Wheeler Hall Auditorium.

...Jim Marinos' famous battle cry: "We don't need no steenking badges."

...On a cold rainy night just before Christmas, the freshman Saints who were running the Ohio State offense against the varsity were asked to entertain a promising recruit from Ventura City College. They were not anxious to leave the fraternity house, The recruit suggested some cards, and a blackjack game ensued.

The Saints were "taken to the cleaners" by this brute of a linebacker who later would inflict further major damage on Johnny O's knee. His name was Pat Cannamela.

The Cal experience, all aspects of it, prepared these men for significant accomplishments while at school and in their subsequent careers. Johnny "O" became a two-time All American, John Peterson a Scandinavian All American and Bill Mais became co-captain of the team. All of the Saints made their contributions in helping the Cal Bears to winning seasons. The Saints were members of the 1951 Rose Bowl team.

Johnny "O" was a player's player, a coach's dream. He asked no quarter and he gave none. He gave new meaning to the words "contact sport." He did everything asked of him, and his performance, leadership, and unselfishness were an inspiration to fellow players. He was the top draft pick of the Chicago Cardinals, and he played for ten-plus years in the NFL. He was All Pro and set a single-game rushing record for the Washington Redskins that stood for 12 years. He is currently retired, living in Long Beach.

Bill Mais retired from IBM Marketing Management and currently is a financial adviser. He and his wife, Jane, have seven children and fourteen grandchildren. He is a member of the St. Anthony Hall of Fame and is on the boards of the St. Anthony Foundation and Palm Desert Tennis Club. He is a resident of Long Beach.

John Peterson recently retired as a City Attorney for Long Beach. He is married with six children and five grandchildren. He is a member of the St. Anthony Hall of Fame and is on the board of the Palm Desert Tennis Club.

Dean O'Hare is an independent securities broker in Glendale, California. Bob Parkin is a Superior Court Judge in Norwalk, California, while residing in Long Beach. He is a member of the St. Anthony Hall of Fame and is on the Board of the St. Anthony Foundation.

HART FAIRCLOUGH

⌘

Being one of "Pappy's Boys" has a slightly different meaning for me than it does for his former players. I believe my association with Pappy and the results of it are unique.

As a veteren leaving the service at the end of World War II, my story might start out much the same as his players. I, too, enrolled at Cal, first in the Engineering Department. Later I switched to education and PE, looking forward to a football coaching career. But---how I arrived at that point and what followed differs from the experiences of his players.

Before the war, I went from an 80-pounder to 105 pounds in four years of high school. Too small for football, I missed out on playing the sport I had loved since I was big enough to pick up and carry a ball. The closest I got to the high school football program was two years as a yell leader.

During several years in the service my weight jumped from 120 to 135, but with no previous football experience, I was hardly big enough to compete against the football turnout at Berkeley following the war. At least, this was the advice others gave me.

Although pre-enrolled in June of 1946 for the fall semester at Cal, my heart was not in Engineering, but on coaching football. However, I received no encouragement in this regard from anyone I confided with, including my former high school vice principal, who had been a long time football coach. Then, fortunately, there came an exception. This was my pre-war high school track coach, and also head football coach, Fred Canrinus. He was an All-American end at St. Mary's College under "Slip" Madigan back in the early 30's. He and "Eggs" Manske were teammates on the College All-Stars in the first Pros vs. All-Stars Game in 1934.

With Coach Canrinus, I discussed my forthcoming year at the University and my real desire for a future in coaching football, and of the discouragement I had experienced. Coach Canrinus not only encouraged me, but also provided some ideas and an approach to follow. This gave me the extra confidence needed to "go for it". His suggestion was to "go see the head coach (then Frank Wickhorst), tell him of your aspirations and maybe he'll help you. Be a manager, a stat man or whatever. Follow the practices, the games, study all aspects of football. Don't just learn a few segments or one favorite position, as I did. It will help you offset the disadvantage of not having played the game."

Within a week, I drove to Berkeley and changed from engineering to education and a PE major. My talk with Coach Wickhorst led to my first year as manager. As many who might read this will recall, the 1946 season was not a very successful one for many players and for one particular manager as well. That summer, somewhat discouraged, I talked again with Coach Canrinus. Again he encouraged me to press on--"Give it another year--go talk to the new coach, Lynn Waldorf."

My world changed after a 20-minute talk with "Pappy." He not only encouraged me, but told me, in effect, "You don't have to play the game to coach it, although it sure does help. But if you study the game thoroughly and you have the drive and the feel for it in your heart--that's what it takes."

He proceeded to make suggestions: If I reported two weeks before school, I could follow all of the team's double practices, meetings, film sessions, etc.--just as if

I were a player. He got me a room with the team in Bowles Hall and even included me in all the training table meals. He said he'd explain to the assistant coaches what I was doing and that I could have copies of plays and all the other information that players received.

Needless to say, Pappy's encouragement was contagious. I started that 1947 season with a singular dedication my life had not had before. As a student in my classes and as a manager on the practice field and at games, I was into it 100% (Well, maybe not every class). At the same time, I was involved in learning every aspect of the game. During managing lulls, or before and after practice I talked with Bob Hemphill about all the essentials of player equipment, with trainers Jack Williamson and Bob Peterson about injuries and their care, and I tried to catch as many as possible of the "chalk talk" sessions by Wes Fry, Bob Tessier and Eggs Manske.

On the field, whenever managing duties permitted, I left sideline areas and stood by group drills to listen, observe and take notes. As much as possible, the same routine was followed as team offense and team defense was practiced.

At games, besides the usual managerial duties, I observed all pre-game team talks in the stadium locker rooms, the on field warm-up drills, sideline coaching, half-time corrections and strategy talks and post-game remarks.

From time to time during the season I was able to have a few words with Pappy. At the end of the season, Sedge Thompson was selected as next year's Senior Manager, so I was through as manager after two years. However, once again Pappy said I was welcome to follow the team in a similar manner, which I did throughout most of the 1948 season.

To this day, I still have notebooks full of all aspects of "the Waldorf T", as well as the many memories of the Rose Bowl teams--the Jensen-to-Keckley pass against Stanford, the train trip back to Wisconsin, the game there where Montagne hit the goalpost head on, Brunk's kickoff return against USC, and on and on.

So my path in football was different from the players of the 1947 and 1948 seasons. For those who graduated and went into high school coaching, our paths were somewhat the same. However, there was one major difference. Most of the players were either hired as head varsity coaches or as key assistants, whereas I had to start down the line as an assistant JV coach. But without "a name" or at least playing experience, I was ready for that and expected it.

To prepare for that first hiring, I helped out as a walk-on volunteer at Oakland Tech High School while still at Cal working on my Master's thesis. Tech had only two coaches so they were glad to get any extra "no pay" help they could get. As assistant to the JV coach in 1950, I had the good fortune of working with a first year sophomore quarterback by the name of John Brodie.

My next break came when Rod Franz and John Ralston went together to head up the football program at Mt. Diablo High School in Concord. Rod knew of my goals and said I could have an open position as assistant JV coach. The head JV coach gave me the choice of line or backs. For the experience, I chose line coach, so as to be able to work more closely with Franz, an All-American expert on "trench warfare".

After two years, Ralston left to become the head football coach at San Lorenzo High. Franz offered me the varsity backfield spot. We finally beat a Tony Knap Pittsburg team, 7-0, in 1953, and won the league championship. After that season, Rod moved on as the first head coach at U.C. Riverside. An experienced coach from Portland, Orv Steffen, was brought in to replace Franz. I would have to wait. But again, the change provided more experience with another fine coach and one who used a different offense, the "multiple T." Two years later he resigned due to some health concerns and to take advantage of some administrative opportunities. It was 1956, and my time had arrived.

One can attribute more than average success in coaching football to many things. Certainly the quality of your players, your coaching staff, circumstances within the league, injuries, officiating, even the "bounce of the ball" are all factors. My teams won better than 60% of their games over the years, winning five titles in six years over one stretch. We experienced some losing seasons, too. I was fortunate in 1961 to co-coach the Shrine North All-Star team to a 7-2 win over the South in the LA Coliseum---with Craig Morton as my quarterback. After six assistant seasons and 14 years as head coach at Mt. Diablo, I reluctantly stepped down after the 1969 season because of a lower back injury.

Looking back, it would be hard to believe that my 20 years of fun and success in football coaching could have been accomplished without the initial encouragement of Fred Canrinus and the understanding and opportunities that Coach Waldorf provided in his first years at Cal. Very few know this story, but Coach Canrinus and Pappy did. Although I never played football for either of them, perhaps others should know how these two men took the time and interest in, and ultimately affected, the life of a non-player.

CHRISTIAN E. MARKEY, JR.

⌘

It will become only too obvious that this writer is much too old to put in chronological order the events he has participated in with those to whom he owes thanks and to whom he wishes to say thanks. So what! Let's give it a try.

I could be wrong, but I think I have awakened almost every morning of my life with a smile on my face; ready to take on the day...or ready to have the day take me on. For this, thanks to Mercy and the "Judge" (my parents). My dad was Justice of the Peace in Calexico, CA., in the Twenties; the title stuck with him. I guess I inherited it.

None of you ever met my father, only a few of you met Mercy. I didn't get to see much of either of them after I turned eleven and they divorced. But something good happened those first few years. Can't think of any other reason for the morning smile.

Thanks to the McCandlesses, the Ternquists, the Kents and the Spiris (the wonderful families I lived with during my four years at Whittier High), there was never a shortage of family love and companionship. Jack Spiri is still my brother.

Because of those folks, some very wise and thoughtful teachers, coaches and administrators at Whittier High and some pretty solid friends and teammates, the "war years" (1944-1947) became a great time to grow up. As I think back, it certainly could have been a mess. Ed Hookstratten and Rod Hills, classmates and teammates from Whittier, are still around, enjoying the good life. Rod and I were law partners for 10 years in Los Angeles, from 1964 to 1974 (when I went on the bench and he went to the White House as Counsel to the President).

Thanks to all the above, and many more, my adolescence was, in reality, a wonderful time.

Adulthood began when Jim Howe and I left the office of Paul Christopulos on a typically beautiful fall day in September, 1947 (I was 17 at the time) and headed for the Sigma Nu House to be greeted by, among others, John Graves and Jon Baker. We stayed for four years.

Jim was a Whittier classmate/teammate whom you'll remember as a baseball and water polo player, and a character. Jim, John, and Jon are no longer with us, but my thanks goes to them and to many others at the "Snake House" for giving me the chance to do some growing up there with them.

Having become quite adept at adopting families, I managed to spend a lot of time with the Conner family of Alameda. Sherry, Barry and Dick were Snakes and talked their parents into believing that I was too skinny to play football and needed some home cooking. Marty and Jim Cullom thought the same and stuffed wonderfully delicious waffles down me every Sunday I showed up.

It didn't work, but thanks for trying...and thanks for being family.

The football years of '47, '48, '49 and '50 were something else. Talk about growing up! I don't think I was cut out to be a football player, but I can't thank Pappy, Wes, Bob, Eggs and Zeb enough for giving me the chance to try.

The Navy paid my way through Cal as a regular in the NROTC, but I showed them. I took a regular commission in the Marine Corps (the fact that I was a chronic seasick case had nothing to do with the choice) and, of course, along came the Korean War.

From Berkeley to Quantico in the fall of '51 was a big step for someone who hadn't spent much time any farther east than Riverside. But Marty and Jim Cullom (and their waffle recipe) found their way to Quantico about the same time. I sat on the bench (again) and watched Truck play for the Quantico Marines the fall of '51. I spent that year on the East Coast and enjoyed every minute of it.

The next time I saw Lt. Cullom was in Korea about 1000 meters south of the front lines. The next time I saw Marty was in June of '53 when she met me at the plane at Alameda NAS and we drove up to the Oak Knoll Hospital to see what was left of the Truck. Thanks to the Good Lord, there was plenty left; a bit rearranged, but nothing had happened to his mouth. As lippy as ever.

I will always love the Marines and the Culloms. Thanks.

The family years, that is, the Markey family years, followed. Sharri, my first wife, and I,* set about to raise our family and were pretty successful. Jill, Christian III, Melinda and Michelle were and are beautiful children who are now good loving, caring adults and my best friends.

Sharri and the kids put up with the stress of getting a husband/father through law school, fifteen years of trial lawyering and fifteen years of trial judging. Sharri and I divorced in 1988 after 34 years, but my thanks go to her and the kids for those years and the obvious good that came from them.

My tour with the Alumni Association and the Board of Regents was the experience of a lifetime. Dick Erickson and Garff Wilson mentored me through thick and thin, and, if you remember Cal in the late sixties and early seventies, things got very thin on a number of occasions.

Pete Schabarum and the late William French Smith somehow managed to convince then Governor Ronald Reagan that I, a life-long Democrat, just might qualify as a Superior Court Judge. In April, 1974, he appointed me. At a party that Eric Schultz put on in my honor soon thereafter, Pappy, who was invited but could not attend, sent a telegram that read,, "Dear Chris: Congratulations: I always knew you belonged on the bench."

My thanks to Pete and many others. I thoroughly enjoyed every minute I sat on the bench. Yes, all the benches!

Well, as can be seen, I've been a very lucky person and recently my luck held. I somehow managed to talk a beautiful young, Irish lass, a lawyer, no-less, into becoming my best friend, companion, partner, lover and wife. Many of you have met her. Martha Carton Byrnes is her name, but she is known as Mickey. Now, if she'll just stop out-driving me (she plays from the men's tees), life will be perfect.

Thanks, Mick, I'll love you forever.

---

* At the wedding, Jim Monachino served as best man, Pete Schabarum and John Olszewski were ushers and a Marine buddy, Eddie LeBaron, stood by. The wedding didn't make too many social pages, but certainly hit a few sports pages.

GEORGE SOUZA

⌘

I was born and raised in Vallejo, California, and entered Vallejo High School in 1938. I played three years of varsity football and lettered two years as an offensive and defensive tackle. In my senior year I was named MVP and Captain and made the All Conference team of the North Bay League. I also lettered in varsity basketball for three years, was an All Conference guard in the NBL two years, Captain and MVP in my senior year and a member of the squad that won 31 straight games and two NBL basketball championships. I also lettered in track for three years as a shot putter and discus thrower. I won the CIF State Meet in 1941 in the shot put. I was Captain and MVP in my senior year.

After high school graduation in June of 1941, I went to work for the Post Office for about six months and then went to the Mare Island Naval Shipyard as a Sheetmetal Apprentice. On November 2, 1942, I enlisted in the Army Air Force. I spent a little over three years in the service, two and a half of them in England on an Air Force ground crew. Near the end of WWII, I played football, basketball, and track on the base teams. I played end for the first time and really enjoyed it. I was an All European guard in basketball and in 1945 I was a member of a US team that went to Ireland to demonstrate American basketball to the Irish in Dublin.

I got out of the service in February of 1946 and returned to Mare Island to continue my apprenticeship. This lasted for about three months, and then I decided to go to Vallejo J.C. I played end on the football team that won two championships and I was All League two years. I was voted MVP and Captain my second year. I also played basketball two years and was All League each year. In addition, I lettered in track those two years. After junior college, I worked in a wholesale tobacco and candy store and then--surprisingly--ended up at U.C. Berkeley.

As I mentioned, my enrollment at Cal was unexpected. After two years at Vallejo JC, I was unsure of what I wanted to do. I really felt insecure. I still had a yearning for sports but no idea what I wanted to do with my life. As a home town boy, I had an allegiance to Vallejo and I felt--for one reason or another--that I was indebted to my friends and the rest of the people there. I did not want to fail--the fact that my mother had died during this time did not help matters.

Then I came up with a plan: go to Cal, try out for football, hang around for a few weeks before getting cut, and then leave. That way I could always tell the people from home that I "gave it the old college try" and that was that! So I had my sister drive me to Berkeley where I began my plan. Things did not work out the way I had expected--I sort of "hung in there" for awhile and after a few minutes playing time against St. Mary's and Santa Clara and after making the trip to play Navy, things kept getting better. I owe a lot of my "hanging in there" to a lot of great guys I met at Cal, including, of course, Pappy and Eggs Manske. You can't go wrong playing with guys like Franz, Van Deren, Jensen, Lotter, Schmalenberger, Begovich, Jones, Hirshler, Montagne, Turner, and Cullom--to mention a few.

I struggled with my studies at Cal. I put in a lot of time with the books, but nothing seemed to sink in. I was majoring in Business Administration but I could see that this was not my forte. I managed to keep my head above water and eventually graduated in General Curriculum.

My mind was still unsettled as to what path I should follow. Even though I had graduated and had had a little success in football, I still felt unsettled! And this is where Pappy played a big part in my attitude and in my life.

I went to Pappy's office just before my final days at Cal and talked with him about my frustrations. I told him I felt uneasy about not knowing what to do with my life--I still felt like I was letting others down. Pappy summed it all up quite simply by saying, "George, there aren't a whole lot of people in this world who readily know what they want to do in life--those who do are very fortunate and are few and far between. When the time is right, you'll know what to do. Don't worry about it."

I really felt good about talking with Pappy--and I must say here that Eggs was a big help too--and I proceeded to get on with things.

I drove an ice cream and milk truck route for a local dairy in Vallejo for a year or so and then took a job as a bread salesman for the Langendorf Co.--a bread driver. I was making good pay and I had good benefits, but I knew this was not the answer. I was with Langendorf for more than a year, but while playing some town basketball, I injured my right knee and was off work for almost two months. I had a lot of time to think, and on my first day back on the job, with my supervisor in attendance, I told him that I had decided to go back to school to get a teaching credential. I'll never forget "Gene's" response--I feared for the worse, but he was so happy for me I couldn't believe it. Now, I knew I had made the right decision! Gene even offered me a job in the summer months to take vacation routes. I will never forget his enthusiasm.

I got my teaching credential at Sacramento State and I began my first teaching and coaching job at Davis High School in 1953. Even though I taught two periods of social studies, one period of math, three periods of P.E. and coached varsity football (by myself), basketball, and baseball--none of which were salaried positions--and had noon duty on the playground, I knew this was what I wanted to do. The time to know had finally arrived! Thanks Pappy.

A year later I married my lovely wife, Katherine Matulich, also a school teacher. We have been married 41 years and we have two children--Matthew and Carrie. We also have three grandchildren--Molly, Nate, and Eli.

I spent 30 years in the education field--two years at Davis, six at El Camino in Sacramento, one at Bella Vista, and 21 at La Sierra, teaching physical education and coaching football, basketball, and baseball. And it was great. I got a late start, but thanks to Pappy, Eggs, Gene and a few other great people (including my dear wife), they were 30 wonderful years.

I retired in June of 1983 in a "Big Hurrah!"--one of my former students at La Sierra High School, Jamie Gittins--also a Cal alumnus--sent Kathy and me to Europe for a month, all expenses paid. That's what I call a "Big Hurrah!" Now we are anxiously waiting and hoping that Reader's Digest will draw our names in the big pay-off contests so we can make another journey. In the meantime, we are spending our retirement years visiting the kids and their children, keeping up the homestead, and helping out at one of the Sacramento area high schools as Girl's Athletic Director.

ROBERT HENRY (STORMY) HILEMAN

⌘

I was born in Perry, Oklahoma on December 18, 1925. My mother was Ruth Carter Hileman; she died in 1992 at age 89. She worked as a housekeeper and cook in Hollywood from 1930 to about 1938. She broke her ankle while working in the Naval Ordinance Depot in Vallejo during WWII. She lived the last 30 years in Montalvo, CA, in the house that Gramma and Grandpa bought in 1931 for about $4500.

One brother, Jack, Cal class of '43, was a chemist for Standard Oil, then a chemistry teacher at El Camino College for 25 years. He is now retired, living in McKinleyville, CA. My father was Charles Hileman, who died in 1956. He was an oil field driller and later operated his own earth moving company in the West Texas boom of the late '40's and 50's. Mother and Father divorced when I was an infant.

I was raised by my grandmother, Nora Summerford Carter in Montalvo. I attended school there and went into town (four miles) for Ventura Junior and Ventura Senior High School. Ventura had a 6-4-4 plan, meaning the junior high included grades 7-10, and the senior high was on the same campus as the junior college. I played football, basketball, track and tennis. I played trumpet in the orchestra and got to carry the instrument of the prettiest girl in school. I was the only guy in the orchestra big enough to carry her harp to her car.

The 1942 football season was cancelled my senior year after a Japanese mini-submarine shot a few shells at Goleta, north of Santa Barbara. The year before, in the 11th grade, we won the league championship. My best-known teammates were Jack Myers, later of UCLA, the Philadelphia Eagles and then the Rams, and V.T. Smith, known later as "Vitamin" Smith, who was a kickoff return specialist for the Rams, having gone to college at West Texas State. He was second string halfback on our team!

I started Cal as a freshman in July of 1943, when they had the original three semesters a year. I made the team that fall, but I was declared ineligible because freshmen had to have at least a "C" in every course, and I only had a "C average." I worked at Standard Oil in Richmond from October, 1943 until I entered the Marine Corps in April, 1944.

After boot camp in San Diego I was sent to Radar School in Chicago and then to Gulfport, Miss. I was assigned to the 4th Marine Regiment, then training on Guadalcanal in December, 1944, where I was a BAR man (Browning Automatic Rifle). Transferred to the 6th JASCO (Joint Assault Signal Company), I became a communications lineman. (They saw on my record that I had gone to Radar school earlier, so they figured that had trained me for operating a switchboard on the beach or stringing telephone lines among the palm trees).

I landed with the second wave on Okinawa, April 1, 1945, and stayed until the island was secured. My outfit went to Guam for rest and recuperation. When the war ended, the 6th Division went to Tsingtao, China for occupation duty. Five or six months later I was transferred to the 1st Division, Headquarters Company in Tsiensien. These officers had seen that I had one year of typing in the ninth grade (with a C+ grade!) and gave me a staff sergeant's job handling the payroll for a whole Marine Company (of course, I got paid at my private's rate!)

I should have been sent home in May, according to the points I had accumulated, but was delayed until late July. I left China fat and sassy and was discharged in San Diego on August 11, 1946.

I entered Ventura Junior College in the fall of 1946. I had stopped by Berkeley, but Coach Frank Wickhorst didn't have time to see me. (I was lucky, someone told me later.) The football team at Ventura had a so-so season, 5 and 5, I think, in the tough Los Angeles Conference. I played fullback, whereas in high school I had been a blocking back at right half, and Myers and I were the linebackers.

When Pappy was named coach at Cal, I transferred there for the spring semester. I think everyone remembers the huge crowd that turned out for spring practice for a new coach. The number I remember is somewhere around 260. After a couple of weeks, I wrote home that I was doing pretty well. I was sixth string fullback out of 22 fullbacks, you understand! After some early scrimmages, Pappy called me in to say he'd like me to move to center where I could continue to be a linebacker and maybe help the team more. (Actually, I think he and Wes said, "We're moving you to center!")

I have moved around a lot since college, but I will always think of the members of my high school championship team and the '47 and '48 Cal teams as my teammates for life. A while back I was trying to explain to a non-athlete just what made teammates so special. "They are more than friends," I said, and "some of them are not even close friends," I added. "But they are what I would call stand-up, forthright people, so trustworthy that you can count on them to get the job done. By the same token, you know that you must do the same for them. The shared activities of training (till it hurt!), the rough humor (of some of the guys), the exhilaration of making a good play, of someone on your side scoring, or winning a game, these all combine to form a bond." We (speaking of the '47 and '48 teams) only lost two games, so we didn't get the benefits of sharing a lot of defeats, but those two (USC 14-39 and Northwestern 14-20) were "lulus." I am confident that today I can walk up to any teammate and feel the shared past as if it were just last season, not almost a lifetime ago. Some I haven't seen since school, yet I like to know about them, and I used to look forward to going to Boots Erb's restaurant, *The Bow and Bell*, to catch up on everyone. Boots, in turn, remembered what I was doing and would pass that on, too. There ought to be a special section for Boots, I think, because he did so much to keep us informed about what was happening with the teammates we never or seldom saw. (Those who formed and nurtured the "Pappy's Boys" group deserve great praise also.)

I married Hypatia Teague in the spring of 1951. She was a valedictorian, along with Chuck Hanger, at UC in 1948, and taught speech and drama at Cal when we met in 1950. After we were married, several football players took her class; the best known was probably Les Richter. After graduation I worked for Beatty Scaffold, in Oakland, Armco Steel and Cutter Laboratories in Berkeley.

I began teaching in 1954 on a provisional credential, when Hypatia took a teaching job in Oakdale, CA. I found one nearby in Ripon, teaching algebra, geometry and trigonometry. I was hired because they wanted a JV football coach and a track coach. They were lucky that I was pretty good in math. Within a couple of weeks, I knew I had found a career. My students and players liked me, I seemed to be able to explain the mathematics so they could understand, and the parents and Principal liked the strict discipline I maintained both in the classroom and on the field.

One of my students was the daughter of Larry Siemering, former coach at COP (now UOP), assistant coach with the Redskins (Eddie LeBaron was there and had played for Larry at COP.) and recently head coach of the Calgary Stampeders in Canada. This led, indirectly, to my taking a teaching position at Santa Cruz High School, where Larry had just been named coach, and being his assistant for two years. Larry, who had assisted Amos Alonzo Stagg for years, is one of the most unusual men I have ever known, and when I saw him last summer, he was shooting great golf at age 80. He is one of three great athletes I have known. I think of them as genius athletes because they do so many things so very well. The other two are Jack Jensen and my high school teammate, Jack "Moose" Myers. Incidentally, Santa Cruz High won its first championship in 12 years in our first year of coaching.

By 1958 I had finished my Master's degree in secondary school administration at San Jose State and was offered the job of Vice-Principal of a new high school in Santa Clara, named Buchser H.S. I was there seven years. When the former superintendent's second son got promoted over me, I left to work in the American School in Teheran, Iran as Junior/Senior High School Principal. The time there was exciting and fulfilling.

Next was a two-year contract as Superintendent/Principal of the Dacca American School in Dacca, E. Pakistan, now Dhaka, Bangladesh. This was a small (K-12, with 360 pupils) school with American dependents of the American Consulate, USAID and Ford Foundation employees, missionaries and some business people. We even had two daughters of the Japanese Consul. I was there during the Hatol (general strike) that preceded the fight for independence and just before the hurricane that killed an estimated 200,000 (yes, that is right--two hundred thousand persons).

Upon returning to the States in 1969 (we watched the landing on the moon by American astronauts from Sorrento, Italy in July, 1969 while on our way home), Hypatia and I separated, then divorced in 1970. I went to Tucson and entered the doctoral program in school administration. I met Alyce Kathleen Godshall, from Gaffney, South Carolina, in graduate school at the University of Arizona. She was completing her masters degree in school counseling. We were married in October of 1971.

We moved to San Manuel, Arizona, about 35 miles northeast of Tucson; Alyce as counselor in the high school and I as Principal of the elementary school in Mammoth, Arizona. San Manuel was, and is, a company town built upon copper mining. As a newcomer I got to ride the elevator shaft down 4000 feet to watch the whole process!

After two years there, I got a job as Superintendent of Schools in Geyserville, California in Sonoma County. Geyserville is about 30 miles north of Santa Rosa and 35 miles south of Ukiah. My only natural child, Caroline Elizabeth, was born in a hospital in Santa Rosa June 15, 1976. I was at Geyserville for eight years as Superintendent/Principal of the small district with a high school, middle school, elementary school and alternative school--about 400 students all told.

In 1985, after Alyce was counseling at Cloverdale Schools and I was unemployed, but trying to be an educational consultant, we decided to move to South Carolina where Alyce's mother and dad were in poor health. We completed the move in the fall of 1985. Her mother died about one year later and her dad died in 1989. I have been retired for more than three years, although I did work part-time for a local computer retailer.

When you marry a younger woman, and become a father at age 50, your life does not follow the typical pattern. I have enjoyed being a father this time because of fewer worries about what I should and should not do as a dad. It is not going to matter an awful lot anyhow, or so it seems.

Caroline Elizabeth Hileman is a tall, good-looking dark blonde--my *California Girl*. I'm sure she is my daughter (in case you are remembering the joke about the old professor whom everyone thought some student had it in for) because she has my dimple in the chin and my hazel colored eyes. She is 5'8" and about 135 pounds. She has played four years of soccer for her high school here and hopes to at least try out for sweeper position at USC. No, that is not the University of South Carolina, as they call themselves here; it is, I regret saying, the University of Southern California, to which she has applied, been accepted and sent the first of what will be an awful lot of money.

I first got interested in computers when I bought several for the business department at school in 1982. I have since become deeply interested. When we went to South Carolina, I joined the local Palmetto Personal Computer Club. There were some neat people in it and I got active in the organization. A couple of years later I was asked to be editor of the monthly magazine, which I was for over two years. After another year as secretary, I now spend time writing on my new 80486 50 Mhz computer with 16 K RAM, 655 MEG hard drive, CD-ROM, tape backup with tons of programs. The computer is a "no-name" clone which I put together.

Retirement is OK, but I have hopes of returning to California soon now that Caroline will be in school there. The weather here is good for about three weeks a year (two in the spring and one in the fall). Most of the time, April/May to October/November, it is hot and humid, and deep winter can get down to 10-15 degrees -- with humidity, that is *cold*! I hate to exercise, and either tennis or golf is too active for me in this heat.

I am currently in fair health. I quit smoking almost five years ago, and what with taking several Caribbean cruises at Christmas, I gained a lot of weight. A month ago my doctor said I might be pre-diabetic and advised me to lose weight. I have lost 14 pounds in the last month and hope to lose 20-30 more. (When I think about smoking, I remember Bob Tessier telling me that if I had to smoke, he guessed that it was OK, but would I please not smoke on the steps to the Gym because it made the coaches look bad.)

Attending Cal when I did, and playing for Pappy and his staff when I did, and with the teammates I had, made it easy to be proud of the University and its teams. We rated highest or next to highest in most academic areas on a national ranking and our athletic teams were champs in football, division winners in basketball and champions of the first World Series of collegiate baseball. We also had great individual track stars and an eight-oar crew team that won the '48 Olympics. I didn't get interested in the so-called "minor" sports until later, but they were probably of equal caliber. I'm remembering Hugh Mumby on the swings, Jack Lampke in boxing and an SAE fraternity brother, Lorne Main in tennis. He was hitting two-handed backhands then and may have been the first to do that. (As a Canadian citizen he played for Canada in the next Davis Cup games.) All this without scholarships! (If there were any under-the-table payments, I never heard of them in all the years I was there.)

We lived in a great era of a great University; we helped make it that way and we left a winning legacy for all to see.

ERNEST B. LAGESON

⌘

It all began for me in Sharon, North Dakota on a snowy December Morning in 1932. At that time I became the only child of Ernest B. Lageson and his wife, the former Eunice McLean. My parents were both teachers, a prestigious but low paying profession in the Depression-ravaged Midwest of the Thirties.

In 1941 we moved to California and Dad worked briefly on the staff of the Federal Penitentiary at Alcatraz. For two years we lived on the Island. While living in San Francisco I attended Lowell High School and began my formal athletic career as a member of the "Goof Squad", the lowest echelon of football humanity.

We moved to Pittsburg, California in 1948 where my parents taught school and I became a member of the high school football team made famous by the legendary John Henry Johnson.

High school football in Pittsburg in the 1950s was viewed by the townspeople as a form of religion. Thousands would attend the games and when we played at Monterey High there were as many Pittsburg rooters as there were fans for the home team. In the two years I attended Pittsburg we were undefeated in conference play, losing only two games in two years, both to much larger schools, Berkeley and Fresno High Schools.

Following graduation I was actively recruited by Cal, Stanford and College of the Pacific, the latter still basking in the glory of the great Eddie LeBaron. Although I had an initial preference for Cal because of my father's contact with the University as a graduate student, any doubt I had as to choice of schools was swept away during my meetings with Coach Waldorf. His warmth and interest in me was genuine and personal. Even discounting his physical size, Pappy was truly "larger than life".

During my sophomore year, when an injury ended my participation in football and rugby, it was a compassionate Pappy who explained how much there was to "life after football" and who made my separation from the game an upbeat experience. Although my formal association with Pappy was a brief one, it is an experience and phase of my life I have never forgotten.

One of the high points of the 1950 season for me was the chance to participate in the preparation for Pappy's final Rose Bowl. I was among the group of freshmen and Ramblers selected to run the Michigan offense and defense, and was thrilled to be a part of it. To this day, however, I still recall my somewhat feeble efforts to get past that human wall of offense known as Les Richter. Our grueling experience during that Christmas vacation was rewarded with a pair of Rose Bowl tickets, more than adequate compensation. Although the tickets would bring $100 from the local scalper, whose name I have forgotten, my pair went proudly to my parents.

As I look back on those days of the Fifties, I recognize how important my athletic experiences were in developing the work ethic and attitudes so important in building a life and a career. Football and the men who coached it taught me that a measure of success could be attained by the application of a few simple concepts: hard, conscientious work with attention to details and fundamentals; a desire to win, but with integrity, poise and class; a willingness to prepare thoroughly for what has to be done; an ability to work with others in an unselfish team spirit; an ability to do the very best of which you are capable without worrying about what cannot be changed; and finally, to learn from your mistakes, and not brood over what might have been done differently, but to go forward, stronger for the experience.

Since my participation in the NROTC Program had kept me in school during the height of the Korean War, upon graduation I paid my dues with two years of service in the Navy. I was ordered to the U.S.S. John R. Craig, DD 885, then home ported in San Diego.

On the Craig I was assigned to the Gunnery Dept. and put in charge of the First Division. This consisted of approximately 60 Boatswain's Mates, Gunner's Mates and seamen responsible for the care and maintenance of the forward half of the ship as well as the various phases of deck seamanship involving that part of the ship. I quickly learned as much as I could about mooring, anchoring, transfers at sea and related activities. Shortly after I reported aboard, the ship deployed for a six month tour of duty in the Far East.

Upon our return I immediately took leave and married Jeanne Lettiere, the girl I had dated in high school and while at Cal. We spent the summer months together in San Diego, after which the Craig left again for the Far East and Jeanne returned to her teaching job in Pittsburg.

Whereas the first cruise was a learning experience, the second was a command experience. I served as the ship's First Lieutenant, which is the officer in charge of all maintenance and deck seamanship activities. In addition to the Departmental duties, there was the ship handling aspect of the job, particularly as Officer of the Deck underway. As such you were in charge of all underway activity, responsible only to the Captain. The responsibility was great and the stress significant.

At the end of my two years, I was offered shore duty at the station of my choice anywhere in the world in exchange for a two-year extension. Although the thought was appealing, I felt that being married and having been accepted to the law school at Boalt, my choice was to return to school and leave the Navy.

My first year of law school was not an enjoyable experience. The Socratic method of teaching was a new and unpleasant experience, and the arrogant, brow beating teaching style of some of the faculty was even more intimidating than the educational experiences I had faced in the military. By the end of the first semester I was satisfied I did not want to be a lawyer, and I repeatedly told myself that the only reason I was still there was to prove to the faculty and administration that I could survive.

One of my friends, now a Superior Court Judge, urged me to "stay with the program". His father was a lawyer who had assured him that the practice of law bore no resemblance to the travails of law school. In addition, Jeanne, whose teaching salary had financed my first year, counseled against quitting and wasting our joint investment. It was sound advice. With the passage of time the faculty proved to be decent souls after all, many of the courses turned out to be interesting and there were even some very happy times over the next two years.

When it came time to consider employment, my first choice was trial work. At that time, the quickest path to success (or failure) as a litigator was as a deputy district attorney. John Nejedly, the recently elected District Attorney for Contra Costa County was in the process of upgrading his office. The situation was perfect for a recent graduate seeking trial experience, and seven of us from my class went to work for John.

I was assigned to the Richmond Office as the junior deputy in a six-attorney office that included five veteran prosecutors. The head of our office was a wily old litigator, whose knowledge of juries, opposing counsel and courtroom skill was vast. Additionally, he was an excellent teacher.

In the year I served as a deputy DA, I was able to try more than twenty-five jury cases to verdict. My skills developed, my trial results were positive, and slightly more than a year after joining the office I was hired by the San Francisco firm of Bronson, Bronson and MacKinnon of San Francisco, one of the premiere litigation firms in Northern California.

At the time, Bronson was a first generation law firm with the founding partners still active in the practice and management of the firm. Founded by Ray Bronson in 1919, the firm consisted of 13 partners and nine associates when I joined them in 1961. This made it one of the ten largest law offices in the City and, although no one realized it at the time, the firm was growing significantly.

By 1964 the firm had 57 attorneys and by the early Seventies over 100. Not only was I handling a significant case load of my own but soon after my arrival there was an extensive list of names below me on the letterhead, suggesting to the outside world that I was more senior than my few years of experience merited. It was indeed an outstanding opportunity and I made the most of it. I became a partner in the firm in 1967.

Over the years my specialties included the defense of civil personal injury, property damage and wrongful death cases. My opposing counsel ranged from the obscure Mission and Market Street plaintiff lawyers to the recognized experts in the field, including Mel Belli, Jim Boccardo and Bruce Walkup. I dealt with lawyers from the small valley and mountain towns of California as well as the prominent plaintiff and defense lawyers from the Los Angeles, Chicago and New York legal communities.

The firm developed a fairly sophisticated aviation practice during this time and I became a part of it for a number of years. We represented most of the major domestic airlines, several foreign carriers and aircraft manufacturers such as Beech and Cessna. To facilitate my handling of these cases I took flight lessons and learned to fly general aviation aircraft.

One of my more memorable cases involved representing Thai International Airlines following the crash of one of its planes into Hong Kong Harbor while attempting to land during a violent thunderstorm. There was clear liability here as to the surviving passengers and the heirs of the deceased, and we were successful in obtaining favorable settlements in all but one of the cases. That case was tried in the Federal Court of San Francisco, and following what I felt was one of my better trial performances, I suffered one of the worst defeats of my career.

Another of the prominent aviation cases I handled was the PSA mid-air collision in San Diego in 1979. That accident involved a light plane colliding with a PSA 727 killing everyone in both planes. We represented the San Diego Airport, which was charged with negligence in controlling the aircraft. Here we were able to extricate the airport, although the case proceeded with the other defendants.

In addition to my litigation responsibilities, as I grew more senior in the firm, I was asked to undertake various administrative duties. I served for eight years as a member of the firm's Management Committee, assisted in the supervision of the litigation department, and, in later years, was a member of the Compensation Committee. My work was recognized in the early Eighties by induction into two national honorary trial organizations. I became a member of The American Board of Trial Advocates in 1983 and was invited to become a Fellow of the American College of Trial Lawyers in 1984.

Over the years, I have lectured on various trial subjects at Boalt Hall Law School, at seminars given by U.C.'s Continuing Education of the Bar, and at courses presented by the Defense Research Institute and various other professional groups. In addition I served on the faculty of the Trial Academy in Boulder, Colorado, sponsored by the International Association of Defense Counsel.

At the request of the firm I became active in the largest civil defense attorneys professional organization in the country, The Defense Research Institute. DRI, as it is known, is dedicated to the improvement of the judicial system and the continuing education of the defense bar. The organization is the national spokesman for the civil defense bar and today has an active membership of 20,000. In 1986 I served as President of DRI and in 1987 as Chairman of the Board of Directors.

In 1986 I left the Bronson office to become a member of the firm of Archer, McComas and Lageson in Walnut Creek, California. It was an amicable parting, motivated principally by my desire to conclude my career in a slightly different atmosphere than then existed at Bronson. The firm had grown to over 150 lawyers, and its large size was incompatible with the attributes I had found desirable during my career there. From 1986 until 1993 I practiced with the Archer firm, handling primarily product liability and construction defect cases. During that time the firm grew from sixteen lawyers to thirty-two. In 1993 I retired from active practice, but I still maintain an Of Counsel status with the firm.

In August of 1987 I had the moving experience of being the guest of John Henry Johnson and his wife at John's induction into the NFL Hall of Fame in Canton, Ohio. A few other members of our high school team were also on hand, making for some happy reminiscing as well as the opportunity to meet and be with some of the greatest players the game has ever produced.

In April of 1995 Jeanne and I celebrated our 40th wedding anniversary. Jeanne graduated from Cal when I did and embarked upon a teaching career at the same time I entered the Navy. She taught until the birth of our daughter Kristine in 1962. Our son Ernie III was born five years later. Jeanne has been a full-time mother and wife since 1962.

Kris attended El Cerrito High School where, among other honors, she was a Merit Scholar. She graduated from Cal in 1983 and the next year married Chas Cardall. The two met during their years as Piedmont Ave. neighbors, Chas in the Kappa Alpha fraternity and Kris in the Chi Omega sorority. Two years later they both entered law school, Kris at Boalt and Chas at Hastings. Following graduation Kris worked as a trial lawyer, then entered the legal publishing field. Since 1992 she has been a full-time mother, looking after the daily needs of young Beau Cardall. Chas is now a senior associate with the San Francisco firm of Orrick, Herrington and Sutcliffe.

Young Ernie entered Cal in 1985 after all-conference recognition as an offensive tackle for St. Mary's High School in Berkeley. In addition to various academic honors, he served as the editor of the yearbook. He followed his brother-in-law as a member of the Kappa Alpha fraternity and upon graduation married the former Natalie Kerckhoff of San Marino, a Kappa Kappa Gamma at Cal. Upon completion of his undergraduate studies, Ernie attended the Pasadena School of Design and presently works as an art director for Satchi and Satchi, an international advertising agency, in its San Francisco office. Natalie teaches 5th grade at the Baldwin Elementary School in Danville.

So, there it is. Three generations of Lagesons at Cal, two still actively tied to the Blue and Gold nostalgia. Hopefully in 2010 history will repeat with the admission of the fourth generation, first Beau, then his yet unborn siblings and cousins. Jeanne and I will be there directing traffic till the end.

GEORGE J. STATHAKIS

⌘

My last football game as a Berkeley Bear was in the 1950 Rose Bowl which we lost to Ohio State on a field goal with only seconds to play. Some 45 years have elapsed since I had the privilege of playing football under Pappy Waldorf, but I remember it as if it were yesterday.

I have often reflected on the Pappy years at Cal throughout my exciting global business career. Among the important messages I absorbed from Pappy is that one must maintain a solid grasp of fundamentals in everything one does and that there is no substitute for hard work. I believe these principles aided me in many successful encounters, both personal and professional. I am sure that the organizational skills and spirit of teamwork exemplified by Pappy and his staff set an excellent example for my years in management.

After I graduated in 1953 with a master's degree in mechanical engineering, I set out with my wife Mary Jo, and our one-year-old daughter, Patty, to join the General Electric Engineering Training Program in Cincinnati, Ohio. GE began training me on several assignments and several months later, we were moved to Lynn, Massachusetts, near Boston.

This was just the beginning of my 30-year career with GE. During that period of time I was promoted to various positions until my final job as a senior executive in New York. Many of the GE years were spent in Saratoga, California, where I rose to be the head of GE's Nuclear Power Business, headquartered in San Jose. The nuclear business was extremely exciting in the 1960's and 70's and allowed me to participate in many interesting ventures around the globe.

During this period, I had many opportunities to meet with notable people. For example, Senator John Pasture, who was Chairman of the Joint Committee on Atomic Energy, Representatives Chet Holifield and Craig Hosman, both from California, and, of course, our own Dr. Glen Seaborg, who was Chairman of the Atomic Energy Commission for many years. Dr. Seaborg and I reminisced about my playing for Pappy at Cal and his representing Cal with the PCC. Another person with whom I crossed paths during the nuclear power years and who was also to become very notable, (particularly to Cal fans), was Chancellor Chang-Lin Tien. Chang-Lin was a nuclear engineer of high standing and did some consulting for GE Nuclear during my tenure.

GE Nuclear Power took me to many places--from Bombay to Fukushima, Japan, to Switzerland, Germany, Italy, Spain, and Taiwan, among others. I was always pleasantly surprised to meet people from all over the U.S. who knew of the Pappy Waldorf Cal teams.

From Nuclear Power and Saratoga, Mary Jo, four of the five children, Susan, Jody, George and Jim, (Patty was living in Geneva, Switzerland) and I moved to the New York City area in 1978. There I headed up the International Trading Operations of GE.

The next several years placed us in Manhattan and Connecticut and had us traveling again to many parts of the globe. Places like Saudi Arabia, Algeria, Australia, Malaysia, Singapore, Thailand, USSR, Turkey, Greece and Egypt--where incidentally I met several times with Ambassador Nick Veliotes, another Pappy teammate.

My international trading responsibility in GE included an international construction company that was then doing close to a billion dollars per year in revenue. This proved to be an especially exciting venture that took me to many remote construction sites. Some of those sites included high-powered transmission lines in the Ecuadorian Andes, a major equipment installation at the Guri Dam in Venezuela, a gas-gathering station in the Sahara Desert in Algeria with a pipeline to the Mediterranean, the Riyadh Hospital in Saudi Arabia, and a power plant in Nigeria.

In these years, I was involved with two international organizations that provided some very fascinating experiences. For two years I was Chairman of the India Chamber of Commerce in the U.S. My extensive travel in the 1960's and earlier association with India gave me the background for this assignment. As Chairman of the organization, I had the honor of meeting Indira Gandhi, a most interesting lady and Prime Minister of India at that time. The second organization was the U.S.-Yugoslavia Business Council which I also chaired. Mary Jo and I made many trips to the former country of Yugoslavia--Dubrovnik, Kosovo, Belgrade, Zagreb, Ljubljana, Lake Bled and Sarajevo.

Another highlight during this time was my appointment by President Reagan to the President's Export Council. This involved considerable time in Washington D.C. working with Secretary of Commerce Malcolm Baldridge and his staff as well as other business executives. The work of the council was very helpful in obtaining government support for U.S. export improvement.

In 1985 I retired from GE to set up my own investment banking business, headquartered in New York City. Through this arrangement, I was asked to manage American Express' two billion dollar loan portfolio to developing countries, mostly in Latin America.

While working with American Express, I set up the International Capital Corporation and invested several hundred million dollars in various Latin American businesses: hotels in Mexico; textiles, a Petrochemical Company, agribusiness in Brazil, as well as an office building in downtown Rio and various businesses in Chile and Argentina. I also set up a bond trading operation to handle developing country debt.

Other investment banking opportunities took me into the high tech industry and Colorado where for several years I was the Chairman and CEO of Ramtron International, a start-up semiconductor (computer chip) company.

Considering the many cities Mary Jo and I have visited, we would rate Rio de Janeiro and Hong Kong high on the list for beauty and natural splendor. Of course, San Francisco was then and still is our favorite city. For natural wonders, we think the Iguassú Falls on the border of Brazil, Argentina and Paraguay are right up there along with Lake Baikal in Central Siberia. By the way, Lake Baikal is the largest body of fresh water in the world (containing over 20% of the world's fresh water), has a surface area about 100 times that of Lake Tahoe and is three times deeper than Tahoe at its greatest depth.

In terms of interesting experiences I would rate meeting Leonid Brezhnev, then President of the USSR and General-Secretary of the Communist Party, among the top. The meeting took place in the late 1970's when I was a delegate to the U.S.-USSR Economic Council meeting in Moscow, which involved about 40 American business executives and government officials and about the same number of Soviets. The main event was a Brezhnev hosted dinner at the Kremlin that started with refreshments and hors d'oeuvres in the Hall of Mirrors. The splendor and magnificence of this hall would stack up very well with the best in the West--such as the Palace of Versailles.

Brezhnev went around the hall and met each American. I must say that at that point Brezhnev did not look well (apparently he was already taken with an illness which was to cause his death in not too many months). After the reception the attendees moved to the Hall of Facts, one of the most famous and beautifully decorated in the Kremlin. The ceiling frescoes of religious scenes could be compared to that of the Sistine Chapel. After many toasts, most of them given by Brezhnev, we enjoyed a lavish meal served by almost one waiter per person. The opulence and grandiose staging of the event was hard to contemplate in the heart of the supposedly egalitarian capital of world communism.

All in all, there have been a lot of exhilarating times since the days at Cal and football, but nothing approaches the thrill I felt in playing for Pappy in the Rose Bowl. Of course, my marriage to Mary Jo and the birth of our five wonderful children are at the top of my great events.

As I limp off the tennis courts, golf courses, and other athletic arenas with my 1950 Rose Bowl knee I am often asked, "If given the chance, George, would you do it over again?" "You bet your life!"

HERB SCHMALENBERGER

⌘

I retired in 1991 as the Supervisor of Physical Education at the University of California, Davis, and since then have kept busy with golf, fishing and enjoying my seven grandchildren. After graduating from Cal in 1950, I worked as a teacher and coach at Pacific Grove High School for five years. My football and baseball teams won championships there, mainly because of Eddie Esteban, who was a truly talented athlete who both pitched and played quarterback. I completed my MA degree in physical education at Cal in 1956 and accepted a teaching position at Davis, where I also coached football, basketball, track and field and swimming. I also conducted coaching clinics at the secondary school level. During the last five years before my retirement, my interests centered on the role of physical education at the university level. I was also a member of the Title IX (women's athletics) Compliance Committee at Davis.

I feel very fortunate to have played football (as a tackle) at Cal when I did, under both Pappy Waldorf and Frank Wickhorst (for whom I retain much respect), and have tried in my teaching and coaching to maintain the high standards set then, in the late 1940's, for student-athletes. I fear, however, that changing attitudes among athletes and the economic crunch at the university level has somewhat eroded that process. I just wish all athletes today could have enjoyed the experiences we had back then.

Finally, and most significantly, I must recognize the contributions of my wife, Maxine, to whatever success I have had in my life, both professionally and privately. I must thank her for putting up with me and for giving us five children and seven grandchildren of whom I am most proud.

BOB CUMMINGS

⌘

I was born October 31, 1925 about 20 miles from Oklahoma University where my Dad, who was a public school teacher and ordained Southern Baptist Minister, took many post-graduate courses. I was number eight of ten children--seven boys and three girls. In high school I played six-man football (state champions two years), basketball and American Legion Baseball. I was active in Boy Scouts and became a Life Scout. We did not have sports my senior year because of World War II.

I qualified for Naval Officers Training but because of a flaw in one eye was not accepted. I later volunteered for the regular Navy and participated in the battles of Saipan-Tinian, Iwo Jima and Okinawa.

After being discharged from the Navy (April, 1946), I made the transition to civilian life by spending several months working for the Continental Can Company in Oakland. By this time my parents and other members of my family had moved to Oakland, thus supplying me with a home base. I was encouraged to attend Cal by my oldest brother, Maj. Charles S. Cummings (a member of the All-Time U.S. Marine Corps Football Team). I enrolled in the fall of 1947, went out for the football (freshman) team and made it!--this after being a scared-stiff young man from Oklahoma on a ship in the heat of battle in World War II.

An enormous change of pace was in store for me. I could sleep through the night without the deadly sound of enemy guns. I had returned in "one-piece" and my feet were once again on good ole Terra Firma...a fact for which I thank God until this very day.

I made first string offensive end but the Friday night before our first game, during dummy scrimmage, a clumsy tackle fell on my ankle and put me out for the season. I lettered in freshman baseball as a pitcher. My sophomore year I played Rambler football but was brought up to the Rose Bowl-bound varsity and participated in all the practices and suited up for the Northwestern game, although I didn't get to play. I was on the varsity my junior and senior years and played in the Ohio State and Michigan Rose Bowls. In the Michigan game I scored a touchdown. In my senior year I was awarded the Andy Smith Memorial Scholarship Award, of which I am very proud and thankful. I was a member of the Lambda Chi Alpha fraternity and made many wonderful friends there.

My work with Cutter Labs and Wyeth Labs in the health field have been both rewarding and challenging. My time at Cal was and is a vital part of my life and I am proud of the University.

JIM CLARK

⌘

I was on the University of California freshman football team of 1949 and the Rambler football teams of 1950 and 1951. I graduated in June of 1953 with a Bachelor of Science degree in civil engineering. I was a member of Chi Epsilon, honorary civil engineering fraternity. I am a life member of University of California Alumni, and a member of Bear Backers.

After graduating from Cal, I went directly into the U.S. Marine Corps Officers Candidate Program, receiving my commission as a Second Lieutenant in September, 1953. After two years of active duty as a platoon leader, I left active duty as a First Lieutenant. I also spent six years in the inactive reserve.

In 1955, I went to work in San Francisco as a structural building designer for the structural engineering firm of John A. Blume & Associates where I became a registered civil and structural engineer. In 1958, I went to work for Continental Heller Construction Company in Sacramento as an estimator and project manager. From 1962 to the present, I have been the General Manager of Tecon Pacific. I have been the President of Clark-Pacific Corporation since 1978 when Clark Pacific Corporation became a General Partner of Tecon Pacific, a large manufacturer and erector of Architectural Precast concrete for high rise buildings in California.

In 1957 I married Sharron Kinch of Madera, California. Sharron is a registered nurse who was graduated from Stanford University in 1959. We have five children, three girls and two boys. All are college graduates. One daughter is an attorney, one is a registered nurse and one is a podiatrist. The two boys are civil engineers and Presidents of corporations which are General Partners in Tecon Pacific.

All of my professional career has been spent in northern California in the engineering and construction business.

DUKE ZENOVICH

⌘

I was 71 years young on May 14th, 1995, and the years have been absolutely magnificent. I anticipate that my fourth quarter, up to the final gun, will be just as good.

I have climbed to the top of a few mountains in my life. One of my most thrilling climbs was going to Cal, earning a Bachelor of Science degree from the School of Business, playing football, and being called up from the Ramblers to the Varsity. Only with motivation supplied by "Pappy," his great assistants, and the wonderful camaraderie from competitive teammates could this have been brought about.

After graduation, Cal Business School's placement bureau secured me an interview with the McKesson Corporation. I spent 33 years of my career with McKesson, starting from the bottom (sales rep) and rising to General Manager of McKesson's Fresno Division. Let me say that on my first interview (1950) with McKesson's top brass, the fact that they knew I was a member of Pappy Waldorf's Golden Bears practically made me an automatic hire.

In closing I thought I would quote a written expression that really touched me, and that was on the "back bar" of one of our famous Bay Area cocktail lounges:

> "In your journey through life, what would life be, if you did not make a few friends along the way?"

After all these years, you must concede that Pappy Waldorf's Golden Bears are friends forever.

RAY SOLARI

⌘

Born and raised in San Francisco, I always had a dream of attending Cal (never called "Berkeley"...), playing football, and beating Stanford. I used to live for Saturday afternoons during the football season when I could listen to the Cal games on the radio. I'll always remember one of my biggest thrills: the 1941 Big Game when Al Derian ran for a touchdown on Cal's first play from scrimmage. Bob Reinhard, All-American tackle, also blocked a punt, which led Cal to an upset 16-0 victory.

My goals were well-met--and then some. As a walk-on freshman in 1947, I experienced the next three years (1948-50) as a member of three conference champions and Rose Bowl teams. Although we lost all three Bowl games (all squeakers), the experience was priceless.

After a year as a graduate assistant under Pappy, I was finally drafted into the Army for two years (1952-54). Upon my return from Korea I was hired for a teaching-coaching position at South Pasadena High School. I never would have guessed that I would be there for seventeen years. My playing and coaching background under the very successful football program at Cal under Pappy Waldorf not only helped me get the job, but also gave me the background for being a successful athletic coach. I had the experience of coaching four CIF championship football teams and several league championship baseball teams (one CIF title). As Director of Athletics I was also kept busy in the total athletic program. In 1960 I had a very rich experience coaching the South Shrine team against the North at the L.A. Coliseum before 50,000 spectators.

A year after my wife died, I remarried in 1972. At this point, I was given the opportunity to coach the football team at Menlo College in Atherton, California. The opportunity to return to my roots was clear in my mind, so although I had enjoyed many rich years at South Pasadena, I did not hesitate to accept the position--a position I held for twenty-three years.

My beautiful wife Connie (UCLA grad) has given me many very happy years and has been an outstanding working mother who has raised two wonderful children, Antonia and Christopher. Antonia is a student at UCLA and Chris graduated from Menlo School and will attend the USC School of Theater...What can I say? If you had told me in 1950 that my son would attend **USC**, I would have said you were insane!

My life at Menlo College has been rewarding for many reasons. The most important is that I have lived a great life with a wonderful family, and have experienced considerable professional success. Retirement for me is very close. Connie and I are losing our "nestlings," so a new life is awaiting--a life of challenging goals.

I owe much to my experience at Cal from 1947-51. My association with such a high caliber of student-athletes (many were WW II veterans) at that time enriched the experience significantly. Also, playing for a great man and a great coach, Lynn "Pappy" Waldorf, and his staff (Bob Tessier, Wes Fry, Eggs Manske, and Zeb Chaney) made it all seem like the very best training in life one could ever have. Also, never to be forgotten---Jack Williamson, head trainer, was a great influence on all of us.

One of my retirement goals is to write a book which will study the past fifty years of collegiate football. What has happened? Where are we going? My ideal model of a healthy football program will be the "Golden Era" of Pappy's Boys.

BRANISLAV YAICH

⌘

It is very difficult to determine what the single most important accomplishment might be in my life. Fortunately, I have had the opportunity to work with high school age people for 37 years in the public schools of California. Needless to say, I have had many pleasant and successful experiences as a teacher, coach, and school administrator. Each position I have held has provided unique opportunities to work with young people. Whether I have contributed or been the beneficiary of such contacts, depends, I suppose, on one's point of view. Nevertheless, I have worked with thousands of students, and each time I see or hear from one of them I feel more than rewarded by my chosen profession.

In my public education career I was both a teacher and coach for 13 years. I taught science and mathematics and coached football and baseball. I was a vice principal at Miramonte High School in Orinda for seven years and then became the principal for eight years. During the last eight years I have been the Assistant Superintendent for personnel in the Acalanes Union High School District.

For 30 of the 37 years that I have worked in public schools I had the opportunity to serve in the U.S. Army Reserve. This too, was a result of my attendance at Berkeley when ROTC was mandatory in the 1950's. In any case, the experiences on active duty during the Korean War and my reserve duty provided additional opportunities for an education second to none. I can say that attendance at the Army War College and at the National Defense University were of immense value in my military as well as in my civilian life. I ended my military career in 1983, holding the rank of Colonel and the position of Assistant Division Commander.

My community life has always been very closely related to my professional life. In 1984-85 while principal at Miramonte High School in Orinda I was also selected to be president of the Orinda Rotary Club. Because of my various activities I was selected as Orinda "Citizen of the Year" in 1985.

I have certainly been fortunate to have had my share of successes as well as to have developed many wonderful friendships and associations. Hopefully, I have helped some young people find their way a little sooner in life than they might have by themselves. The challenges and the opportunities have been tremendous and generally rewarding.

GEORGE PELONIS

⌘

Forty five years ago, a non-stop train traveling from Arizona to Oakland slowed down long enough at 3:00 a.m. in the little town of Banning, California to pick up a 17-year-old kid holding one suitcase and big hopes of playing football for Cal.

Well, time flies when you're having fun, and after three football seasons (frosh, soph, and redshirt) with Pappy, I was relocated to San Diego, having been activated as a Naval Reservist. My return to Cal in 1954 as an ex-G.I. gave me further opportunity to play for Pappy. Unfortunately, the knees gave out, ending my football career. I did, however, meet the girl who was to become my wife, and three years later we were married in her home town of San Francisco. We settled down in southern California and joined the family business, which is restaurants.

During the Sixties and Seventies when the flower children were spreading joy to the world, we were busy raising and educating our six children, doing our share of church, school and community activities, coaching and sponsoring little league teams and other sports, expanding the restaurants in number and size, and developing a catering business, which continues to grow.

In the Eighties and Nineties we have seen all of our children come of age, complete their education, and start out on their own, with hopes they're a little smarter than that 17-year-old kid from Banning.

Our oldest daughter, Cappi, has completed two masters degrees from Loyola-Marymount University, is an educational psychologist, is married to Mark, has two young teenagers, Caprice and P.J., and lives in Laguna Niguel.

Our oldest son, Pete, graduated from Cal State Long Beach with a major in business, has worked as a stock broker, is currently working in the family business, is married to Cathy and has three beautiful pre-school-age daughters, Claire, Emma and Paige.

Our son Jim graduated from Cal State Long Beach, is a physical therapist, and has been associated with Long Beach sports medicine for eight years.

Our son Matt, a twin, graduated from Cal State Long Beach with a major in business, is employed at Enertech in sales, is married to Lisa, and has coached 8th grade parochial school football and basketball teams for ten years.

Our daughter Kerri, a twin, is a graduate of UCLA, has been in advertising for seven years, and is in the process of relocating from Chicago back to Los Angeles, where she will be a supervisor with the D.M.B. & B. Agency.

George Jr., our recent graduate and the only one to attend Cal Berkeley, is a film major with interests in special effects and directing.

My wife Arline and I have lived in the same home in the same community of Los Alamitos for 35 years, and we continue to enjoy it. We are grateful to all of the people who contributed so much to our formative years: good parents, good teachers, and good coaches, which brings me back to Pappy.

It is an honor and a privilege to be counted among the many ex-jocks who were fortunate enough to have played ball for Pappy Waldorf and the Golden Bears during the Golden Years.

GLENN GULVIN

⌘

It was late August, the year 1950. The place, Berkeley, California. There were almost a hundred prospective footballers who showed up at Memorial Stadium for that first day of fall practice.

I had just turned 19 that summer and was probably even naive for that age. I didn't really weigh enough to play the position I was seeking, tackle, but I lacked the speed and agility to play a more skilled one.

The morning began with the Head Coach, Lynn "Pappy" Waldorf, addressing the assembled players. He proceeded to explain his plans, hopes and expectations for his team in 1950. As he neared the finish of his remarks, he said: (increasing the volume of his deep resonant voice) "Now if some of you are wondering just who is going to be on this football team, I'll tell you. The first eleven men who play for me will be the eleven best football players. The next eleven men will be the ones who want to play football the most." With whatever doubts I had regarding my level of skills, I knew, inside, that there was a place for me on his team.

I played on Pappy's teams and missed only two games (due to injury) in the ensuing three years. In my senior year, my teammates selected me for the "Ken Cotton Award" as the "Most Courageous Player."

Pappy made one proud to play for him. He also commanded respect by example. His integrity was aptly demonstrated in a half time talk to the team at the Cal vs. USC game in 1951, at Memorial Stadium. Several SC players had been more than zealous in the first half. An SC linebacker had tackled our fullback and appeared to deliberately try to injure him (which he did). Our team, to a man, was incensed, and during the half-time break, you could feel the anger escalating. Pappy waited until almost the end of the break and then addressed the team. He was brief, urging us to go out on the field in the second half and play a hard, good and clean football game. Sensing that this language was perhaps not strong enough considering the tense atmosphere of the locker room, he concluded by saying: "and any man on this team who elects to play in an unsportsmanlike manner, will never play football for me again," We didn't win that game, but, each of us won something far more important in our lives.

Other than my father, Pappy Waldorf probably was the strongest influence on the way I lived my life. He made you prove to yourself that you could compete if you wanted to compete badly enough and that success can be found honestly without playing dirty. Pappy's principles were a positive in my business life. I thank him, in part, for much of my success. Hopefully I have been able to be a positive influence for others along the way.

On those occasions when some of Pappy's former players are together, we tend to reminisce about the "Grand Old Man". One of my favorite stories dates to some twenty years after I had graduated from Cal. I was attending a dinner, honoring Joe Kapp, at a hotel in San Francisco. Following the dinner Joe had an informal reception in his suite. As I entered the elevator, so did Lynn Waldorf. He looked terrific for his age and I complimented him by saying, "Pappy, you don't look a day older than when you were coaching." He smiled and in that beautiful deep voice said, "Glenn, how does a fat man have wrinkles?"

HERBERT S. (SEDGE) THOMSON

⌘

As purveyor of jocks and socks to the '47 and '48 football teams--as varied a group of athletes as has ever been assembled--I learned more about individual foibles and behavior than was ever taught in a classroom. Handing out towels, shagging balls, dispensing meal and movie money, and even locating misplaced contact lenses, enabled me to enjoy vicariously as football manager the success and fame of those teams. The truly great athletes were a pleasure to serve; those who merely thought they were great could be a pain!

As a working companion of the players, the coaches, trainers, ticket and equipment managers, and indeed Athletic Directors, I learned much about human relationships, organization, politics, and even the "system". I also developed lifelong friendships and enjoyed a camaraderie experienced by few.

Pappy, for example, taught me two important principles of management. First, hire a fine staff, give it authority with concomitant responsibility, and hold the reins lightly but firmly. The second was to hold all people in high regard no matter their station, their capability, or their aspirations.

Since graduation, I have enjoyed more than forty years in university business administration. Beginning at Berkeley I quickly became involved in such matters as physical plant operations, residence hall management and the negotiation and administration of research contracts at the state and federal levels, as well as the ever present problems of parking.

Thence to UC Santa Barbara where I was the chief business officer and helped that minor campus grow beyond the expectations of the early Fifties. The building program became my responsibility along with town and gown and governmental relationships. Of course there was still the hand-holding of students and parents, and the ever present problems of parking. I enjoyed being the spokesman for the campus as well as lobbying long and hard for its growth before both local and state authorities.

Moving to the University of Washington as Business Manager in the early Sixties I endured the sometimes sphincter-tightening demonstrations and confrontations so characteristic of the Sixties and Seventies. Again, the whole menu of services was on my platter, including the ever present problems of parking! The U/W had a huge building program which became my baby, as did the task of presenting to state and local officialdom, to community clubs and to anyone interested, the University's position on growth, environmental impact and all those related items which have become buzz words in modern day construction.

Some would call it a prosaic life, but my career has been devoted to making the institutions I have served a more pleasant arena for students and faculty. While I never became "rich and famous," I have the satisfaction of knowing I made a difference in the quality of the campus and in the teaching and learning environment. To me it has been challenging and rewarding--it began with jocks and socks and ended with laboratories and libraries!

I must mention two very proud moments. First, when Pappy at a banquet introduced me as "The finest senior manager I've ever had!" and the next when I was awarded The Distinguished Business Officer Award, the highest honor the National Association of College and University Business Officers bestows.

Now, if we could only solve the ever present problems of parking!

DWIGHT A. CARLSON

⌘

At 139 pounds wringing wet and with an Alumni Academic Scholarship tucked in my wallet, you'd think I'd have had more sense than to play football at Cal. But I've been a survivor since beating death from whooping cough in my first year, so the thought of scrimmaging against Johnny Olszewski, Les Richter, Al Talley, Bob Karpe and the other "room and board" players was a challenge not to be ignored. My high school coaches taught, "The bigger they are the harder they fall." And they fell! Hard!! Before the platoon system and I were history I received my Freshman Letter and Rambler Sweater that still hangs proudly in my closet, and sometimes on my 155-pound frame.

After graduating in January 1955 I served two years as Personal Affairs and Casualty Officer at Castle Air Force Base in Merced, California before returning to U.C. to earn a degree of Doctor of Jurisprudence from Boalt Hall. The day after the Bar Exam our daughter Nori Jo and my wife, Virginia, who had received her M.S.W. Degree and her PHT (Putting Hubby Thru) Degree, embarked on a 30-state auto/camping tour of the U.S.

On returning I associated with the Shepard & Shepard law firm in Selma before opening my practice in Dinuba in 1964. I ran unsuccessfully for Justice Court Judge and for Tulare County Supervisor, but was elected to the Dinuba School Board. I became active in Kiwanis International and served as my club's President and as Lt. Governor of Division 18 of the CAL-NEV-HA District and was privileged to give the nomination speech for Governor Ernest Korte. In my early general practice, if a body, warm or cold, walked in, I represented it. My only capital punishment client was found not guilty. My last 15 years of practice were limited to Real Estate, Corporation law, Probate law and Estate Planning.

I was raised in a Primitive Baptist home. In comparison, Fundamental Evangelists are flaming religious liberals if not heretics. It was my mother's conviction that "If God intended man to be on the moon he would have put him there." But I had come to believe God was much greater than my parents' understanding of Him and was baptized into Jesus Christ at the Berkeley University Christian Church on Easter Day 1951. I served as President of the college Disciples' Club and later served as an Elder in the Christian Churches in Selma, Dinuba and Visalia. In 1967, I became legal counsel for the Christian Churches (Disciples of Christ) of Northern California-Nevada and served in that capacity for 21 years. When the Jim Jones Guyana incident occurred, I and others helped the authorities and potential claimants to determine that the CCNC-N was not an appropriate party to any possible litigation.

In 1968 I became one of six founders of ESKATON, a non-profit health, housing and educational corporation sponsored by the CCNC-N. I served as a Director, donating one week a month, for 15 years, during which ESKATON acquired or constructed eight acute care hospitals, 1600 low income housing units in Richmond and San Diego, seven Senior Housing Projects and five convalescent hospitals. ESKATON has since merged with Alta Bates Hospitals of Oakland.

In November 1983, I suffered an incident of cardiac arrhythmia and had two cardiac "near death" experiences. Though since then I have had a pacemaker and am tied to four daily medications, I am blessed because I have no dietary or physical limitations and continue to enjoy golf, bowling, backpacking, fishing and tennis.

By 1987 I could no longer reject God's call to enter into full-time ministry and entered the Mennonite Brethren Biblical Seminary in Fresno. I received my degree of Master of Arts in Theology and Virginia her second PHT Degree in June, 1991. I was ordained on December 16, 1990 and was called as Associate Pastor of the Hanford Christian Church in June 1991. In my two and a half years of ministry there it welcomed 75 new members, 27 through baptism. Since April 1, 1994, I have been the Pastor of the First Christian Church of Watsonville, California.

God has blessed Virginia and me with five children, Nori Jo Naylor, Ralph, Daniel, Heidi Hoelson and Michael. Our three adopted children are bracketed by our biological daughter and son. Our lovely, vivacious Heidi, age 26, having just graduated from U.C. Davis, suffered a fatal asthma attack and passed into new life with her Lord on July 12, 1992.

Our God is a good and great God whose call to servanthood never ceases. This "Old Blue" is living evidence that He can make our life to become "Gold" even after we reach three-score years.

JERRY SCOTT

⌘

In 1948 I made the right decision to go to Cal. It was a visit by Pappy and John Graves (a fullback on the 1947 team) to Long Beach that clinched my decision.

I was part of Pappy's Deep Freeze. Coming out of Long Beach City College, I had to learn the system and prove I could compete with the established players. And believe me, we did compete!

With Pappy and his staff you felt you would be given every chance to succeed. It was hard work, but they made it fun. And it is always more fun to win. In the two years I was lucky enough to play at Cal, the only games we lost were in the Rose Bowl; so we were 20 and 2. Pappy and his staff had the conviction that hard work and fair competition can bring success in any endeavor.

After graduation I worked for the Ford Motor Company for 13 years and was one of the youngest chassis superintendents in the country. After Ford, I sold insurance securities. For the past 27 years, I have served as California Probate Referee.

I have been happily married to a wonderful woman for 46 years and have four children, all of whom are married and leading very successful lives. They have given us eight grandchildren.

I am happy that I have been able to stay in good health and to support my family. We have many friends from the Pappy years and we still keep in touch with the university.

Wealth is determined in different ways. Some will say by the size of your estate in dollars. I believe it is to be found in a happy family, in friendship and in good health.

NORM PRESSLEY

⌘

After graduation in February, 1950, I worked in Sales and Sales Management for International Harvester Co., in the Motor Truck Division, for ten years, the last five as manager of the San Diego Branch.

I left International to become a General Motors truck dealer, with most of the money supplied by the company. I added the Peterbilt franchise two years later. Before turning this business over to my oldest son, I served on the President's Council of both Peterbilt and General Motors and was Pacific Truck Dealer of the Year in 1976, as selected by Business Week Magazine.

I am a past president of the San Diego Boys Clubs, and was responsible for bringing the Unlimited Hydroplane races to San Diego. I am currently heading a national fund-raising program for the U.S. Olympic Committee.

I retired from the truck business in 1983, and became an almond grower, and currently am farming about 1700 acres in 10 different locations and am active on the Almond Board of California. I fly my own plane to supervise these orchards.

I often refer to lessons I learned from Pappy and Eggs that have helped me in all phases of my life. It still seems unbelievable to me that I was able to make the team and play in two Rose Bowls.

I am still active in golf, tennis, skiing (snow and water), fly fishing, body surfing, and scuba diving.

DOUG DUNCAN

⌘

I left Cal with a BA in Criminology and returned to the Navy for a short hitch with the Office of Naval Intelligence. In 1950 I transferred to the Secret Service in San Francisco and during the next 30 years I served in various locations throughout the U.S. as an Agent and Agent in Charge. I was assigned to protective details for Presidents Truman and Eisenhower at the White House in the early 1950's and through the years had occasional assignments with all the Presidents through Ronald Reagan. These assignments, along with the criminal investigative work under our jurisdiction, made for a busy and active life, complemented by a wonderful wife, Mary, three children and now eight grandchildren.

Since my retirement in Sacramento in 1980, I have done some real estate development work plus a lot of RV fishing adventures.

For me, raised in Berkeley and having spent a lot of Saturdays sneaking into Memorial Stadium to watch Herwig, Bottari, Reinhardt et al, being a Pappy's Boy was a dream come true. In my work I saw a lot of prominent people and historic events but none ever topped the thrill of heading out that tunnel with all the great players I was lucky to be associated with. Those relationships and the leadership of our coaches have been a lifelong inspiration for me and I am thankful that Pappy's Boys exists so we can continue to enjoy those memories and the teammates we shared them with.

BOB BAGLEY

⌘

Absolutely, California and Pappy Waldorf had a great influence on my life. To begin with, I was steeped in U.C. tradition, as my family all attended Cal, starting with my eldest uncle, a baseball player, in the late 1890's. I was born and raised in Oakland and spent much time at Memorial Stadium. I too, wanted to represent Cal, and to run out from that North Tunnel and play on that field.

On the road to Cal, I attended University High School in Oakland, played football and was named to the All-City First team both my junior and senior years.

World War II was going strong, so I enlisted in the Marine Corps. As a result, I was left with irreparable leg damage. I was too young at the time to realize that was really the case. I was finally admitted to Cal in the spring of '49.

At this point, Pappy, Wes, Bob and Eggs made a major impact on my life. That first spring practice was a memorable occasion. I was a walk-on, not recruited, and older than most other team members. I was given a football and instructed to line up as the 17th center...a long way to go!

Through Pappy's great skills as a teacher and coach and through his ability to motivate people to rise to the occasion, I was able to mature as a person and football player. To be voted captain for the '51 Pennsylvania game was a thrilling experience, one due largely to Pappy's skills and patience with me. Unfortunately, that game resulted in a leg injury and because of the previous leg damage, made it impossible for me to continue.

However, Pappy provided me with the great opportunity to be part of his coaching staff. It was there that I was able to acquire those skills so necessary in coaching and education. Most notable among these were organizational techniques, the discipline to focus on detail and the ability to motivate young men. Without these attributes I could not have had such a successful career.

I moved on to coach at San Ramon High School and Santa Rosa High School. We never experienced a losing season and had several championship years. The wonderful relationship I shared with the young people I had associated with as their coach came to fruition when, 25 years after retiring from coaching, these men gathered and put together a great reunion and banquet in my behalf. What a great experience and reward. Pappy's message did indeed get across.

PETE MERING

⌘

After my undergraduate days at Berkeley I served two years in the Army and could not resist returning to Berkeley--this time to attend the School of Law (Boalt Hall). Teammates Dwight Ely and Dick LemMon were there at the same time. The high point of my law school years was winning the campus-wide two-man volleyball tournament in 1958. Not bad for a slow-footed lineman.

After law school I returned to Sacramento and was in private practice for one year. Out of a desire to do more trial work, I joined the office of the Sacramento District Attorney. For various reasons, I switched to the Public Defender's office after a few years. I remained a public defender for 13 years. In both offices I tried a great many jury cases, running the gamut from misdemeanors to major felonies and death penalty cases.

In 1977, Governor Jerry Brown had the good judgment to appoint me to the Municipal Court and four years later, in another flash of brilliance, he elevated me to the Superior Court. I was fortunate to be available during his term of office, since few other governors have given much consideration to public defenders.

I have now logged 18 years on the bench. Most of my assignments have been in departments that primarily handle criminal cases, although I was assigned to the juvenile court for five years. While I have handled many interesting and challenging cases, I will mention two that I consider particularly significant or noteworthy. In 1992, I handled the death penalty proceedings concerning Morris Solomon, a serial killer responsible for the deaths of seven women, and likely a few more whose bodies were not found. In 1993, I ruled that the Sacramento County Board of Supervisors could not lawfully impose drastic reductions in the level of health care services provided to indigent persons who are maintained on general assistance. This ruling is still on appeal.

Trying to make the varsity football team taught me some valuable lessons. One is that success or unexpected progress can occur if you don't give up. Another is that your adversaries are not as tough as they look, or as you may imagine them to be. Even big name lawyers put on their pants, or skirts, one leg at a time.

DANIEL V. BEGOVICH

⌘

It seems like just a few years ago, yet it is almost half a century that the bells of the Campanile were ringing and I was hurrying to class. I left the University after the fall semester of 1949 just seven units short of graduation and it wasn't until 1956 that I completed the additional courses for my degree in economics.

I had met Emma, the lady of my life, the summer of 1949 and we were married the following June. I was working in the family restaurant business when I purchased my first home and then became interested in the real estate brokerage business. Subsequently I worked in real estate sales and management and founded my own firm, Danco Real Estate Inc. I have been in the real estate brokerage business in the Westlake area of Daly City for 40 years now. We branched out into the building-development of homes and small income properties and today we are one of the largest independent brokerage firms in North San Mateo County. My son Daniel has recently taken over the business.

Our greatest accomplishments, though, are our three children. All are UC system products and grads. Ann received her degree at UC San Diego and went on to obtain her doctorate in genetic immunology at the University of Pennsylvania and is presently working in research. Dan was a UC Berkeley grad and was on the '77-'78 basketball teams. Patrice has degrees from UCLA and the Art Center in Pasadena and operates her own design business.

Athletic competition has always been dear to me from the days of playing touch football on the streets and playgrounds to tackle football at the Saturday morning pick-up games at the Marina Green.

The first important mentor in my life was my junior high school track and soccer coach, Frank Zanazzi. He instilled confidence in me and gave me direction. His teams were always of championship caliber. It was on these teams that I first met my lifelong friend and teammate, Rod Franz. Incidentally, Bob DiGrazia, the UC soccer coach for many years, was also a teammate.

Galileo High is just a few blocks from the Bay so crew was a tremendously invigorating sport that I thoroughly enjoyed. Rod Franz was our port stroke and I rowed the starboard bow in the 1942 league championships. We practiced on the bay each afternoon and on Saturday mornings in calm, rough or rainy weather. Henry Lewis was our dedicated coach and it was Mr. Lewis who first brought us to Memorial Stadium to usher the Cal football games. One of my great joys yet remains crossing the bay and walking up to Memorial Stadium to watch the Bears and the Cal Marching Band.

Just one week after my 16th birthday I played in my first football game at Kezar Stadium. I began as a substitute end who then stepped up to play the entire season after the veteran starter went out with a season ending injury. I was also the punter. My very first punt at Kezar traveled from our fourteen yard line over the opponent's goal some 86 yards away. I could punt for distance with the best and I also had touch and was able to kick to the corners.

Red Schfelin was our first football coach, a true gentleman who made the game fun. Louis Haas was our coach the following year. He was a fiery man with loads of enthusiasm. He moved me to the backfield where I received "All City" mention. These were the war years and many seniors enlisted or went to work in the defense industries. I skipped my senior semester and high school football and took a scholarship to USF where I was the tailback on the 1943 team. We had a very competitive schedule with opponents such as Cal, USC and the service teams of St. Mary's and Del Monte pre-flight. We were pulverized each week.

I enlisted in the Army Air Corps and was allowed to complete the fall semester reporting for duty in January 1944. I spent 28 months in the service attending different mechanical schools. I was discharged in the spring of 1946. Rod Franz and I both wanted to attend a major university. We met with then Cal assistant coach, Irv Uteritz and decided that Berkeley was the place for us. Rod had grown to large and muscular proportions and possessed that consistent drive and fire. He had only one speed--full speed--and he rose from an obscure reserve to a four-year starter and three time Consensus All American.

I did not compete in football in 1946 but concentrated on my studies. In early 1947, Lynn Waldorf became the new Cal coach and the 1947 spring practice was my first introduction to Cal football. I recall there were more than 200 students who turned out for our first spring practice. The majority were, like me, older war veterans. Waldorf's program was one of detailed planning and preparation. A schedule was posted the first of each week outlining each minute of our daily practice sessions. Our offensive and defensive schemes were very basic and simple but we practiced each detail over and over and over. One-on-one blocking---ends on tackles and line backers, guards and tackles one-on-one---was emphasized. The lead blocker or flanker back would block the defensive end depending on how the end reacted. Simplicity but always with repetition---repetition and more repetition. Quickness and getting off the ball were essential elements in Waldorf's coaching philosophy. Pappy was a master organizer, and his assistants complemented him effectively. Ed Manske, Bob Tessier and Wes Fry were great teachers and communicators. Manske and Tessier particularly had a zest and enthusiasm that they passed on to the entire team.

My first season at Cal was at fullback where I saw action behind Johnny Graves and Jackie Jensen. After a knee injury in the Wisconsin game, I saw most of my action and competition with the "Monday Mudders," those players who saw limited action in the previous Saturday's game. In the Spring of 1948 Ed Manske approached me about switching from the backfield to end. It was agreeable to me. I just wanted to compete and be a part of the team. Manske spent a great deal of time making me aware of blocking angles, leverage and the advantage of quickness and balance. He had a capacity for making all his ends feel special. We obtained the very best and newest equipment. He made each of us tough. One-on-one with the tackles day after day--"Get off!" "Hit!" "Maintain your balance, keep your feet moving, control your opponent." "Again!" "Set!" "Hike!"

My junior year I saw limited action behind Bud Van Deren, a truly great athlete. I got to look forward to the Monday Mudders contest where you showed your abilities and relieved your frustrations. These were great teams and we had enormous talent. My senior year I stepped into the left end position and was the leading receiver of Bob Celeri's and Boots Erbs' passes and did a competent job of blocking those big tackles and line backers. We were a team even more explosive than the previous year's conference champs. Each and every play could be a touchdown from any position on the field. It didn't matter who carried the ball--all our backs had great talent! When injuries occurred, the player stepping in rose to the occasion, knowledgeable and prepared for the task at hand. I marveled at our detailed scouting reports prepared by Ed Manske and the staff. They were masterpieces.

There was then and there remains today a sense of humor that pervades our gatherings and makes them special events. Yet, when it was or is time to tend to the business at hand, there was and is leadership and singleness of purpose. Great young men--great men--all winners! Pappy's Boys!

FORREST KLEIN

⌘

I can recall that I always wanted to attend Cal and to play football and become a football coach.

My mother, Klara Klein, was an avid Cal supporter, both for the school and the football program. She never attended Cal but she always said to me, "You will attend Cal." In 1944 I was accepted to Cal but World War II said No. Into the service I went--Navy.

Discharged July, 1946, I registered at Cal and was accepted for the fall of that year. The 1946 season was not the best for the team, the school or me. I blew out my knee just before the first game and did not play the rest of the season.

In the spring of 1947, Pappy Waldorf became the football coach at Cal. Spring practice--my first ever--was something. There were more than 200 players on the field. The atmosphere at spring practice was unbelievable.

In the 1949 season Cal was picked fifth in the conference. We had lost a number of players we thought would come to play that year. The team had great spirit and became as close and focussed on winning as any I ever played for or coached.

After the 1949 season I was named All-American, an honor I will treasure all my life. I was voted Player of the week--All Bay Area--after our game with USC. That was the game in which Frank Brunk ran 102 yards for a touchdown. It led us to the Rose Bowl. The Rose Bowl stands out most in my mind. Many players never get the chance to play in one; I played in two.

Ever since I was 13 years old I had wanted to be a football coach. Cal and Pappy Waldorf prepared me to do just that.

I coached football for 38 years---junior high, high school, junior college, college and the pros. My overall record as a head football coach is 125-20-2. In 10 years as head football coach at Alameda High School my teams compiled a remarkable 81-7-2 record, including five undefeated seasons and 34 straight victories over four years. In 1968 the Alameda High Hornets were voted the Number One Prep Football team in California. I was voted Coach of the Year for 1967 and 1969 and in 1968 was named Head Coach of the North Team in the annual Shrine All Star Football game in Los Angeles.

As an assistant coach at Cal in 1955, Pappy gave me some sound advice. He said if a player is not doing well and you have to get his attention DO IT. But always find something good he has done and tell him about it before you let him go back to practice.

In other words find the good in people.

In my coaching and in my life I strived to follow that philosophy.

PAUL ANDREW

⌘

All my life as a kid in San Francisco, I wanted to play football for Cal. In my family, if you didn't go to Cal, you supported those who did. My uncles, one aunt, stepfathers, and many cousins went to Cal. My real father, Paul McCoy, lettered in football in 1919. We were a musical family. At Thanksgiving and Christmas, we had two pianos going at all times with my Aunt Elizabeth, Aunt Esther, and Uncle Henry banging out rag-time tunes, carols, and Cal songs. By the time I was five, I knew the words to "Fight for California," "The Stanford Jonah," and "Big C," better than "Silent Night", and "Deck the Halls". I knew that red was a bad color, and I hated Stanford.

I went to my first Cal game at about age six. I listened to Cal play-by-play on the radio on Washington Street while playing "Kick the Can", and "Tap the Finger." My father's photo, in his Cal football suit was over my bed. I was ingrained. My life's ambition was to play football for Cal.

As I got older, my friend, Lud Renick, and I would take the Key System to Cal games on Saturday, and watch men like Bob Reinhard, Jim Jurkovich, Al Derian, and George Nicholau. On Sunday we'd be at Kezar Stadium watching the Catholic schools, U.S.F., St. Mary's, and Santa Clara. After these games, we'd spill out onto the field with all the rest of the kids, and check the size of those guys. They seemed massive.

My hope to grow that size seemed remote, but there was always the "dream". My "sandlot" peers felt that Billy Baer, (future Poly High, St. Mary's great), and I were destined for better things, subject, of course, to God-given gifts such as physique and speed. Billy had a lot more of both, so ambition had to be my main suit.

I had a silver and green leather helmet, and shoulder pads. We played pick-up games at Alta Plaza Park, and Julius Kahn Playground daily from August to December. It went like clockwork without parental, or "Little League" supervision. In fact, many of us did it on the Q.T., as there was this prevailing theory that football was bad for young bones, and we better not get caught out there, tackling someone!

After eighth grade at Grant Grammar School, we went to Lowell High on Hayes and Masonic. Because I couldn't climb a rope, I couldn't make the Freshman team at Lowell, the "Goofs." I kind of walked-on anyway, but never got a chance to play. As I was struggling in the classroom, playing football for Cal seemed an impossibility. The following summer, a Grant classmate, Dick Pischell came back from a year at Cate School down near Santa Barbara. My mom was more than willing to send me there, and I had great fun playing soccer in the fall, basketball in the winter, and baseball in the spring. There was a lot of discipline there, and it helped a lot.

After battling what may have been dyslexia at Cate, I then moved to Drews School, and finally to Cal Extension, before I finally got into Cal in the fall of 1949. After enrolling in a class down at L.S.B., I must have turned towards Harmon Gym five times before mustering the courage to sign up for freshman ball. I was given the last of the football uniforms issued, and took the field looking more like W.W. Heffelfinger, Class of 1892.

Two things boosted my morale. 1) I reported to Bud Van Deren, the Freshman end coach, and he asked, "where did you play high school ball?" I said, "I didn't." He said, "Good, you don't have any bad habits." 2) My friend, Lud Renick, who was on the Ramblers, either got serious about grades, or had a bad experience opposite Rod Franz and quit football. I forget which, but I got Lud's "state of the art" uniform and the next day went out feeling confident, and no one was laughing.

It was great to be a Freshman with the "Saints". The "Saints" were six or seven newly recruited stars from St. Anthony High School, Long Beach. They included the likes of Johnny Olszewski, Bill Mais, John Peterson, and Dean O'Hare. The Freshmen beat the Ramblers handily with the Saints using St. Anthony's plays. After that the dream came true as I ran out of the tunnel in Memorial Stadium for the "preliminary game." There were a few Freshman jerseys without numbers. I had one of them, but it didn't matter.

For the next four years I became a part of the "Waldorf era". Looking back on it becomes more and more special. Playing for Pappy, Eggs Manske, and the rest of Pappy's staff gave me some needed self-esteem. Although football wasn't important to Ginger Chubb, I got to meet, and marry a great gal because of what it did for me. Also, there's no doubt football gave me the courage to go into the Marines, and to overcome any fear of responsibility, such as starting a property management, and hotel company, being a Receiver and Bankruptcy Trustee in over 300 cases, or running the Monterey Rugby Tournament/Pebble Beach Rugby Classic, which lasted 32 years. Above all, the lifelong camaraderie that we all feel, and my continued love of Cal, has led to involvement with the Bear Backers, Big C Society, Cal Rugby, Big C Career Day, and the Grid Club Career Counseling Committee for active Cal football players.

RALPH KRUEGER

⌘

On special occasions with friends and family, I find myself reminiscing about the exciting times spent starting at right tackle during the 1950 season and the 1951 Rose Bowl. A sophomore at the time, I learned the meaning of performance goals and self-discipline from Pappy Waldorf and Line Coach Bob Tessier.

After graduating from Cal (Class of '52), and fulfilling my military commitment, I entered a life of corporate sales. After living in several locations, my wife, Bobbie, and I settled in Sacramento where I now manage a wholesale roofing material company.

My three children and their families all live in the Sacramento area as well, which allows me to stay in close contact with my seven grandchildren. They are a great joy to me.

BOB WITTER

⌘

My biggest thrill from Cal Football came approximately 40 years after I had taken my uniform off for the last time in 1951.

My family had been third generation Cal Berkeley people, so there was never any question as to where I was going to go to college. I graduated from Grant Union High School in Sacramento in 1947. I had been an "All City" tackle. I was big for my age and as it turned out, was fully grown at that time. I didn't get any bigger and I sure didn't get any faster. I was told I was a great runner, except that it was too long in the same place.

I first met Pappy Waldorf at a recruiting gathering in Stockton. It was his first year. Coming to Cal as a 17-year-old freshman in 1947 was an awesome experience for me. Cal seemed filled with veterans from World War II, in their early or mid twenties. Full grown men! As a young athlete, I was terribly intimidated by veteran All Americans like Rod Franz and Jim Turner. Fighter pilots and flame thrower marines from Iwo Jima were fraternity brothers! My cousin had been killed on the SS San Francisco off Guadalcanal. How could I possibly measure up against such Idols? Quite frankly I never ever did get over the intimidating feelings about older players.

Cal football was at the beginning of a four-year heyday---full freshman football program, huge varsity program which included a subdivision of the varsity roughly as follows:

First 3 squads-Varsity
Squads 4 through 6-Ramblers
Squads 7 and up-Scramblers

each with their separate schedule of games.

I played a lot of freshman football and with the Ramblers as a sophomore. That was the process: hopefully, to then progress to the varsity for your junior and senior years. My junior year was the turning point. I stayed on the Ramblers. There was no organized weight-training or year-round conditioning then as there is now, and I personally got neither bigger nor faster. I had reached the limit of my football ability. Younger better players, the Karpes, the Richters and the like began passing me by. This is the point where most marginal players usually recognize their situation and move on to other activities. I liked to play, and pride and family tradition kept me showing up. I thought that surely I would get enough playing time somewhere to earn my letter. So I played my sophomore, junior and senior year as a first-string Rambler, which also makes you fourth string on the varsity.

Now that's not all bad! Got to play a lot of Rambler football. We mostly played state college, junior college and military teams. We played many preliminary games in Memorial Stadium in the late mornings prior to the varsity game.

What made it especially nice was that after the Rambler game, many of us would put on a varsity jersey and run on to the field as the fourth string varsity, knowing perfectly well we would probably never see any action. By the time we might ever get in a game, Cal would either be so far ahead that we couldn't do any harm or so far behind that we couldn't do any good. Cal was never behind for long. In my four years, Cal was 38-1-1 in regular season play.

My perception was that under Cal's great line coach Bob Tessier, Cal had three strings of guards and tackles so strong that it really didn't matter who started. We Ramblers got to play a lot of "Monday Mudders", full game scrimmages against the varsity players who didn't get in the game on Saturday and were really pissed off about it and were out to kill somebody on Monday to show the coaches that they should be playing more. Ramblers were pure dogmeat! We had a good time. Cal was winning and we were a part of it.

We had some good laughs as Ramblers. The best one I'll always remember was one day Rambler guard Augie Mara (his nose looked like it had been hit with a coal shovel) got knocked right on his back. Rambler coach Zeb Chaney ran over and yelled at Augie in his southern accent, "Augie, you ain't neva' gonna be nothin' but a Rambler!" Augie, flat on his back, looked up and said, "Zeb, you ain't neva' gonna be nothin' but a Rambler coach!" That finished the day. Nobody could get serious after that.

"Ramblers go to the Rose Bowl" and we did! We ran out onto the Rose Bowl on New Year's Day just like the big kids!

Looking back, there are countless ex-football players in this country who would have given their right arm for the privilege of running out on that field. Three years in fact. Not all bad.

In preparation for the Rose Bowl, the Ramblers were important. We were the scout team and ran the opponent's defense. The freshman team ran the opponent's offense. We were treated as first class citizens so it was all a great event. Losing the three Rose Bowls was equally painful to us all.

Speaking of the Rose Bowl games, it is my personal feeling that the wait between our last regular season game with Stanford in late November, and the Rose Bowl, some five or six weeks later, somehow damaged Cal far more than it seemed to hurt the Big Ten teams. I think if we had played the Rose Bowl the week or next week after the Big Game, we would have won.

My last game was the Rose Bowl on January 1, 1951. We were losing. Pappy kindly put me in for a few minutes at the end. In the locker room after the game, he came by, shook all of our hands, and said a few words to each of us individually. I don't recall what; maybe, "I'm sorry," or something like that.

We left our gear in the middle of the floor. I stole my helmet, the leather type (plastic wasn't in yet). It had a face mask which you put on after you got your front teeth kicked out, which I did as a freshman. They are smarter now. Everyone wears a mask before the fact. Many years later I proudly showed this helmet to my young sons, and they really put me in my place by innocently saying, "Gee, Dad, what a great old-fashioned helmet." So it goes.

I never did get enough playing time for a Big C letter award. I'd be a liar if I said that it didn't hurt a lot for a long time. I had some good successes in other areas which helped to offset the pain. I was a three-year letterman in Rugby. Rugby doesn't demand great speed of its forwards. I played first-string lock as a 19-year-old sophomore and played on the first two American teams that ever won the World Cup series from the University of British Columbia. Jim Cullom, then Les Richter, were our big guns.

I liked ROTC and earned the top rank of Cadet Colonel in the UC Corps Unit. I graduated in 1951, and the ROTC commission gave me instant employment since the Korean War was on. I became a Field Artillery Forward Observer with the 49th FA BN, and then the Fire Support Control Officer for the 2nd BN 17th Inf Reg. Bronze star medal on Pork Chop Hill. Didn't get wounded. I was 23.

In 1953 I came home from Korea, farmed and ran some sheep. My 1500 sheep got the first diagnosed case of the Australian Blue Tongue disease found in America and died. Fact: the average young farmer goes broke in three years. To show my superiority, I went broke in two and a half!

Went into the stock and bond business and have been there since, some 35 years. I thank my lucky stars that those damned sheep died. Had they not, I might still be irrigating in hot mosquito-ridden pasture fields and castrating sheep in the ancient and honorable manner made much more difficult because of the loss of my front teeth.

I married a lovely woman named Marilyn Affleck in 1958. She was a pharmacist who went to Stanford, then on to USC for her doctor's degree in Pharmacy. Can you imagine that? Thank goodness she doesn't grind me about the Big Games or wear red too often. I probably love and appreciate her more now than ever before. We have had some great times: children, the outdoors, hunting and shooting competitive trap together. Marilyn was California State PITA champion one year. We had some terrible and tragic years, too. It is truly amazing that we are still married.

From 1951 graduation to the early 1980's, some 30 years, I had very little meaningful contact with the University. Football games, local alumni association, but that's all. Too busy with the things that supposedly reasonably successful family people do between the ages of 30 and 50: Rotary, Boards of Red Cross and Boy Scouts, Boy Scout outings with my sons, 4-H and horse stuff with my daughter.

I was manager of a stock brokerage office from 1968 to 1981, a very stressful period of time. The early 1970's were something else, with the worst stock market decline since 1929. Hundred-year low in bond prices. Massive failures of securities firms. The stockbroker population went from 80,000 to 40,000. Jokes about driving cabs. Our office did very well in spite of the lousy market.

Whatever it was or whenever it started, I began to abuse myself and stopped taking care of myself in all ways, physically, mentally and emotionally. It's a long process.

In 1983, our lovely, bright, talented 20-year-old daughter saw fit to take her own life. For the next 18 months, the anger, guilt, remorse and resentment were overwhelming. In 1985, my family insisted I get help, and I was ready.

Things turned around. I stopped the abuse and started taking better care of myself, lost about 40 pounds, and from that point to now my life has gotten progressively better and better. My wife and sons are truly fine. Both boys graduated from Cal. Bob Jr. played a little rugby in his day. He is married and has two fine children. He is currently a heavy-duty government bond trader in New York. My other son, Rick, is married and recently joined Dean Witter & Co. as a stockbroker. Starting with my father in 1932, Rick will be the third generation of my immediate family involved in the securities business in Sacramento, some 60 years to date! This pleases me no end as you can well imagine. Both sons are great guys. I could not want for a better family. I am a very lucky man.

The University of California came back into the picture. In the middle 1980's, Athletic Director Maggard told all non-revenue sports departments that there were tough financial times ahead and if that sport planned to stay around it would have to earn its own money. My sport was Rugby. Paul Andrew, Tom Witter, Ron Witter and a few of us resurrected the old George Witter Fund and started to run with it. I am proud to say that the now Witter Rugby Endowment Fund has a book value of $770,000 which supplies rugby with about 60% of its annual income. I am so very happy and proud of that. In 1988 I was awarded the Trustee Citation from the UC Alumni Association for the rugby fund-raising efforts.

Somewhere in there my dear friend, Boomer Andrew, finagled me and my cousin, Tom, an honorary Big C membership, which quite frankly is like kissing your sister. Recently the retroactive awarding of the Big C letter to all previous rugby Circle C and deserving players was far more meaningful.

Other current Cal activities include membership on the Bear Backers Council, specifically the "Friends" of the committee.

Of paramount importance is fund-raising for the tremendous Strawberry Canyon Grass Field project. This world class grass field area is big enough to contain one and one-half full-sized practice football fields in the fall, then it can be realigned in the winter and spring for a regulation-sized official rugby field. It is named Witter Rugby Field in honor of the three generations of my family who have attended, supported and played athletics at Cal and of rugby, the University's oldest competitive sport. At one time or another 13 members of my family played rugby at Cal. In 1951, five of us were on the same team.

Coach Jack Clark kindly appointed me an official member of the Rugby traveling team. I have been to Houston twice and to Colorado Springs for the final four national championships of 1991, 1992 and 1993. Cal Rugby is three-peat winners as you know, and won ten national championships in 14 years. My duties include driving a van, helping Dave Stenger with washing the uniforms and acting as all-around "gofer". I really love it. What a joy to be associated with such a fine group of young men.

What the hell does all this have to do with Lynn O. "Pappy" Waldorf, and playing Rambler in the late '40's and early '50's? Really quite a lot.

In 1987, along came Bob Karpe again with Dick Erickson and a few more who thought it would be a good idea for all old football players who played under Pappy to form an organization dedicated to (1) getting together once a year for a reunion good time, (2) being helpful to the football program in unique and meaningful ways, and (3) to further Pappy's principle of athletic and academic excellence at the University. To date some really good projects have been accomplished.

I was asked to be on the board. Later to my horror, I was elected first Vice President which is the chair before the Presidency. All my Rambler inadequacies rushed back, and I could not believe that the board or the membership would stand still for having a non-letter winning Rambler as their president. I was deadly serious. The board rejected my refusal and convinced me I was being foolish in such thinking.

Rod Franz and I have become great friends these past years. I told him of my anxiety. Rod most sincerely told me that as far as he was concerned, Cal would never have gone as far as it did had it not been for the constant quality pressure to excel put on the varsity players by the Rambler organization. What he said helped, and I would like to think it is so. I hope other old "veteran" Ramblers who might read this will get some satisfaction and peace from Rod's remarks.

So there we are. The fall of 1992, the biggest football event of my life took place. I humbly and gratefully became president of the Pappy's Boys organization, an unparalleled football thrill for this old Rambler.

What did I receive from Cal athletics, football, rugby and Pappy's Boys?

1. The source of so many of my very best friends.
2. Being associated with the winners. Quality men and women who do good things, keep their word, do their best and can be counted on in a pinch.
3. Code of honor and teamwork. Of being a good leader and a good follower.
4. Being able to return from defeat. To get up one more time. The will to live and the will to win.
5. And from my teammates and friends, the peace of mind that comes from being accepted simply for what I was and am.

For me the classic quote by Calvin Coolidge seems to sum it up:

> "Nothing in the world can take the place of persistence. Talent will not: nothing is more common than unsuccessful men with talent. Genius will not: unrewarded genius is almost a proverb. Education will not: the world is full of educated derelicts. Persistence and determination alone are omnipotent. The slogan 'Press On' has solved and always will solve the problems of the human race."

All of these gifts and lessons learned are, of course, priceless.

In closing, to me, the Pappy's Boys organization is like a shooting star, a brilliant flash of light with a defined beginning and a predictable end. I sincerely hope, however, that the spirit, energy and innovation of "Pappy's Boys" will catch on with players, coaches and teams of all seasons so that one day there will be a mighty force of all Cal football players dedicated to the principles of having fun together, helping the football program and promoting athletic and academic excellence.

Appendix

PAPPY'S BOYS
RECOGNITIONS

CALIFORNIA ATHLETIC HALL OF FAME

Jon Baker
Rod Franz
Jim Cullom
Jack Jensen
John Olszewski
Nibs Price
Les Richter
Carl Van Heuit
Lynn O. (Pappy) Waldorf
Jack Williamson

BAY AREA SPORTS HALL OF FAME

Jack Jensen
Lynn O. (Pappy) Waldorf

NATIONAL FOOTBALL FOUNDATION HALL OF FAME

Rod Franz
Jack Jensen
Edgar (Eggs) Manske
John Ralston
Les Richter
Lynn O. (Pappy) Waldorf

GLENN T. SEABORG AWARD

Rod Franz

PAPPY'S BOYS
ALL AMERICAN PLAYERS
1948, 1949, 1950 TEAMS

Bob Celeri

Rod Franz

Jack Jensen

Forrest Klein

Jim Monachino

John Olszewski

Les Richter

Jim Turner

Carl Van Heuit

PAPPY'S BOYS WHO COACHED*

Many of Pappy's Boys undertook football coaching responsibilities at the conclusion of their playing careers at Cal. Thus the football coaching philosophy and traditions established by Coach Waldorf were carried on to future generations.

Those men who coached football at the high school, college and/or professional levels are:

Bob Bagley
Paul Baldwin
Bob Brooks
Joe Kapp
Bill Cooper
Jim Cullom
Ray DeJong
Bill Dutton
Tom Dutton
Dick Erickson
Hart Fairclough
Rod Franz
Pat Gelardi
Mike Giddings
Jim Hanifan
Ed Hart
Jack Hart
Stormy Hileman
Frank Humpert
Richard Stevens
Forrest Klein
Will Lotter
Vince Maiorana
Roy Muehlberger
Rube Navarro
Hal Norris
John Pappa
Roy Parker
Lukie Phillips
John Ralston
Charlie Sarver
Herb Schmalenberger
Ray Solari
George Souza
Bob Celeri
Jim Turner
Lloyd Torchio
Bud Van Deren
Carl Van Heuit
Staten Webster
Harry West
Mike White
Jim Whitley
Ray Willsey
Branislav Yaich
And Others

Individuals who achieved head coaching status at the college or professional level are:

Jim Hanifan - St. Louis Cardinals
Joe Kapp - Vancouver B.C. Lions, University of California, Berkeley
Will Lotter - University of California, Davis
Vince Maiorana - Contra Costa College
Luke Phillips - Monterey Peninsula College
John Ralston - Utah State, Stanford, Denver Broncos, San Jose State
Herb Schmalenberger - University of California, Davis
Ray Solari - Menlo College
Bud Van Deren - Humboldt State University
Mike White - University of California, Berkeley, University of Illinois, Oakland Raiders
Ray Willsey - London Monarchs, University of California, Berkeley

* Submissions by Ray DeJong, Jack Hart, Dick LemMon, Roy Muehlberger, Carl Van Heuit. Compiled by Carl Van Heuit. Includes players from all Waldorf teams.

IN MEMORIAM*

Name	Position (s)	Rose Bowl Year (s)
Jon Baker	Left Guard/Linebacker	1948
Henry Bakken	Manager	1948
Pete Brewer	End	
Eddie Byrne	Trainer	1948, 1949 and 1950
John Cadenasso	Fullback	1949 and 1950
Bob Celeri	Quarterback	1948 and 1949
Don Cox	Left End	1948
John Cunningham	Right End	1948
Walt Davis	Tackle	1948 and 1949
Don Edmonston	Right Guard	1949
Greg Engelhard	Asst. Athletic Director	1948, 1949 and 1950
Don Feuerstein	Center	
Wes Fry	Backfield Coach	1948, 1949 and 1950
Steve Glagola	End	
Don Grant	Guard	1949
John Graves	Fullback	
Brutus Hamilton	Athletic Director	1948, 1949 and 1950
Jim Harkness	Team Physician	1948, 1949 and 1950
Ed Hart	Left Guard	
Matt Hazeltine	Center/Linebacker	
Jack Jensen	Fullback	1948
Len Jones	Right Tackle	1948 and 1949
Hal Keenan	Manager	1948 and 1949
Wally Laster	Fullback	1949 and 1950
Jim Lawson	End Coach	
Billy Main	Left Half	1948
Gus Manolis	Center	
Augie Marra	Right Guard	1949 and 1950
Pat Martin	Right Half	1948
Ed Michelsen	Halfback	1950
Brick Muller	Team Physician	1948, 1949 and 1950
Rube Navarro	Fullback	1948 and 1949
Lyle Nelson	Right Tackle	1948 and 1949
Bob Peterson	Trainer	1948, 1949 and 1950
Dick Porter		
Don Robison	Fullback	1949 and 1950
Bob Tessier	Line Coach	1948, 1949 and 1950
Howard Thayer	Center	1948
Don Tronstein	Tackle	
Lynn Waldorf	Coach	1948, 1949 and 1950
Joe Wardlaw	Right Guard	1950
Staten Webster	Right Half	1948
Sam Williams	Quarterback	
Jack Williamson	Trainer	1948, 1949 and 1950
Tom Witter	Halfback	1948

*Includes known Pappy's Boys from the 1947 - 1956 Teams

The 1948 Team

No	Name	Pos.	Age	Wt.	Ht.	Class	Exp.	Home Town
69	Baker, Jon*	LG	25	207	6.1	Senior	3-V	San Francisco
87	Begovich, Dan*	RE	23	193	6.1	Junior	1-V	San Francisco
75	Borghi, Hank*	RT	23	212	6.4	Senior	4-V	Niles
21	Brown, Don*	Q	23	175	5.11	Junior	1-V	Stockton
32	Brunk, Frank*	F	22	182	5.11	Junior	1-V	Berkeley
60	Bynum, Gene*	RG	24	190	5.9	Soph	1-JC	Pomona
22	Celeri, Bob*	Q	21	170	5.1	Junior	2-V	Fort Bragg
84	Cox, Don*	LE	21	193	6.2	Junior	2-V	Glendale
64	Cullom, Jim*	LT	22	224	5.11	Junior	1-V	Piedmont
89	Cunningham, John*	RE	23	232	6.4	Junior	2-V	Richmond
45	Dal Porto, Bob*	LH	24	182	6.0	Senior	2-V	Oakley
66	DeJong, Ray*	LG	22	200	5.10	Junior	1-V	Enumclaw, WA
65	Dodds, Bobby*	LG	22	200	5.11	Junior	2-V	San Francisco
53	Duncan, Doug*	C	22	205	6.1	Junior	2-V	Berkeley
25	Erb, Charles*	Q	22	175	5.10	Junior	1-V	Los Angeles
20	Erickson, Dick*	Q	22	166	6.1	Senior	2-V	Stockton
61	Fox, Charles*	RG	23	213	6.1	Junior	1-Tr	Statesville, NC
67	Franz, Rod*	RG	23	208	6.1	Junior	2-V	San Francisco
76	Frassetto, Gene*	RT	26	219	6.0	Senior	2-V	San Francisco
50	Hileman, Bob*	C	22	205	6.0	Junior	1-V	Montalvo
80	Hirschler, Dave*	LE	23	185	6.1	Senior	3-V	So. Pasadena
44	Houston, Dick*	LH	20	170	5.10	Junior	1-JV	Glendale
85	Humpert, Frank*	LE	22	179	5.11	Junior	2-JC	Napa
36	Jensen, Jack*	F	21	192	5.11	Junior	2-V	Oakland
73	Jones, Len*	RT	27	212	5.9	Junior	1-V	Junction City, KS
42	Keckley, Paul*	LH	24	160	5.9	Senior	2-V	Pomona
68	Klein, Forrest*	LG	21	211	6.0	Junior	2-JV	San Francisco
14	LemMon, Dick	RH	18	198	6.0	Soph	F	Berkeley

*veteran

No	Name	Pos.	Age	Wt.	Ht.	Class	Exp.	Home Town
55	Lenz, Wilbur*	C	22	190	6.1	Senior	1-JV	Stockton
46	Losey, Bob*	LH	23	182	6.0	Junior	2-JV	Berkeley
33	Lotter, Will*	F	23	190	6.0	Senior	2-JV	Alameda
43	Main, Billy*	LH	24	160	5.8	Junior	2-V	Alamo
10	Martin, Pat*	RH	23	189	5.11	Junior	1-JV	Riverside
81	Minahen, Bob	RE	19	195	6.0	Soph	F	Stockton
23	Minahen, Tim*	Q	22	177	6.0	Senior	2-V	Stockton
35	Monachino, Jim	F	19	189	5.10	Soph	F	Redondo Beach
11	Montagne, Billy*	RH	22	180	5.11	Junior	1-V	Forestville
78	Najarian, John	LT	20	237	6.3	Junior	1-V	Oakland
31	Navarro, Rube*	F	23	190	6.0	Junior	1-JV	Santa Barbara
72	Nelson, Lyle	RT	20	202	6.2	Junior	1-JV	Fullerton
77	Orr, Bob*	LG	21	180	5.11	Junior	2-JC	Long Beach
54	Papais, Lou*	C	21	207	6.3	Junior	1-V	Sacramento
63	Poddig, Herb*	RG	25	218	6.2	Senior	2-V	Daly City
82	Pressley, Norm*	RE	22	196	6.0	Junior	1-JV	Salinas
70	Price, Jim*	LT	22	218	6.0	Soph	1-JV	Fresno
41	Sarver, Charles	LH	20	153	5.7	Junior	2-JC	Bakersfield
12	Schabarum, Pete	F	19	180	5.11	Soph	F	Covina
74	Schmalenberger, Herb*	RT	23	209	6.0	Junior	1-JV	Albany
30	Schultz, Eric	C	25	213	6.2	Junior	2-JC	Middletown, CT
37	Solari, Ray	F	20	198	6.0	Soph	1-JC	San Francisco
83	Souza, George*	LE	25	195	6.2	Junior	2-JC	Vallejo
13	Swaner, Jack*	RH	23	198	5.11	Senior	3-V	Coalinga
56	Thayer, Howard*	C	21	180	6.0	Senior	2-JV	Los Angeles
79	Turner, Jim*	LT	23	230	6.4	Senior	2-V	Oakland
86	Van Deren, Frank*	LE	23	195	6.1	Senior	1-V	San Leandro
40	Webster, Staten*	RH	20	176	5.10	Senior	1-JV	San Francisco
62	Zenovich, Duke*	RG	24	202	6.0	Senior	2-JV	Fresno

*veteran

The 1948 Record

SEASONAL RECAP
(California figures listed first)

Opponent	Score	Rushing	Passing	Total
1. Santa Clara	41-19	412-183	118-70	530-253
2. Navy	21-7	312-95	40-142	352-237
3. St. Mary's	20-0	212-82	81-94	293-176
4. Wisconsin	40-14	190-94	181-112	371-206
5. Oregon State	42-0	367-39	169-92	536-131
6. Washington	21-0	280-61	44-0	324-61
7. USC	13-7	258-169	68-138	326-307
8. UCLA	28-13	139-67	35-195	174-262
9. Washington St.	44-14	353-73	147-129	500-202
10. Stanford	7- 6	257-85	55-96	312-181
11. Northwestern	14-20	194-274	83-17	277-29
	291-100	2974-1230	1021-1082	3995-2312

Won 10 -- Lost 1 (Rose Bowl Game)
Attendance: 675,000 in 11 games

The 1948 Record
(cont.)

TEAM STATISTICS
(Including 1949 Rose Bowl)

	Bears	Opps.
Total yardage gained from running plays	**3407**	**1611**
Number of yards lost from running plays	433	381
Net yardage gained from running plays	**2974**	**1230**
Forward passes attempted	170	201
Forward passes completed	64	73
Forward passes had intercepted	25	30
Forward passes incomplete	81	98
Total yardage gained from forward passes	1021	1082
Total yards intercepted passes returned	428	383
Total net yards gained--running and passing	3995	2312
First downs from running plays	136	60
First downs from forward passes	44	39
First downs from penalties	3	4
Total first downs	**183**	**103**
Total number of scrimmage plays	800	700
Number of kickoffs	52	27
Average length of kickoffs	51.60	50.55
Average length of kickoff returns	18.75	19.24
Number of punts	41	69
Total yardage of punts	**1438**	**2487**
Average length of punts	35.07	35.89
Total yardage of punt returns	572	240
Average length of punt returns	12.71	9.60
Number of penalties against	59	37
Yards lost on penalties	432	280
Ball lost on downs	16	19
Total number of fumbles	28	26
Own fumbles recovered	10	11
Ball lost on fumbles	18	15
Touchdowns	42	17

The 1948 Record
(cont.)

INDIVIDUAL STATISTICS

RUSHING

Player	Pos.	TCB	YG	YL	NYG	Aver.
Brunk, Frank	FB	10	50	4	46	4.60
Celeri, Bob	QB	39	250	160	90	2.31
Dal Porto, Bob*	LH	15	54	4	50	3.33
Erb, Charles	QB	1	0	0	0	0.00
Erickson, Dick*	QB	17	39	39	0	0.00
Houston, Dick	RH	1	1	0	1	1.00
Jensen, Jack*	FB	148	1183	103	1080	7.31
Keckley, Paul*	LH	49	195	26	169	3.45
Main, Billy	LH	57	308	23	285	5.00
Minahen, Tim*	QB	4	3	1	2	0.50
Monachino, Jim	LH	11	40	5	35	3.18
Montagne, Bill	RH	8	18	0	18	2.25
Navarro, Rube	FB	4	5	23	-18	-4.5
Sarver, Charles	LH	27	118	10	108	4.00
Schabarum, Pete	FB	9	23	2	21	2.33
Schultz, Eric	FB	1	7	0	7	7.00
Scott, Jerry	RH	1	20	0	20	20.00
Swaner, Jack	RH	137	811	27	784	5.70
Webster, Staten*	RH	49	282	6	276	5.62

PASSING

Player	Pos.	Att.	Comp.	Int.	YG	Pct.	TD's
Celeri, Bob	QB	69	27	9	470	39.1	3
Erb, Charles	QB	4	0	2	0	00.0	0
Erickson, Dick*	QB	52	25	3	311	48.0	0
Jensen, Jack*	FB	28	6	9	150	21.4	1
Minahen, Tim*	QB	8	4	2	47	50.0	1
Monachino, Jim	LH	2	0	0	0	00.0	0
Navarro, Rube	FB	2	1	0	16	50.0	0
Schabarum, Pete	FB	5	1	0	27	20.0	1

*Not returning in 1949

The 1948 Record
(cont.)

INDIVIDUAL SCORING

Player	Pos.	TD's	PAT's Att.	PAT's Made	Total Points
Celeri, Bob	QB	1	0	0	6
Cullom, Jim	LT	1	42	37	43
Cunningham, John	RE	1	0	0	6
Duncan, Doug	C	1	0	0	6
Erickson, Dick*	QB	1	0	0	6
Jensen, Jack*	FB	7	0	0	42
Keckley, Paul*	LH	2	0	0	12
Lotter, Will*	FB	1	0	0	6
Main, Billy	LH	2	0	0	12
Minahen, Bob*	RE	1	0	0	6
Montagne, Bill	RH	2	0	0	12
Pressley, Norm	RE	1	0	0	6
Sarver, Charles	LH	6	0	0	36
Souza, George	LE	1	0	0	6
Swaner, Jack	RH	12	0	0	72
Webster, Staten*	RH	2	0	0	12

PASS RECEPTIONS

Player	Pos.	Caught	No. Yards	Net TD's
Brunk, Frank	FB	1	17	0
Cunningham, John	RE	14	222	1
Dal Porto, Bob*	LH	1	15	0
Hirschler, Dave*	RE	1	13	0
Houston, Dick	RH	1	16	0
Jensen, Jack*	FB	1	23	0
Keckley, Paul*	LH	7	130	0
Main, Billy	LH	4	8	0
Minahen, Bob	RE	1	12	0
Montagne, Billy	RH	1	27	1
Pressley, Norm	RE	6	77	0
Sarver, Charles	LH	5	124	3
Souza, George	LE	8	159	1
Swaner, Jack	RH	1	9	0
Van Deren, Frank*	LE	11	172	0
Webster, Staten*	RH	1	4	0

*Not returning in 1949

PUNTING

Player	Pos.	No. Punts	Total Yardage	Average
Brunk, Frank	FB	2	70	35.0
Celeri, Bob	QB	4	106	26.5
Erickson, Dick*	QB	4	115	28.75
Jensen, Jack*	FB	27	980	36.3
Navarro, Rube	FB	1	47	47.0
Schabarum, Pete	FB	3	124	40.0

BEST OFFENSIVE PLAYERS

	Jack Jensen*	Jack Swaner	Paul Keckley*	Bob Celeri	Billy Main	Charley Sarver
Yards on Rushing	1080	784	169	90	285	108
Yards on Passing	150	0	0	470	0	0
Yards on Passes Caught	23	9	130	0	8	124
Yards on Interceptions	19	0	54	39	0	0
Yards on Punt Returns	32	56	245	0	162	35
Yards on KO Returns	158	96	47	12	67	0
Total Yards	1462	945	645	611	522	267

*Not returning in 1949

FINAL PCC STANDINGS

Team	W	L	T	Pts.	Opp. Pts
California	6	0	0	155	40
Oregon	7	0	0	125	48
USC	4	2	0	94	53
WSC	4	3	1	164	172
OSC	2	3	2	101	125
Stanford	3	4	0	124	69
Washington	2	5	1	89	123
UCLA	2	6	0	129	201
Idaho	1	5	0	92	123
Montana	0	3	0	7	126

The 1948 Record (cont.)

NEW ALL-TIME CALIFORNIA MARKS SET IN 1948

Jack Jensen broke Arleigh Williams' all-time California running record by amassing the huge total of 1703 net yards in his three years on the varsity for an average of 5.80. Williams' previous record set in 1932-33-34 was 1404 net yards for a 2.77 average.

Jensen and Jack Swaner broke the one-year running record held by Vic Bottari who netted 578 yards in 1938. Jensen this year netted 1080 yards while Swaner netted 784 yards.

Jim "Truck" Cullom set a new PCC conference record for number of conversions in one conference season by "toeing" 21 out of 22 attempts through the uprights. The old record was held by Tommy Walker of Southern California with 15. Cullom's season record was 37 out of 42.

The Bears set a new California offensive record this year by collecting 2974 yards rushing and 1021 yards passing for a total of 3995 yards. This broke last year's record of 3625 yards. In 10 regular-season games the Bears ran up 3718 yards.

NATIONAL RANKINGS
(Rose Bowl not included)

Cullom ranked SIXTH in the nation among the point after touchdown kickers.

The Bears placed NINTH in the nation in total offense averaging 372.6 yards per game.

The Bears placed SIXTH in team rushing, averaging 278.8 yards per game.

Jensen ranked THIRD in the nation in rushing with an average of 7.38 for 1010 yards.

Swaner ranked NINETEENTH in the nation in rushing with 705 yards for a 5.86 average.

The Bears ranked NINTH in the nation in rushing defense, allowing only 95.7 yards per game.

The Associated Press poll Monday after the Big Game showed California ranked FOURTH in the nation.

The 1948 Record
(cont.)

PACIFIC COAST CONFERENCE STATISTICAL RANKINGS

TEAM

RUSHING OFFENSE--FIRST with net of 2788 yards, averaging 5.2 for 536 plays and 27.8 per game in 10 games.
PASSING OFFENSE--NINTH with net of 938 yards, off 58 completions in 156 attempts for 37.8 percentage, 938 yards gained, an average of 93.8 per game.
TOTAL OFFENSE--FIRST with net of 3726 yards, averaging 5.4 for 692 plays, and 372.6 per game. Led in first downs with 171.
RUSHING DEFENSE--FIRST, limiting opponents to 957 yards, an average of 95.9 per game and 2.5 yards per play.
PASSING DEFENSE--SIXTH, limiting opponents to 1065 yards, an average of 106.5 per game. Opponents pct. was 38.1, off 77 completions in 202 attempts.
TOTAL DEFENSE--FIRST, limiting opponents to 2022 yards, an average of 202.2 per game and 3.5 per play. Opponents made 97 first downs.
PUNTING--SIXTH, averaging 35.3 yards per kick off, 1306 yards from 37 punts.

INDIVIDUAL

RUSHING--Jensen led PCC with 1010 yards on 137 carries for 7.4 average. Swaner was SECOND with 705 yards on 120 carries for 5.7 average.
PASSING--Celeri was THIRTEENTH with 420 yards on 24 completions in 61 attempts, a percentage of 39.3. Erickson was FOURTEENTH with 278 yards on 22 completions in 46 attempts, a percentage of 47.8
TOTAL OFFENSE--Jensen led PCC with 1060 yards, 1010 from rushing, 150 from passing in 161 plays. Swaner was SIXTH with 705 yards all from rushing. Celeri was THIRTEENTH with 539 yards, 119 from rushing, 420 from passing in 97 plays.
PASS RECEPTION--Cunningham was ELEVENTH with 13 caught for 208 yards. Van Deren was TWENTY-SECOND with 10 for 156 yards, and Souza was THIRTY-FIRST with 8 caught for 159 yards.
PUNTING--Jensen was SIXTH, punting 24 times for 889 yards, an average of 37.0
PLACE-KICKING--Jim Cullom led PCC with 35 kicks after touchdown in 40 attempts, a percentage of 87.5
PASS INTERCEPTION--Paul Keckley led PCC by intercepting 7 for 54 yards.
SCORING--Swaner led PCC with 66 points on 11 TD's Cullom was FOURTH with 41 points on one TD and 35 placements, with Jensen and Sarver tied for FIFTH with 36 points on six touchdowns.

The 1949 Team

No	Name	Pos.	Age	Wt.	Ht.	Class	Exp.	Home Town
55	Bagley, Bob	C	21	214	6.1	Soph	1-JC	Oakland
34	Baldwin, Paul	LH	22	178	5.10	Junior	2-JC	Bakersfield
84	Bartlett, Ed	L-RE	21	195	6.1	Soph	Fr	Berkeley
87	Begovich, Dan	LE	23	192	6.1	Senior	1-V	San Francisco
21	Brown, Don	Q	23	174	5.11	Senior	1-V	Stockton
40	Brunk, Frank	LH	22	177	5.11	Senior	2-V	Willows
37	Cadenasso, John	F	20	191	6.0	Soph	HS	Oakland
22	Celeri, Bob	Q	21	173	5.10	Senior	3-V	Fort Bragg
77	Cullom, Jim	LT	23	230	5.11	Senior	2-V	Piedmont
80	Cummings, Bob	RE	23	183	6.2	Junior	1-JV	Oakland
66	DeJong, Ray	LG	23	198	5.10	Senior	2-V	Enumclaw, WA
65	Dodds, Bobby	RG	23	198	5.11	Senior	2-V	San Francisco
63	Edmonston, Don	RG	18	210	5.11	Soph	Fr	Sacramento
25	Erb, Charles	Q	22	178	5.9	Senior	1-V	Winters
67	Franz, Rod	RG	24	196	6.1	Senior	3-V	San Francisco
61	Fox, Charley	RG	24	214	6.1	Senior	1-JV	Concord
52	Groger, Dick	C	18	202	6.1	Soph	Fr	San Francisco
54	Harris, Charles	C	18	200	6.1	Soph	Fr	Pomona
10	Hibbs, Joe	RH	18	176	6.0	Soph	Fr	West Covina
51	Humpert, Frank	F	23	195	6.0	Junior	1-JV	Napa
73	Jones, Len	RT	27	218	5.9	Senior	2-V	Junction City, KS
68	Klein, Forrest	LG	22	210	6.0	Senior	1-V	San Francisco
38	Laster, Wally	F	24	196	6.0	Junior	2-JC	San Anselmo
89	LemMon, Dick	LE	19	191	6.1	Junior	1-JV	Berkeley
23	Marinos, Jim	Q	19	175	5.11	Junior	1-JV	San Diego
24	Markey, Chris	Q	19	164	5.11	Junior	1-V	Whittier

No	Name	Pos.	Age	Wt.	Ht.	Class	Exp.	Home Town
81	Minahen, Bob	RE	20	197	6.2	Junior	1-V	Stockton
35	Monachino, Jim	L-RH-F	19	187	5.10	Junior	1-V	Redondo Beach
11	Montagne, Bill	RH	22	180	5.11	Senior	2-V	Piedmont
75	Muehlberger, Roy	LT	21	210	6.2	Senior	2-JV	Hollywood
31	Navarro, Rube	F	24	195	6.0	Senior	2-JV	Santa Barbara
72	Nelson, Lyle	RT	20	190	6.2	Senior	2-JV	Fullerton
88	Norgren, Roger	LE	20	180	6.2	Soph	1-JC	Redondo Beach
20	Ogden, Brent	Q	19	165	5.10	Soph	Fr	So. Pasadena
42	Pappa, John	LH	19	171	5.10	Soph	1-JC	Sacramento
82	Pressley, Norm	RE	22	196	6.0	Senior	1-V	Salinas
70	Price, Jim	LT	22	206	6.0	Junior	1-JV	Fresno
50	Richter, Les	C	18	210	6.2	Soph	Fr	Fresno
33	Robison, Don	F	18	193	6.0	Soph	Fr	Martinez
71	Rush, Bill	LT	22	220	6.5	Junior	2-JC	Santa Rosa
41	Sarver, Charles	LH	20	152	5.7	Senior	1-V	Bakersfield
32	Schabarum, Pete	F	20	181	5.11	Junior	1-V	Covina
74	Schmalenberger, Herb	RT	24	198	6.0	Senior	1-V	Albany
30	Schultz, Eric	F	25	195	6.2	Senior	1-V	Middletown, CT
12	Scott, Jerry	RH	21	185	6.0	Senior	1-JV	Long Beach
69	Solari, Ray	LG	21	198	6.0	Junior	1-JV	San Francisco
83	Souza, George	LE	25	190	6.2	Senior	1-V	Vallejo
53	Stathakis, George	C	19	198	5.11	Soph	HS	Vallejo
85	Stern, Glenn	RE	24	185	6.0	Junior	1-JV	San Francisco
13	Swaner, Jack	RH	24	190	5.11	Senior	3-V	Coalinga
79	Turner, Jim	RT	24	234	6.4	Senior	3-V	Oakland
45	Van Heuit, Carl	LH	21	170	5.8	Junior	1-JV	Berkeley
86	Ward, Roy	LE	19	170	5.10	Junior	1-JV	Newport Beach
76	Witter, Bob	RT	19	201	6.2	Junior	Fr	Sacramento

The 1949 Record

SEASONAL RECAP
(California figures listed first)

	Opponent	Score	Rushing	Passing	Total
1.	Santa Clara	21-7	227-134	132-20	359-154
2.	St. Mary's	29-7	198-118	121-56	319-174
3.	Oregon State	41-0	304-101	205-95	509-196
4.	Wisconsin	35-20	247-142	126-103	373-245
5.	USC	16-10	196-105	50-136	246-241
6.	Washington	21-7	277-158	140-93	417-251
7.	UCLA	35-21	193-181	230-151	423-332
8.	Washington St.	33-14	284-166	99-107	383-273
9.	Oregon	41-14	134-159	85-72	219-231
10.	Stanford	33-14	390-167	70-189	460-356
11.	Ohio State	14-17	133-221	106-34	239-255
		319-131	2583-1652	1364-1056	3947-2708

Won 10 -- Lost 1 (Rose Bowl Game)
Attendance: 656,963 (third straight year over the 600,000 figure)

The 1949 Record
(cont.)

TEAM STATISTICS
(Including 1950 Rose Bowl)

	Bears	Opps.
Number of rushing plays	558	522
Yards gained, rushing	3017	2016
Yards lost, rushing	434	364
Net yards gained, rushing	**2583**	**1652**
Passes attempted	163	220
Passes completed	65	95
Passes had intercepted	19	22
Yards returned intercepted passes	257	328
Total yards gained, passing	**1364**	**1056**
Number of rushing, pass plays	721	742
Total yards gained, passing and rushing	**3947**	**2708**
First downs, rushing	124	96
First downs, passing	35	48
First downs, penalties	2	0
Total first downs	**161**	**148**
Number of kickoffs	58	32
Average length, kickoffs	49.2	48.1
Average length, kickoff returns	20.9	18.9
Number of punts	59	68
Total yards	**2140**	**2542**
Average length, punts	36.27	37.38
Yardage, punt returns	541	464
Average yards, punt returns	12.5	13.6
Number of penalties against	72	62
Yards lost, penalties	511	483
Total number of fumbles	38	40
Own fumbles recovered	16	23
Touchdowns	46	18
Total points	**319**	**131**

The 1949 Record (cont.)

INDIVIDUAL STATISTICS

RUSHING

Player	Pos.	TCB	YG	YL	NYG	Aver.
Brown, Don*	QB	1	0	0	0	0.0
Brunk, Frank*	LH	91	438	38	400	4.39
Celeri, Bob*	QB	61	336	204	132	2.16
Erb, Charles*	QB	12	36	38	-2	-.17
Monachino, Jim	RH	138	821	40	781	5.66
Montagne, Bill*	LH	7	26	4	22	3.14
Navarro, Rube*	FB	10	10	27	-17	-1.7
Ogden, Brent	QB	1	0	6	-6	-6.0
Pappa, John	LH	16	54	14	40	2.49
Robison, Don	FB	29	191	1	190	6.55
Sarver, Charles*	LH	32	328	11	317	9.90
Schabarum, Pete	FB	94	458	38	420	4.46
Scott, Jerry*	RH	45	202	13	189	4.20
Swaner, Jack*	RH	21	117	0	117	5.57

PASSING

Player	Pos.	Att.	Comp.	Int.	YG	Pct.	TD's
Celeri, Bob*	QB	117	48	12	1081	41	9
Erb, Charles*	QB	41	16	5	253	39	3
Ogden, Brent	QB	1	0	1	0	–	0
Sarver, Charles*	LH	1	1	0	30	100	1
Schabarum, Pete	FB	3	0	1	0	–	0

*Not returning in 1950

The 1949 Record
(cont.)

INDIVIDUAL SCORING

Player	Pos.	TD's	PAT's Att.	PAT's Made	Total Points
Baldwin, Paul*	LH	1	0	0	6
Begovich, Dan*	LE	3	0	0	18
Brunk, Frank*	LH	4	0	0	24
Celeri, Bob*	QB	3	0	0	18
Cullom, Jim*	LT	0	46	39	39
Erb, Charles*	QB	2	0	0	12
Minahen, Bob	RE	1	0	0	6
Monachino, Jim	RH	15	0	0	90
Montagne, Bill*	LH	1	0	0	6
Norgren, Roger*	RE	1	0	0	6
Robison, Don	FB	1	0	0	6
Sarver, Charles	LH	6	0	0	36
Schabarum, Pete	FB	2	0	0	12
Schultz, Eric*	FB	1	0	0	6
Scott, Jerry*	RH	2	0	0	12
Swaner, Jack*	RH	3	0	0	18

PASS RECEPTIONS

Player	Pos.	No. Caught	Net Yards	TD's
Begovich, Dan*	LE	14	273	3
Brunk, Frank*	LH	10	348	2
Cummings, Bob	RE	2	44	0
Minahen, Bob	RE	5	61	1
Monachino, Jim	RH	8	190	3
Montagne, Bill*	LH	1	19	0
Norgren, Roger*	RE	3	35	1
Pappa, John	LH	2	22	0
Pressley, Norm*	RE	2	19	0
Robison, Don	FB	2	15	0
Sarver, Charles*	LH	6	174	2
Schabarum, Pete	FB	5	85	1
Scott, Jerry*	RH	2	17	0
Ward, Roy	LE	3	62	0

*Not returning in 1950

The 1949 Record (cont.)

PUNTING

Player	Pos.	No. Punts	Total Yardage	Average
Brunk, Frank*	LH	7	223	31.9
Celeri, Bob*	QB	33	1140	34.5
Navarro, Rube*	FB	5	191	38.2
Robison, Don	FB	9	392	43.6
Sarver, Charles*	LH	1	26	26.0
Schabarum, Pete	FB	4	168	42.0

LEADING OFFENSIVE PLAYERS

	Bob Celeri*	Jim Monachino	Pete Schabarum	Frank Brunk*	Charley Sarver*	Don Robison
Yards on Rushing	132	781	420	400	317	190
Average per carry	2.16	5.66	4.46	4.39	9.90	6.55
Yards Passing	1081	0	0	0	30	0
Yards on Passes Caught	0	190	85	348	174	15
Points scored	18	90	12	24	36	6
Number of Punts	33	0	4	7	1	9
Average Punts	34.5	0	42	31.9	26	43.6
Yards on Punt Returns	0	46	6	48	22	19
Yards on KO Returns	18	81	145	295	49	0
Total Plays	178	138	97	91	33	29
Total Yards	1231	1098	656	1091	592	224

*Not returning in 1950

FINAL PCC STANDINGS

Team	W	L	T	Pts.	Opp. Pts
California	7	0	0	220	80
UCLA	5	2	0	186	149
Stanford	4	2	0	185	67
USC	4	2	0	159	105
OSC	5	3	0	180	161
Oregon	2	5	0	153	164
Washington	2	5	0	126	203
WSC	2	6	0	116	205
Idaho	1	4	0	85	193
Montana	0	3	0	40	123

The 1949 Record
(cont.)

NEW ALL-TIME CALIFORNIA MARKS SET IN 1949

Individual--Single Game

Most Yards Passing: 214 in UCLA game, Bob Celeri.
Most Yards, Total Offense: 225 in UCLA game, Bob Celeri.
Most Pass Completions: 12 in UCLA game, Bob Celeri.

Individual--Single Season

Most Yards Gained Net from Passing: 1081, Bob Celeri
Most Pass Completions: 45, Bob Celeri.
Most Consecutive PAT's, 19, Jim Cullom.

Three Year Career Records

Most Yards Gained Net from Passing, 2186, Bob Celeri, 1947-48-49.
Most Yards Gained, Total Offense: 2423, Bob Celeri, 1947-48-49.
Most Consecutive Games Scored In: 25, Jim "Truck" Cullom, 1947-48-49.
Most Number of Conversions: 103, Jim "Truck" Cullom, 1947-48-49.

Single Game Records--Team

Most Yards Gained Passing: 230 in UCLA game.

Single Season Records--Team

Most Yards Gained Passing. 1064 yards
Highest Average Gain Per Play: 5.48 yards.
Most Pass Completions: 64.

Miscellaneous Team Records

Most Consecutive Games Scored In: extended by 1949 team to 34 games, includes 8th game (Oregon State) of 1946 through 11th and last (Ohio State) game of 1949.
Largest Crowd to Witness a Single Game: 100,963 (1950 Rose Bowl).

1949 NATIONAL RANKINGS
(Rose Bowl not included)

Brunk ranked TWENTY-THIRD in the nation in kickoff returns with a 32.8 yard average and 295 yards.
The Bears ranked NINTH in the nation on kickoff returns, averaging 22.6 yards per return and garnering a total of 588 yards.
Monachino ranked THIRTY-SECOND among the rushing leaders with 694 yards, a 5.55 yard per carry average.
The Bears ranked FIFTEENTH in rushing offense, averaging 245 yards per game.
The Bears ranked FOURTEENTH in total offense averaging 370.8 yards per game.
Celeri ranked TWENTY-THIRD among individual players in total offense with 1135 yards, 975 passing and 160 rushing.
The Bears ranked TWENTY-EIGHTH in the nation in total defense, allowing an average of 245 yards per game.
The Associated Press poll Monday after the Big Game showed California ranked THIRD in the nation.

The 1949 Record
(cont.)

PACIFIC COAST CONFERENCE STATISTICAL RANKINGS

TEAM

RUSHING OFFENSE--THIRD with net of 2450 yards, averaging 245 yards per game and 4.73 yards per play for 518 plays.
PASSING OFFENSE--SIXTH in the conference on the basis of 1258 yards gained on 62 completed passes for an average of 125.8 yards per game, 20.3 yards gained for each completed pass and a completion record of 41 per cent.
TOTAL OFFENSE--SECOND with 3708 yards, 2450 rushing and 1258 passing, for a 370.8 yard per game average and a 5.55 yard per play average for 688 plays.
RUSHING DEFENSE--California was FIRST in this department, limiting the opponents to a total of 1428 yards gained on rushing, an average of 142.8 yards per game given up, 3.1 yards per play.
PASSING DEFENSE--FOURTH, having allowed 1022 net yards by passing, a 102.2 yard per game average and a 4.9 yard gain per total passes atempted average.
TOTAL DEFENSE--FIRST, allowing a total of 2450 yards to the opponents, a total identical to the net rushing offense mark posted by the Bears. The average gain per play for the opponents was 3.7 yards per play, including passes completed only, for 661 plays.
PUNTING--FOURTH, with a total of 2005 yards on 53 punts for a 37.8 yard per punt average. One punt was blocked in regular season play.

INDIVIDUAL

RUSHING--Monachino was THIRD in the PCC with 694 yards gained, on 105 plays for a 6.6 yard per carry average. Schabarum was THIRTEENTH with 393 yards and a 4.5 average. Brunk was EIGHTEENTH with 361 yards, a 5.1 yards per carry average.
PASSING--Celeri was EIGHTH in the PCC in passing with 45 completions out of 106 attempts for 975 yards, nine TD's and a 42 per cent completion mark.
TOTAL OFFENSE--Celeri was SECOND with a total of 1135 yards, 975 passing and 160 rushing in 159 plays. Monachino was TENTH with 694 yards, all from rushing. Schabarum was TWENTY-SIXTH with 393 rushing yards, and Brunk was TWENTY-EIGHTH with 361 rushing yards.
PASS RECEPTION--Begovich, the top Bear receiver, was NINETEENTH in the PCC. He received 13 passes for 258 yards and three touchdowns.
PUNTING--Celeri was SEVENTH with 1002 yards on 27 kicks and a 37.1 average. Robison and Schabarum placed SECOND and THIRD among those with less than 20 punts during the season.
PASS INTERCEPTION--Van Heuit ranked FOURTH in interceptions with five. He returned for a total of 35 yards. Klein was NINTH with four interceptions and 66 yards returned. Montagne also had four and was ranked ELEVENTH on the basis of his 42 yards returned.

The 1949 Record
(cont.)

PAT's--Cullom again placed FIRST in the conference, converting 37 out of 44 during the regular season. Set a new PCC mark, kicking 26 of 32. His toe was good for an .841 percentage mark.
SCORING--Monachino placed FIRST in the conference, duplicating the performance of Jack Swaner in 1948. Monachino scored 13 touchdowns for 78 points during the regular season. (He boosted his total to 90 with two TD's against Ohio State in the Rose Bowl.)

The 1950 Team

No	Name	Pos.	Age	Wt.	Ht.	Class	Exp.	Home Town
87	Andrew, Paul	LE	21	190	6.0	Soph	Fr	San Francisco
77	Bagley, Bob	RG	23	210	6.1	Junior	1-JV	Oakland
14	Baham, Bob	RH	23	185	5.10	Junior	1-JV	Vallejo
84	Bartlett, Ed	LE	22	195	6.1	Junior	1 V	Berkeley
82	Beal, Bob	RE	20	200	6.3	Soph	Fr	Los Angeles
13	Cadenasso, John	F	22	192	5.11	Junior	1-JV	Oakland
80	Cummings, Bob	RE	24	201	6.2	Senior	1-V	Oakland
74	Cunningham, Bill	LT	23	215	6.2	Soph	1-Col	Vallejo
71	Curran, Don	RT	19	220	6.2	Soph	Fr	Berkeley
55	Ely, Dwight	RG	18	210	6.2	Soph	Fr	San Anselmo
85	Firzgerald, Bob	LE	21	210	6.2	Senior	2-JV	Concord
26	Forbes, Bob	RH	20	170	6.0	Junior	2-JC	San Bernardino
25	Greenleaf, Tom	QB	19	170	5.11	Soph	Fr	Berkeley
52	Groger, Dick	C	20	200	6.1	Junior	1-V	San Francisco
76	Gulvin, Glenn	LT	19	205	6.4	Soph	Fr	Long Beach
50	Hahn, Leighton	C	19	200	6.2	Soph	Fr	Vallejo
54	Harris, Charles	C	19	200	6.1	Junior	1-V	Pomona
66	Hart, Edward	RG	21	185	5.10	Senior	2-JV	Oakland
83	Heltne, Bruce	RE	20	200	6.2	Junior	1-JV	Berkeley
72	Karpe, Bob	LT	19	226	6.2	Junior	Fr	Covina
10	Hibbs, Joe	RH	19	180	6.0	Junior	Fr	Bakersfield
47	Keough, Tom	LH	18	155	5.10	Soph	Fr	Pomona
56	King, Gordon	C	19	175	5.10	Soph	Fr	San Diego
73	Krueger, Ralph	RT	20	220	6.3	Soph	Fr	Oakland
65	Laster, Wally	RG	25	205	6.0	Senior	1-V	San Anselmo
21	Lee, Dick	Q	20	178	6.1	Soph	Fr	Oakland
89	LemMon, Dick	FB	20	195	6.1	Senior	1-V	Berkeley
61	Maiorana, Vincent	G	19	201	5.9	Soph	1-JC	Monterey

No	Name	Pos.	Age	Wt.	Ht.	Class	Exp.	Home Town
22	Mais, Bill	Q	19	175	5.10	Soph	Fr	Long Beach
23	Marinos, Jim	Q	20	185	5.11	Senior	2-JV	San Diego
24	Markey, Chris	Q	20	170	5.11	Senior	2-JV	Whittier
62	Mering, Pete	LG	19	210	6.0	Junior	1-JV	Sacramento
75	Miksits, John	G	22	240	6.0	Junior	1-JV	Copley, PA
81	Minahen, Bob	RE	21	195	6.2	Senior	2-V	Stockton
35	Monachino, Jim	LH	21	185	5.10	Senior	2-V	Redondo Beach
41	Nysteun, John	LH	19	170	5.10	Junior	1-JV	Oroville
20	Ogden, Brent	Q	21	175	5.10	Junior	1-JV	So, Pasadena
36	Olszewski, John	F	20	185	5.11	Soph	Fr	Long Beach
42	Pappa, John	LH	20	180	5.10	Junior	1-V	Sacramento
11	Parker, Roy	F	24	180	5.10	Senior	2-JV	Pacific Grove
44	Peterson, John	LH	20	183	5.9	Soph	Fr	Long Beach
46	Phillips, Lukie	LH	22	160	5.7	Senior	1-JV	Monterey
31	Powell, Bill	F	23	180	6.0	Junior	1-JV	Sanger
32	Ralston, John	FB	23	187	5.10	Senior	2-JV	Norway, MI
67	Richter, Les	RG	19	225	6.3	Junior	1-V	Fresno
79	Rieger, Tom	RT	20	220	6.2	Soph	Fr	Berkeley
33	Robison, Don	F	20	190	6.0	Junior	1-V	Martinez
70	Rush, Bill	LT	24	218	6.4	Senior	1-JV	Forestville
12	Schabarum, Pete	RH	21	187	5.11	Senior	2-V	Covina
69	Solari, Ray	LG	22	205	6.0	Senior	1-V	San Francisco
88	Stern, Glenn	LE	25	190	6.0	Senior	2-JV	San Francisco
45	Van Heuit, Carl	LH	23	161	5.8	Senior	1-V	Berkeley
86	Ward, Roy	LE	21	175	5.10	Senior	1-V	Newport Beach
68	Wardlaw, Joe	RG	23	195	5.11	Senior	2-JC	Vallejo
15	West, Harry	RH	21	173	5.8	Junior	2-JC	San Diego
64	Witter, George	LG	20	185	5.10	Junior	1-JV	San Marino

The 1950 Record

	Opponent	Score	Rushing	Passing	Total
1.	Santa Clara	27-9	311-226	99-164	410-390
2.	Oregon	28-7	257-199	77-51	334-250
3.	Pennsylvania	14-7	335-64	21-47	356-111
4.	USC	13-7	214-114	24-83	238-197
5.	Oregon State	27-0	267-101	48-122	313-223
6.	St. Mary's	40-25	292-180	167-159	459-339
7.	Washington	14-7	189-115	81-125	270-240
8.	UCLA	35-0	321-39	68-73	389-112
9.	USF	13-7	163-80	12-23	175-103
10.	Stanford	7-7	243-55	49-217	292-272
11.	Michigan	6-14	175-145	69-146	244-291
		224-90	2767-1318	715-1210	3482-2528

Won 9, Tied 1, Lost 1 (Rose Bowl Game)
Attendance: 611,607 (fourth straight year over the 600,000 figure)

The 1950 Record
(cont.)

TEAM STATISTICS
(Including 1951 Rose Bowl)

	Bears	Opps.
Number of rushing plays	592	422
Yards gained, rushing	3040	1595
Yards lost, rushing	275	277
Net yards gained, rushing	**2765**	**1318**
Forward passes attempted	108	202
Forward passes completed	48	105
Passes had intercepted	11	18
Yards returned intercepted passes	318	121
Net yards gained, passing	**715**	**1210**
Number of plays, rushing and passing	721	742
Total yards gained, rushing and passing	**3482**	**2528**
First downs, rushing	128	67
First downs, passing	29	52
First downs, penalties	5	3
Total first downs	**162**	**122**
Number of kickoff returns	22	44
Total yards kickoff returns	351	881
Number of punts	52	67
Total yardage of punts	**1767**	**2532**
Average length, punts	34.0	37.7
Number of punt returns	45	21
Average length of punt returns	8.5	8.5
Number of penalties	78	58
Total yards penalized	290	362
Total number of fumbles	41	33
Total fumbles lost	21	15
Number of touchdowns	33	13
Conversions attempted	33	13
Points after touchdown	26	10
Safeties	0	1
Total points	**224**	**90**

The 1950 Record
(cont.)

INDIVIDUAL STATISTICS

RUSHING

Player	TCB	YG	YL	NYG	Aver.
Olszewski, John	167	1047	39	1008	6.03
Monachino, Jim*	153	773	19	754	4.93
Schabarum, Pete*	141	667	20	647	4.59
Pappa, John	24	186	8	178	7.41
Robison, Don	12	105	2	103	8.58
West, Harry	11	52	0	52	4.73
Cadenasso, John	8	39	2	37	4.62
Lee, Dick	10	46	18	28	2.80
Hibbs, Joe	4	18	0	18	4.50
Nystuen, John	3	11	0	11	3.67
Philips, Lukie*	6	12	5	7	1.16
Minahen, Bob*	1	5	0	5	5.00
LemMon, Dick	2	5	0	5	2.50
Keough, Tom	2	3	0	3	1.50
Cummings, Bob*	1	2	0	2	2.00
Ogden, Brent	7	14	24	-10	-1.42
Mais, Bill	2	0	7	-7	-3.50
Marinos, Jim*	36	41	126	-85	-2.36

PASSING

Player	Att.	Comp.	Int.	Pct.	Yards
Marinos, Jim*	49	28	3	.571	298
Ogden, Brent	25	9	4	.360	134
Mais, Bill	13	8	2	.616	128
Lee, Dick	15	3	1	.200	70
Schabarum, Pete*	4	0	1	.000	–
Markey, Chris*	2	0	0	.000	–

INDIVIDUAL SCORING

Player	TD's	PAT Att.	PAT Made	Points
*Schabarum, Pete	11	0	0	66
*Monachino, Jim	6	2	2	38
Olszewski, John	6	0	0	36
Pappa, John	4	0	0	24

*Not returning in 1951

PAPPY'S BOYS
1947 THROUGH 1956

Ackerman, Dave
Adams, Jed
Adams, Sam
Agier, Harry
Agliano, Ag
Agorastos, Manny
Alfano, Jim
Anderson, Bob
Anderson, George
Anderson, Jack
Anderson, John
Andrew, Paul
Arata, Ray
Archibald, Norman
Arnold, Carl
Artero, Pete
Atkinson, Bob
Atkinson, Dick
Autenrieb, Jack
Babros, Joe
Bacigalupi, Andy
Bagley, Bob
Baham, Bob
Baker, Jon
Baldwin, Paul
Baranco, Vic
Barker, Dwight
Bartlett, Ed
Baxter, Jim
Beal, Bob
Beale, Pax
Beaver, Jim
Becker, Norm
Beeson, Bill
Begovich, Dan
Belenis, Bill
Bender, Allen
Bergron, Willard
Bernhardt, Paul
Bianchi, Dwight
Binkley, John
Blake, Wilson
Blanchard, Jim
Bohlke, Russ
Boone, Dan
Boone, Stan
Bordonaro, Sebastian
Borghi, Hank
Bradhoff, Lloyd
Brandt, Ed
Brazill, Nat
Brewer, Pete
Briggs, Asa
Broadbent, Don
Brooks, Bob
Brooks, Jere
Brown, Barry
Brown, Clark
Brown, Don
Browne, Mike
Brunk, Don
Brunk, Frank
Buffington, Lee
Burns, Ross
Bush, Hal
Bynum, Gene
Cadenasso, John
Calendar, Dick
Campbell, Tru
Caraballo, Hector
Carian, Harry
Carlson, Dick
Carlson, Dwight
Carmichael, Jim
Casey, Mike
Celeri, Bob
Chambers, Roland
Chan, Albert
Cherry, Eugene
Cherry, Jim
Chiappone, Bob
Clarke, Bob
Clark, Dick
Clark, Jim
Clarke, Hank
Cochran, John
Contestabile, Joe
Cooper, Bill
Cooper, Dan
Copeland, Joel
Corey, Bill
Coste, Lionel
Cox, Don
Crandall, David
Cranmer Jr., Lee
Crebbin, Pete
Cullom, Jim
Cummings, Bob
Cunningham, Bill
Cunningham, John
Curran, Don
Currie, Bob
Currie, Ron
Dahlgren, Charles
Dahlin, Ron
Dal Porto, Bob
Dal Porto, Don
Darracq, Dal
Davis, Charles
Davis, Frank
Dawson, John
Dawson, Wayne
Day, Dick
DeBell, Bill
DeJong, Ray
Deloney, Thurman
Denton, Don
Dillon, Jim
Dimeff, Steve
Dodds, Robert
Domoto, Pete
Donnelly, Ray
Doretti, Frank
Dossa, Al
Drew, Jerry
Duff, Jim
Duffle, Fred
Dumke, Dick
Duncan, Doug
Dunlap, Al
Dutton, Bill
Dutton, Tom
Edmonston, Don
Edwards, Art
Elliott, John
Ellis, Hal
Elworthy, John
Ely, Dwight
Engle, Wayne
Erb, Charles
Erdelatz, John
Erickson, Dick
Erickson, Jerry
Escano, John

Fackrell, Carlos
Fandl, Hal
Faulkner, Jim
Fay, Harold
Feuerstein, Don
Fink, Don
Finn, Gordon
Fiorina, Marvin
Fites, Larry
Fitzpatrick, Jim
Fletcher, Ed
Fong, George
Forbes, Art
Forni, Jay
Fortune, Dick
Fournier, Joe
Fox, Charley
Fox, Gerald
Franklin, Oran
Franz, Rod
Fraser, Tom
Frasetto, Gene
Frentzen, Joe
Frey, Ed
Fristoe, Ken
Fuller, Kenneth
Galbraith, Huxley
Gallagher, John
Garlinger, Howard
Garroli, John
Garthwaite, Jed
Garzoli, John
Gelardi, Pat
Ghilarducci, Henry
Gianulias, Gus
Gibbs, George
Giddings, Mike
Giers, Paul
Gilkey, Charles
Gilkey, Don
Gillespie, Gerald
Gillespie, George
Giudice, Hank
Glagola, Steve
Glick, Mike
Glick, Steve
Godfrey, Pearce
Gonsalves, Ronald
Gonzales, Bob
Goodrich, Russ
Gordon, Doug
Gosling, George
Gottlieb, Gary
Gove, Jim
Granger, Ted
Graves, Clark
Graves, John
Gray, Richard
Greenleaf, Tom
Greife, John
Greub, Ed
Groefsema, Kenneth
Groger, Dick
Groudine, Harvey
Gulvin, Glenn
Gurvitz, Howard
Hagen, Ken
Heggerty, Gene
Hahn, Leighton
Halajian, Harry
Hale, Max
Hallinan, Kayo
Hanifan, Jim
Harkness, Don
Harper Jr., Dave
Harris, Charles
Harris, Don
Harris, Ozzie
Harrison, Fred
Hart, Ed
Hart, Jack
Hartman, Dick
Hatzis, George
Hazdovac, Nick
Hazeltine, Matt
Heltne, Bruce
Henderson, Thelton
Hendrix, Fred
Henze, Tom
Herring, John
Herrling, Bob
Hibbs, Doug
Hibbs, Joe
Hildebrand, Noel
Hileman, Robert
Hillebrand, Bill
Hinton, Jerry
Hirschler, Dave
Hodge, Fred
Hoffelt, Merrill
Hoffman, Ralph
Holsten, Don
Hofstetter, Bill
Holl, Ed
Holston, Charles
Homuth, Dick
Honea, Milt
Hood, Dave
Hoppe, Hal
Hops, Al
Hotle, Joe
Houston, Dick
Howard, Don
Hubbard, Ron
Huber, Allan
Huber Jr., Skip
Hudson, Dave
Hughes, Mike
Humpert, Frank
Hyin, Dmitri
Iaukea, Curtis
Innis, Joe
Irvine, Ed
Irwin, George
Jackson, Herb
Jackson, Jim
Jacobes, Roy
Jacobs, Proverb
Jacobsen, Dick
Jacuzzi, Remo
Janopaul, Dick
Jarvis, Bob
Jensen, Jack
Jiu, James
Jobe, Gordon
Johnson, Charlie
Johnson, Dick
Johnson, Don
Jones, Leonard
Jones, Robert
Jordan, Zack
Kalamaras, John
Kapp, Joe
Karpe, Bob
Katsura, Yosh
Kavanagh, Dennis
Keckley, Paul
Kehoe, Larry
Kenfield, Ted
Kenyon, Clark
Keough, Tom
Kern, Dick
Kidder, Jim
Killeen, Bill
Kincade, Don
King, Dick

King, Gordon
Kitchin, Bill
Klehn, Henry
Klein, Forrest
Kniptash, Bob
Knutson, Dave
Knutson, Walt
Kolte, Dick
Kotler, Jim
Kramer, Tom
Krueger, Ralph
Kuhl, Chuck
Lacey, Marv
Lacey, Tom
Lackey, Jim
Lagana, Larry
Lageson, Ernie
Laird, Ray
Lamke, Jack
Langan Jr., Bill
Larson, Paul
LaRue, Jene
Laster, George
Laster, Wally
Lawyer, Dick
Lee, Dick
LemMon, Dick
Lenz, Wilbur
Linck, Donald
Logan, Bob
Lom, Bob
Long, Dave
Lorenz, Jim
Losey, Robert
Lotter, Will
Lutz, Dick
MacBeath, Bill
Machado, Charles
Maguire, Hugh
Main, Bill
Main, Tim
Maiorana, Vince
Mais, Bill
Manolis, Gus
Maples, Roland
Marinos, Jim
Markey, Chris
Marks, Don
Marra Augie
Martin Jr., Charles
Martin, Gerald
Martin, Harley
Martin, Pat
Martin, Sennie
Martin Jr., Tevis
Martucci, Charles
Mascarin, Ed
Math, John
Mathews, Art
Mathews, Don
Mathews, Ted
Mattarocci, Frank
Mayberry, Doug
Mayer, Gene
McCandlish, Bill
McDermon, Chuck
McDonald, Bruce
McFarlane, Jim
McGrath Jr., Tom
McKee, Stuart
McKnight, Paul
McLaughlin, Tom
McLean, Fred
McManigal, Ken
Melbye, Dick
Mering, Pete
Merlo, Frank
Merrill, Edward
Meserve, Keith
Michael, John
Michelsen, Ed
Mickens, Ed
Miksits, John
Miller, Bud
Miller, Dick
Mills, Dave
Minahen, Bob
Minahen, Tim
Mitchell, Don
Moldenschardt, Bill
Monachino, Jim
Montagne, Bill
Morris, Delton
Morton, Jim
Muehlberger, Roy
Muir, Jim
Murray, Eric
Myers, Ken
Najarian, George
Najarian, John
Nankeville, Bill
Navarro, Rube
Nelson, Gene
Nelson, Gil
Nelson, James
Nelson, Lyle
Nelson, Vic
Newell, George
Newell, Minton
Nicholson, Andy
Nicolson, Murdo
Nordland, Bill
Norgren, Roger
Norris, Hal
Nystuen, John
Obler, Bruce
Obradovich, John
O'Brien, Joe
Obuhoff, Olie
Ogden, Brent
O'Hare, Dean
Oliva, Joe
Oliver, Bob
Olson, Gary
Olszewski, John
Orr, Bob
Osorio, Richard
Paige, Dick
Pallas, Christom
Panttaja, Bill
Papac, Nick
Papais, Lou
Pappa, John
Parker, Dick
Parker, Roy
Parkin, Bob
Patton, Bill
Paul, Lowell
Paynter, Dick
Paynter, Tom
Pearson, Howard
Pelonis, George
Perrin, Tony
Perry, Gerald
Peterson, John
Phelan, Mike
Phillips, Bo
Phillips, Don
Phillips, Lukie
Pieper, Harry
Peistrup, Don
Pihl, Don
Piunti, Ernie
Pland, Dick
Poddig, Herb
Popin, Jim

Poppin, Nick
Powell, Bill
Pressley, Norm
Price, Jim
Prindiville, Terry
Pringle, Don
Radcliffe, Gary
Ragatz, Dexter
Ralston, John
Ramseier, Roger
Ramsey, Robert
Range, Don
Richardson, Roy
Richter, Les
Rieger, Tom
Rigby, Dick
Riggs, Manford
Roberts, Darrell
Robison, Don
Rocker, Gene
Rodgers, Don
Rogers, Jim
Rogers, Tom
Roush, Ken
Rush, Bill
Russell, Renny
Sarver, Charles
Savage, Mike
Schabarum, Pete
Schmalenberger, Herb
Schmeiser, Alan
Schultz, Eric
Schwocho, Ken
Scott, Jerry
Seaver, Don
Senior, Walt
Shore, Nate
Short, Phillip
Silverthorne, Wil
Simkins, William
Siracusa, Louis
Slauson, Sam
Sliwayder, Dave
Smidt, Joe
Smith, Charles
Smith, Donn
Smith, Dudley
Sockolov, Ron
Solari, Ray
Solvin, Howard
Souza, George
Souza, George L.
Stanley, Bob
Stathakis, George
Stellern, John
Stern, Glen
Stern, Roland
Stevens, Dick
Stevenson, Frank
Stevenson, Ozzie
Stewart, John
Stirton, John
Stone, Andy
Stone, Bill
Stone, Jim
Stowell, Doug
Stroud, Otis
Sullivan, John
Swaner, Jack
Taber, Larry
Takeuchi, Roy
Talley, Al
Thayer, Howard
Thinger, Byron
Thompson, Charles
Thompson, Ira
Thomson, Bill
Timmerman, Don
Tinay, Ronald
Tinkham, Frank
Tipton, Dale
Toner, John
Toombs, Frank
Torchio, Lloyd
Towle Jr., Charles
Trant, Allen
Tronstein, Don
Trost, Art
Troughton, Dave
Trutner, Tom
Tryon, Tom
Tullsen, Dick
Tunik, Ira
Turner, Jim
Valerga, Jack
Vallotton, Bill
Van Deren, Frank
Van Heuit, Bob
Van Heuit, Carl
Veliotes, Nick
Vevera, Godfrey
Vial, Sergio
Vohs, Jack
Voigt, Ernest
Vukasin, George
Wallace, Ralph
Ward, Roy
Wardlaw, Joe
Warren, T.H.
Wash, Don
Washington, Sam
Waste, James
Weber, Art
Webster, Staten
Weed, Les
West, Harry
Wheatcroft, Ron
White, Mike
Whitley, Jim
Whyte, Don
Willback, Mel
Williams, Floyd
Williams, Kenneth
Williams, Sam
Williamson, John
Willsey, Ray
Wilson, Don
Wilson, Jim
Wilson, John
Wilson, Ken
Witter, Bob
Witter, George
Witter, Phelps
Witter, Ron
Witter, Tom
Wong, Jike
Wong, Mynin
Worrell, Bob
Wright, Cliff
Wright, Hank
Wuth, Lewis
Yaich, Branislav
Yerman, Jack
Young, Bill
Young, John
Young, Pete
Young, Ray
Zavadil, Dave
Zenovich, Duke
Zorbas, Andy
Zumstein, Harry